12-95

Sheffield Hallam University
Learning and IT Services
Adsetts Centre City Campus
Sheffield   S1 1WB

101 515 407 7

D1390866

Gender relations in German history

KEY TEXT
REFERENCE

N 1997   -9 MA

.0V 1998

SHEFFIELD HALLAM UNIVERSITY
LEARNING CENTRE
WITHDRAWN FROM STOCK

-4 NUV 2002

28 NOV 2001
29 NOV 2002

Women's History

General Editor
June Purvis
Professor of Sociology, University of Portsmouth

Published
Carol Dyhouse
No distinction of sex? Women in British universities, 1870–1939

Bridget Hill
Women, work and sexual politics in eighteenth-century England

Linda Mahood
Policing gender, class & family: Britain, 1850–1940

June Purvis (editor)
Women's history: Britain, 1850–1945

Barbara Winslow
Sylvia Pankhurst: sexual politics and political activism

Lynn Abrams and Elizabeth Harvey
*Gender relations in German history:
power, agency and experience from the sixteenth to the twentieth century*

Forthcoming
Shani D'Cruze
Sex, violence and working women in Victorian England

jay Dixon
The romantic fiction of Mills & Boon, 1909–95

Wendy Webster
Women in the 1950s

Gender relations in German history

Power, agency and experience from the sixteenth to the twentieth century

Edited by

Lynn Abrams
University of Glasgow

Elizabeth Harvey
University of Liverpool

© Lynn Abrams and Elizabeth Harvey and contributors, 1996

This book is copyright under the Berne Convention.
No reproduction without permission.
All rights reserved.

First published in 1996 by UCL Press

UCL Press Limited
University College London
Gower Street
London WC1E 6BT

The name of University College London (UCL) is a registered trade mark used by
UCL Press with the consent of the owner.

British Library Cataloguing in Publication Data
A catalogue record for this book is available from the British Library.

ISBN: 1-85728-484-4 HB
        1-85728-485-2 PB

305.30943
AB

Typeset in Classical Garamond.
Printed and bound by
Biddles Ltd, Guildford and King's Lynn, England.

Contents

Preface

When German historians gathered in Lancaster in the spring of 1994 for a regional conference of the German History Society on the topic of Gender Relations in German History, they probably did not anticipate the sense of coherence and historical continuity that would emerge in view of the chronological breadth and thematic diversity of the papers on offer. Although discussions spanned the sixteenth century to the 1930s and themes ranged from sex with the devil, the execution of female criminals, liberal dissenting thought, to pregnancy, abortion, domestic violence, homosexuality and wartime experience, it was clear from the emergence of common themes and preoccupations that gender relations in history might most profitably be considered over the *longue durée* in order to highlight the continuities in historical experience as well as the changes.

In this collection we have attempted to reproduce and develop this line of enquiry by publishing six of the original conference papers and commissioning three more. Although the issues considered by the contributors retain the diversity of the conference, thus reflecting the wide range of research currently being undertaken in the field of gender relations in historical scholarship, as editors we have sought to achieve an overall coherence in the collection by locating the essays within a context in which norms of political, social and sexual behaviour for both sexes are the object of regulation and control, but also a matter of conflict, debate and negotiation.

In our introduction we have explored this context in more detail. In doing so we were greatly assisted by the eight contributors who through their research have stimulated us to think more deeply about the gendering of German history. We would also like to thank all those who attended and wholeheartedly participated in the conference, and especially those contributors whose work does not appear in this collection. As editors we are grateful to those who agreed to comment upon individual papers, the anonymous readers who supported the collection, and the sponsors of the original conference, the German History Society, and the host, Lancaster University. The Goethe Institute Manchester and the British Academy also provided generous financial support, and Steven Gerrard at UCL Press has been a patient and encouraging editor.

Lynn Abrams and Elizabeth Harvey

Notes on contributors

Lynn Abrams lectures in German history and women's history at the University of Glasgow. She is the author of *Workers' culture in imperial Germany* (1992) and is currently researching marriage, divorce and the law in nineteenth-century Germany.

Elizabeth Harvey lectures in German and European history and women's history at the University of Liverpool. She is the author of *Youth and the welfare state in Weimar Germany* (1993) and is currently carrying out research on women's involvement in National Socialist Germanization policies in the "German East".

Dagmar Herzog teaches German history and the history of sexuality at Michigan State University, and is the author of *Intimacy and exclusion: religious politics in pre-revolutionary Baden* (1996). Her current work is on anti-fascist memory and identity in post-Holocaust West Germany.

Kate Lacey is Lecturer in Media Studies in the School of European Studies at the University of Sussex, and author of *Feminine frequencies: gender, German radio and the public sphere, 1923–1945* (forthcoming).

Katherine Pence is writing her doctoral dissertation at the University of Michigan, Ann Arbor, on the politics and culture of consumption and gender in East and West Germany from 1945 to 1961.

Ulinka Rublack is Research Fellow at St John's College, Cambridge. She is currently writing a book on women and crime in early modern Germany and preparing a collection of essays on the history of the body.

Claudia Schoppmann lives in Berlin and writes on German women's history. She is the author of *Nationalsozialistische Sexualpolitik und weibliche Homosexualität* (1991) and of *Days of masquerade: life stories of lesbians during the Third Reich* (1996). She is co-editor of *Nach der Shoa geboren* (1994) on second-generation Jewish women in Germany.

Regina Schulte is Professor of Modern History and Gender History at the Ruhr-Universität Bochum. She has published widely in the field of women's studies, peasant studies and the history of crime and is the author of *Sperrbezirke: Tugendhaftigkeit und Prostitution in der bürgerlichen Welt* (1979) and *The village in court: arson, infanticide, and poaching in the court records of Upper Bavaria* (1994).

Cornelie Usborne is Lecturer in European History at the Roehampton Institute, London. She is the author of *The politics of the body in Weimar Germany* (1992) and is currently working on lay healing in nineteenth- and twentieth-century Germany.

Heide Wunder is Professor of History at the Universität-Gesamthochschule Kassel. She has published widely on the history of early modern Germany and is the author of *Die bäuerliche Gemeinde in Deutschland* (1986) and *"Er ist die Sonn', sie ist der Mond": Frauen in der Frühen Neuzeit* (1992).

Chapter One

ᴥ

Introduction: gender and gender relations in German history

Lynn Abrams and Elizabeth Harvey

Women's history – gender history – German history

Writing on the history of German women – by German historians and by historians outside Germany – has, like women's history elsewhere, undergone a remarkable expansion since the 1960s.[1] As is the case with the historiography of other countries too, since the beginning of the 1980s there has been an increasing emphasis on writing the history of German women as part of a broader history of gender. While work declaring itself as women's history continues to flourish alongside gender history – indeed, the two are complementary – the overall process can be seen as a gradual displacement of women's history by gender history, which has been widely noted, and in some cases lamented, by feminist historians.[2] Many, however, have welcomed the shift in emphasis, recognizing the wisdom of Joan Scott's assertion that not only is gender a "constitutive element of social relationships based on perceived differences between the sexes", but that "gender is a primary way of signifying relationships of power".[3] By focusing on gender relations we have attempted to illuminate not only the ways in which the two genders were formed, negotiated and contested over time through discourse, language and social action, but also the ways in which such analyses may contribute to our understanding of the structures and relations of power.

It is for this reason that we decided to focus upon gender as opposed to women, in the hope that an analysis of the power relations between men and women might produce some new thoughts and interpretations for German historians to work with. The pieces gathered here do, to a considerable extent, address the experience of women in a variety of contexts; at the same time, men are present too – as

1

husbands, fathers, soldiers, workers, clergymen, doctors and so on. Neither men nor women, however, are treated as an unproblematic, static category. Instead, the construction of gender identity is seen as being dependent upon variables such as social class, ethnicity and access to power.[4]

The collection does not attempt to provide coverage, or a complete synthesis, of the topic of gender relations in German history: rather, its focus is the construction of gender norms in German society, the enforcement of those norms by the state, the church, social institutions, the law and the community, and conformity and resistance by individuals and groups to the norms guiding female and male behaviour. Including contributions over the long timespan from the sixteenth to the twentieth century enables questions to be raised about continuity and change over the *longue durée*. It is perhaps surprising in the context of a (political) history as turbulent and discontinuous as Germany's – the essays included here traverse the Reformation, the revolutionary 1840s, the First World War, the Weimar Republic, the Third Reich and post-1945 reconstruction – that many of the norms governing relations between the sexes in marriage and in the family, in their sexual relations, in the street and the marketplace, even at the front in wartime, were extraordinarily persistent despite repeated attempts to subvert and challenge them. In this respect, then, gendering German history may suggest a revision, or at least a rethinking, of conventional periodization.[5] The boundaries of, say, 1918 and 1945, appear a little less fixed in the light of gendered discourses on, for instance, maternity, employment and consumption.

Yet it would be misleading to emphasize the continuities at the expense of real and concrete change in the ways in which gender relations have been defined and enforced. Over longer periods of time, change was wrought by social and economic forces, by political and religious movements and intellectual currents. And in the shorter term, the conventional periodization of German history has in some cases marked important watersheds in the history of gender relations – the 1840s, for instance, the First World War, the National Socialist regime. Within this context, in every period, women and men have often negotiated greater freedom of action than seemingly restrictive norms permitted.

Three major themes recur through the contributions: power, the body, and the relationship between public and private. In order to place the contributions in context, in the following sections of this chapter we provide a brief survey of the historiography relating to each of those themes.

Gender and power

All of the chapters in this collection force us to think about the relationship between power, authority and gender norms. Many historians would now concur that gender categories have been built in terms of power relations. This is the case not only in respect of the modern period but the early modern too when, as Merry Wiesner points out, "not only did the maintenance of proper power relationships between men and women serve as the basis for and a symbol of the larger political system, but also for the functioning of society as a whole".[6] Further, relations between the sexes "provided a model for all dichotomized relations which involved authority and subordination".[7] In the sixteenth century, social organization was dependent upon sexual categories: an individual's social position and identity was bound up with his or her sexual position and productive function.[8] At the centre of this web of economic and sexual relations was marriage, in which order was supposedly based on patriarchal authority and female subjection sanctioned by the law, the state and the church. Thus, heterosexual relations have commonly been regarded as the most fundamental site of female oppression and in the specific context of German history it is not difficult to see why. From the Reformation when paternal authority was strengthened within the household (and by extension, within society as a whole), to the nineteenth century when the oppression of women within marriage was legitimized by civil law, and the Third Reich that could only conceive of women within hierarchical heterosexual relationships, the gendered notions of domination and subordination appear to have been firmly embedded in the social and political fabric.

Until recently, most feminist historians would have described such a society, in which women were subordinate to men in almost all areas, including the law, citizenship rights, ownership of property, education, marriage and divorce, as patriarchal. However, "patriarchy" always posed problems as a heuristic concept in that it seemed to denote an undifferentiated system of male domination, relatively unresponsive to historically contingent change. Moreover, there appeared to be little space within a patriarchal model of society to account for women's agency, leaving an impression of unbounded female oppression and subordination. But feminist historians and historians of gender should perhaps pay heed to Carole Pateman's warning that to abandon the concept altogether would mean that "feminist political theory would then be without the only concept that refers specifically to the subjection of women".[9] Recent studies, then, have tended to use patriarchy in a more flexible sense and have regarded it as a historical phenomenon embodying structures of domination that have been subject to change and have affected women in different ways in different social, economic and political contexts. In the words of Judith Bennett, "patriarchy clearly has existed in many forms and varieties and its history will in fact be a history of many different historical patriarchies".[10]

While it is undeniable that the subordination of women within marriage, the economy and the political sphere was an objective reality throughout our period, the study of gender has forced a reappraisal of women's and men's access to power and the wielding of authority. As Anna Clark points out, gender history highlights different forms of male power while also drawing attention to the instability of that power.[11] The "script of male domination"[12] does not permit differentiated and nuanced analysis of patriarchal power as long as that power is always used in a static and repressive sense that renders women passive and docile.[13] Gender history, on the other hand, "requires us to look at how men and women construct their 'experience' within a dialectic of power".[14] This is an especially valuable insight in the context of German history, where political power has traditionally been seen as particularly authoritarian and repressive, permitting women limited agency and possibility of resistance.

In exploring the nature of power and power relations, some feminist historians have found Foucauldian theories valuable, whereby a juridical theory of power is rejected in favour of the theory of a disciplinary society informed by new knowledges that in turn bring forth new modes of surveillance and regulation. In rejecting the notion that individuals and groups may *possess* power, Foucault emphasizes the mechanisms of power and in particular the ways in which power is exercised. By examining the mechanisms of surveillance and regulation, for instance, we can begin to see how the exercise of power creates resistance and produces new forms of knowledge.[15] Foucault has posited that power relations operate primarily through the body. Feminists have taken this a step further by demonstrating how social hierarchies have been created by the construction of gender inequality from biological difference. As Kathleen Canning writes, "when it rejected biological essentialism as an explanation of gender inequalities, feminist history discovered in its own right the power of language, of discourses, to socially construct these inequalities and to anchor them in social practices and institutions".[16] According to Foucault, then, power is a productive and therefore a positive force: power is not always repressive and negative.[17]

We agree that Foucault's understanding of power might be helpful to historians attempting to unravel the power dynamics of gender relations. In particular, the idea of the resistance that arises "at the point where relations of power are exercised"[18] may help us to uncover resistances that have been silenced owing to the apparent force of disciplinary or coercive power. Moreover, Foucault's emphasis on the production of power through discourses and knowledges helps us better to understand different modes of domination. His rejection of the notion that all power is dependent on the state apparatus is similarly valuable.

However, it is still necessary to explain why power is unequally distributed and to understand the place of agency. We would suggest that the wholesale acceptance of poststructuralist theory that subordinates the story of what happened to women and men in the past to the analysis of the construction of "subjective and collective meanings of women and men as categories of identity"[19] – an approach that arguably silences experience and marginalizes agency – presents some major problems.[20] Anna Clark has recently prompted us to address anew what she describes as the problem of how to link the "postmodernist play with language" to "the grubby historical question of power".[21] Clark is primarily concerned with how gender structures class and power relations, and in the context of Britain in the late eighteenth and early nineteenth centuries she asserts that "relations of power were always shifting, but they shifted because real political actors, including women, negotiated and contested them".[22] Clark is surely correct to integrate the language of gender into the political economy, and her emphasis on "real political actors" draws attention to how women and men experienced class formation and the construction of new hierarchies of power. For instance, within the household, the "struggle for the breeches" (as the conflict between husband and wife over authority in marriage and the household economy is termed by Clark) arose as wives asserted greater authority derived from their wage-earning, while husbands who desired to maintain patriarchal power within marriage found their justification for this power being undermined.

For historians examining gender and power in German history, a crucial starting point has been the Reformation. As Lyndal Roper has noted, most historians of early modern Germany agree that the Reformation presaged, if not a crisis in relations between the sexes, then a fundamental reordering of gender relations that saw the emergence of a patriarchal society.[23] The different forms of power exercised by the church, the state and the guilds allocated men and women to fixed but unequal positions in a hierarchical society. As Heide Wunder observes in Chapter 2, secular and religious authority reinforced each other in regulating economic and social life: "social order was imagined as having been created by God himself": fundamental to this order was the hierarchy of gender. Marriage, the household and production were closely entwined and both the personal and the economic relationship between man and wife were predicated upon a gender hierarchy that defined women's tasks as "reproduction" and men's work as "production". A man's position within the community was dependent upon his productive role, his ability to provide materially for his wife and family. Merry Wiesner has illustrated how, in early modern Germany, the exclusively male craft guilds systematically excluded women from artisanal production, hindering women's access to economic power.[24] Clearly, the gendered division of labour so prevalent in the nineteenth and twentieth centuries was not an invention of the industrial era. The guilds devalued all productive activity associated with women's work (labelled *häusliche Arbeit* as opposed to *Erwerbsarbeit*), defined occupations as skilled or unskilled according to the gender of the workers rather than the level of training, dexterity and expertise required, and promoted the notion that women were the source of disorder and dishonour so that so-called "masterless" women – those who worked for wages but were not married or did not live in a male-headed household – were treated suspiciously and sometimes ordered to live with their parents, employer or some other male guardian.[25] A journeyman's notion of honour was defined entirely by his association with the guild (and his disassociation from women in the economic sphere). The concomitant of this identification of male honour and power with his economic role was, however, the loss of a man's power within marriage and the community when he was no longer able to fulfil this function. A woman's social position, on the other hand, was largely determined by her marital status and her sexual reputation which in turn reflected upon the honour and status of her husband. A man who could not control his wife's conduct was deemed unlikely to be able to control his workshop, and the plethora of ballads and woodcuts depicting dominated husbands bears testimony to the early modern disapproval of a marriage "turned upside-down".[26]

Women who appeared to possess independent economic and especially sexual power were regarded as destabilizing influences on the community. It is surely no coincidence that men who taunted and abused their wives with defamatory words such as "whore" and "slut" were frequently marginal characters whose social status had deteriorated owing to a dissolute lifestyle. Having lost their claim to dominance (*Herrschaft*) within marriage, such men turned to physical violence and besmirching the public honour of their wives as a means of restoring order to the marriage. In the early modern period, when honour and status were so dependent on reputation, words carried considerable power.[27] However, Joy Wiltenburg, in her analysis of early modern street literature, suggests that in contrast with England where a woman's tongue was her "primary weapon", in Germany in the sixteenth and seventeenth centuries, "while women's scolding is considered a plague, the female tongue does not attain the same status as an invincible weapon and a symbol of female power".[28] Neither does the German woman emerge on top. "Even the tongue, though powerful enough to make husbands miserable, usually earns the German woman no permanent power".[29] In fact, it was more likely to earn the woman a beating, the ultimate assertion of male power within marriage.

The contributions to this collection suggest that the Reformation left a powerful legacy of strongly delineated gender norms within the household and in the workplace that placed men and women in unequal positions within the power hierarchy. As Heide Wunder reminds us in Chapter 2, enforcing such norms was not a simple matter of indoctrinating a passive population, and the degree of repetition and elaboration of models of proper behaviour for men and for women in the prescriptive literature alerts us to the possible extent to which these models were being ignored. Nevertheless, the Protestant belief that woman's ideal role was as mother and the man's was as father and worker had long-term repercussions for women's legal position and their access to education, the skilled trades and professions. If we are to begin to rethink the traditional historical narrative in German history, this emphasis on the continuity in ways of speaking about gender roles may point the way forward.

The Reformation can also be read as a paradigm of a process of crisis, upheaval and restabilization in gender relations that is echoed at other moments in German history. In Germany, as in other countries, during periods of disruption – social, economic, religious or political – reordering gender relations has been one symbolic means of restoring cultural and social stability.[30] In the nineteenth century, during the upheaval of rapid industrialization, a reordering of gender relations was carried out within the "private" sphere as illicit unions were policed and single women subjected to intense scrutiny, culminating in the 1900 Civil Code.[31] In the economic sphere, distinctions between men's and women's work were reinforced and a discourse of danger emerged related to the supposed effects of women's work on the social fabric.[32] In the aftermath of the First World War and revolution, a major plank of Weimar government policies to restore order and social stability was the restoration of traditional gender roles in the home and workplace.[33] And as Katherine Pence illustrates in her contribution to this volume, the post-Second World War decade in East and West Germany was characterized by an attempted return to "traditional" discourses on gender relations and gendered power structures. As Lyndal Roper suggests, "concepts of gender may display extraordinary volatility at certain moments . . . yet little may actually change in the relations between the sexes".[34]

There may seem little that is peculiarly German in this examination of power relations: relations between the sexes were determined by other variables that had similar resonances elsewhere.[35] And yet, given that Germany has in its history experienced more than its fair share of major transformative moments, the volatility identified by Lyndal Roper is something that has at a number of crucial historical junctures – the Reformation, defeat and revolution following the First World War, the Third Reich and its aftermath, division and (re)unification – particularly characterized the German experience in comparison with that of its European neighbours.

The body and sexuality

Feminist historians, and perhaps especially historians of Germany, have used the concept of the body as a way to understanding the complex ways in which women (and men) were positioned by discourse and legislation in a variety of political and cultural contexts. However, as Kathleen Canning observes, "in much feminist theory and historiography the body has figured as a feminist site of lived experience that serves to ground agency and resistance, to give it concrete origins".[36] Such an emphasis is useful in that it permits one to view the experience of gender in historical perspective as more than just the result of linguistic or cultural practice, and to move towards an approach that views sexual difference as possessing its "own physiological and psychological reality".[37] Take the following narrative from a nineteenth-century divorce court as an example of the ways in which gender was lived and experienced through the perception of the cultural significance and physical reality of the body.

In a Hamburg courtroom in November 1830, Albrecht Ketting attempted to divorce his wife of less than three years, Catharina, on the grounds that she was totally unable to perform intercourse. Albrecht was a widower with three young children and in his lawsuit he made much of the fact that he had hoped, with this second marriage, to provide a happy home for his children. Yet he had been disappointed. "Hardly into his forties, at the peak of his virility, he felt an irresistible urge to satisfy his sexual desire." Although the couple had been formally separated for some time, Albrecht said he was prepared to reunite with his wife if she "would establish for him a new serene domestic happiness by the procreation of children". But this was not possible owing to his wife's "physical condition". Albrecht went on to allege that intercourse was impossible because Catharina's vagina was too narrow. And besides, he alleged, she suffered from such evil-smelling breath, that "when she gets close all desire for intercourse disappears".[38] Catharina, not willing to accept these allegations, countered by stating that the issue was not necessarily *her* ability to have intercourse, but that of her husband.

In this scenario the body, its physicality and the relationship between the biological body and gender identity is clear to see. Catharina's corporeality was represented in terms of her sexuality and her gendered role as wife and mother. The two were intimately related. Similarly, Albrecht staked his identity as a man upon the consummation of his marriage. His sense of masculine identity, which was also constituted by his representation as an "upright citizen who is committed to the strictest observation of the law", was seriously undermined by sexual failure and Catharina was fully aware of this.

It was not always so. That is, gender difference was not always predicated solely upon the observation of biological difference. Before the late eighteenth century, according to Thomas Laqueur, "biological sex, which we generally take to serve as the basis of gender, was just as much in the domain of culture and meaning as was gender".[39] "Maleness and femaleness did not reside in anything particular."[40] In the early modern period, as Alison Rowlands has shown, "Gender, as a cultural definition of appropriate roles, was created and maintained . . . by outward appearance and observable behaviour."[41] It was not until the late eighteenth century that body image and sex roles came to be aligned and, further, became one of the primary determinants of social roles.[42]

Evidently, the body is not a historical constant. The body has a history in terms of the ways in which it was understood and defined by a culture, and the ways it was perceived and imagined by an individual. Approaches that treat bodily phenomena as unchanging over time because of their naturalness have been overtaken by those that seek to understand the instability of notions of corporeal reality and that make a distinction between what Barbara Duden calls the "historicity of matter and the body experience itself".[43]

Historians of early modern Germany have provided numerous insights into ways in which the body was perceived and experienced, and have reinforced the view that early modern concepts of the body differed from the modern in a number of important ways. We know that early modern understanding of anatomy and the sexual organs in particular rested upon the belief that there was only one sex, that is, the female sexual organs were the inversion of the male.[44] It was a world where "the reproductive organs are but one sign among many of the body's place in a cosmic and cultural order that transcends biology".[45] Outward signs of status, of one's place in the sexual-social order were often just as, if not more, important. A woman's status, for instance, could be determined by outward signifiers such as the wearing of her hair long and uncovered (a virgin) or covered (a married woman). As Alison Rowlands points out, a woman's virginity was hidden and she could only demonstrate it symbolically by, in this case, wearing the traditional "virgin's wreath" on her wedding day.[46] Another of these differences was the set of beliefs centred on the relationship between the physical body and the divine.[47] And the symbolic understanding of the functions of the body was of significance in early modern belief systems.[48] For instance menstruation, which was popularly understood as the purging of excess blood or a purification process, invested women with certain powers. And the female sexed body could be imagined as containing magical properties and demonic forces, embodied in the figure of the witch.

This early modern conception of the body began to change in the late seventeenth and early eighteenth centuries as the body's value as a repository of symbolic meaning began to be challenged. The Scientific Revolution revealed the body, and especially the female body, as a natural phenomenon, thus divorced from culture, to be understood through medical and scientific investigation. Woman's body, uniquely unruly and resistant to disciplining before, now became sexualized, pathologized, medicalized and thus liable to exploitation, intervention and control.[49] A good indicator of this shift is the changing official attitude towards infanticide. Before the early eighteenth century the deliberate killing of a child had been interpreted as an evil, devilish and unnatural act and the punishment (and in some cases execution) of the offender reflected this understanding. However, during the course of the eighteenth century executions of women for infanticide dramatically declined owing to the fact that the infanticidal mother was now perceived as weak, desperate and a victim of circumstance.[50] Her "crime" was a means to maintain her honour whereas in the early modern era it was precisely this attempt to conceal the loss of honour, that is the loss of her virginity, which condemned her.[51] Thus, the modern body was defined; a body for which sex determined identity and destiny.[52] "Women's bodies", writes Laqueur, "in their corporeal, scientifically accessible concreteness . . . came to bear an enormous new weight of meaning."[53] This meant that a woman's sexual functions determined her behaviour; her physical but also her mental state was determined by her nature, her reproductive function.[54]

It is important to remember that there has always been a close relationship between cultural perceptions of the body, what is done to the body, and how this is experienced. While we should recognize the power of discourse to define and control the body, at the same time we should not marginalize the physicality of the experience of control and regulation or the ability of the individual to resist or act in a creative way.[55] For example, while taking account of the power of National Socialist discourse on the reproductive body, we also need to explore the different experiences and reactions of those women who were sterilized, forced to have abortions or vilified as homosexuals. Barbara Duden's analysis of one eighteenth-century doctor's relationship with his female patients illustrates the importance of this multi-layered approach. Johannes Storch's perception of the female body was based on observation of bodily secretions and deductions made about the inner process. He treated his patients in accordance with his (not their) perception of the cause of the illness.[56] By the nineteenth century it is just as important to recognize the relationship between perception of the body and medical practice. The belief that a woman's physiology was linked to her psychological condition could result in surgical intervention (ovariotomy, hysterectomy, etc.) to "cure" hysteria for example.[57]

The two chapters in this book that examine practices and policies relating to abortion – Ulinka Rublack's on the sixteenth and seventeenth centuries (Ch. 3), and Cornelie Usborne's on Weimar Germany (Ch. 7) – provide interesting points of contrast and comparison, shedding light on how women's bodies were subjected to scrutiny and control in the "emergency" situation of an unwanted pregnancy. In the medicalized world of the twentieth century, as Cornelie Usborne shows, the medical profession played a key role as a "policing" instance: doctors pursued a twin strategy of seeking to minimize the incidence of abortion while striving to monopolize the practice of such abortions as were carried out. Women seeking abortions often avoided doctors and sought lay assistance instead, not only on the grounds of cost but also on the grounds of doctors' lack of empathy with the woman's situation and their evident distaste for her "polluted" physical condition. By contrast, the medical profession as a factor is relatively unimportant in the early modern context. In the "pluralistic" world of early modern medicine, the influence of the medically trained practitioners was limited: folk knowledge of abortifacient herbs was widespread and women could potentially consult a whole range of male or female healers or knowledgeable acquaintances. Nevertheless, widespread knowledge of herbal remedies for "late periods" did not mean that a woman seeking an abortion in early modern society necessarily found it easy to gain assistance and sympathy from the community or from female networks. As Ulinka Rublack argues, the act of aborting a foetus after it was presumed to have "quickened" was not only subject to criminal penalties but also to growing disapproval and stigmatization by the community: and midwives also played a role in upholding norms of respectability against other women.

The above examples show very direct and sometimes crude forms of intervention and disciplining. But women's bodies were also disciplined and controlled in more subtle ways. Beginning in the sixteenth century, female sexuality in particular was subjected to control on two fronts. As greater emphasis was placed on the stability of the conjugal unit, secular courts were energetic in their policing of sexual relations and indiscipline.[58] Female transgressions were more harshly punished than male, and single women faced stricter sanctions than married men whose punishment was often mild in comparison.[59] Sexual indiscipline in Reformation Germany was defined as engaging in prostitution, concubinage or adultery, that is, engaging in sexual relations that threatened the morality and the stability of marriage. By the nineteenth century, although much of the Protestant reformers' rhetoric had dissipated, the "doubled vision" of woman as wife and mother and a source of sexual danger persisted. As Dagmar Herzog argues in Chapter 4, even the Protestant and Catholic dissenters of the 1840s, although calling for greater equality within marriage, failed to escape from the language of difference that bound women's destiny to that of their bodies. At the state level, the disciplining of the sexual woman continued. The nineteenth century, it has been argued, witnessed various coercive and legislative attempts to regulate "unruly sex" focusing on the instability located within the body of woman.[60] The repeal of restrictive marriage laws in 1868, while making it easier for the lower classes to contract a marriage, also deliberately elevated marriage as the only legitimate expression of social/sexual relations. Mothers of illegitimate children were disciplined by a decree of 1854 that removed the right of a woman who had knowingly had a relationship with a married man to compensation. The laws on concubinage were tightened, permitting the police to prosecute co-habiting couples who "offended public decency".[61] And the unruly sexuality of woman was further controlled in 1871 with the implementation of Paragraph 361/6 of the new Imperial Criminal Code. Prostitutes were subjected to a system of police regulation that restricted their movements and insisted upon compulsory medical examinations. Underlying this new regulatory framework was a medical and socio-psychological discourse addressing demographic and social hygiene concerns. Finally, in 1900 the new unified German Civil Code, the *Bürgerliches Gesetzbuch* (BGB), was implemented following vigorous opposition from feminists on the grounds that it was more hostile to women than the codes it superseded, particularly in the clauses relating to divorce. The ideal of the indissoluble marriage had triumphed and the notion of the legal protection of woman by her husband was given precedence over the protection of the individual by the state.[62]

In the modern period, then, the body of woman was disciplined and regulated both discursively and physically. As long as her body was discursively constructed as dangerous and unruly and above all natural, the female body lost an element of the autonomy/power it had assumed in the early modern era. The body that had formerly housed powerful forces was now pacified and disciplined in order to legitimate certain regimes of domination.[63] During the Weimar Republic the female body became highly politicized within the context of the politics of reproduction. Heightened concern about the declining birth rate from 1900 onwards, the effects of the war on men and women, and the concomitant fear of a shift in power relations between men and women as women chose to have fewer children and the spectre of the "new woman" threatened to rupture traditional gender roles, legitimated – in the state's view – intervention in the realms of fertility and birth control.[64] Cornelie Usborne argues that attempts to limit access to birth control and abortion while promoting eugenic policies to improve the health and quality of the *Volkskörper* necessitated intervention in the body of woman (*Frauenkörper*).[65] During the Third Reich, the congruence between woman's reproductive body and her social destiny as a wife and mother was taken to the ultimate conclusion. Sterilization, involuntary abortion, incarceration and extermination of the "hereditarily unfit" and the "racially impure" contrasted with the propaganda and financial inducements to "Aryan" women to marry and bear children.[66] The Nazi state signalled the end to any possibility of fluidity/instability between material, corporeal reality and gender identity. "Biology" was destiny and sexual ambiguity was not countenanced. The blurring of gender differences was deemed to be damaging to the *Volk*. Within the context of Nazi racial and population policy, as Claudia Schoppmann shows in Chapter 8, male homosexual acts were explicitly criminalized, but female homosexuality was not because a woman was defined by her reproductive capacity and lesbians were still deemed capable of intercourse. Indeed, all childless women were regarded as somehow abnormal and not truly "womanly" by the Nazi state and such women's experience of the regime was to some extent determined by the ideological fixing of the relationship between biology and gender identity.[67] During the period of restructuring after 1945, both East and West Germany spoke the language of "social crisis and biological disorder" as a means of carrying out surveillance of the *Volkskörper* via public health and welfare measures.[68] The attempts to fix that which constantly threatens to be unstable is a continuous theme in historical scholarship on the (female) body and in the essays gathered here. From the sixteenth century, when the institution of marriage was regarded as the basis of the early modern moral order and thus the ideal social system for placing restrictions on woman's sexual behaviour, to the 1930s and 1940s when the Nazi state refused to acknowledge unstable meaning inscribed upon the body and sought to fix gender identity by means of forced intervention, there appears to be a continuum of attempts by the state, the church, the law and other co-opted interest groups to gain control over matter and meaning.

Nevertheless, in the ways they experienced their own bodies, women did resist dominant discourses and forms of coercion and control. Whereas in early modern German culture a woman's body was imagined as inherently powerful, in the post-Enlightenment era this power was no longer culturally imagined/constructed but reverted back to the gift of the individual who had to mark out her own autonomy. So, for example, in cases of domestic violence, while a husband may have attempted to assert his control over the body of his wife by beating and verbally abusing her, a woman might have challenged his authority by divorcing him on the grounds of cruelty. Women who were desperate to terminate a pregnancy in Weimar Germany, despite legislation forbidding abortion except in so-called "therapeutic" cases, took control of their fertility by seeking the help of lay abortionists who were also mainly female.

Clearly, a combination of representations of the body and various procedures of discipline and control was a key element in the maintenance of unequal social relations in Germany. It was primarily the female body that was subjected to procedures and regulations relating to desire, sexuality and fertility, although we should not discount the concomitant disciplining of the male body that involved the definition and enforcement of norms of masculinity and male behaviour.[69] But whereas discourses and actions around the body are characterized in many respects by historical continuity, the forms taken by those discourses and actions were historically contingent.

Gender and the public/private divide

The distinction between public and private has been described as one of the "great dichotomies" used to distinguish between different types of social activities and social spaces.[70] The usage of such a distinction in a general sense to differentiate between matters relating to the wider community or the state, and matters relating to the particular household or individual, can be traced back to antiquity, when the distinction clearly privileged the realm of the *polis*, the realm of politics, law and justice, over the sphere of private economic and social activity.[71] However, it is since the Enlightenment that the terminology of public and private has been characteristically used and refined. At a time of challenges to hereditarily based authority and established orthodoxy, of the emergence of civil society and the formation of "public opinion", it became all the more urgent for political theorists to produce a model of politics and society as it was then evolving, to work out the relationship between the state and its subjects (or citizens), and to propose how the increasingly distinct activities of production and reproduction could and should be organized and regulated. This entailed mapping precisely the areas of social, economic and political life that could neither be assigned clearly to the domain of the state and state policy nor to that of the domestic household. Definitions were needed of what was and what was not a matter of the collective as opposed to the individual interest, what was and what was not accessible to the general population or restricted to an exclusive group, what tasks were to be carried out by or on behalf of the state as opposed to a private agency, and so on. Notions of a "public sphere" and a "private sphere" – with neither term ostensibly privileged over the other – therefore became important concepts in liberal political theory.[72] As concepts structuring the way society has been perceived and organized, they have also become objects of investigation for historians exploring mentalities and analyzing social change in the period from the eighteenth century onwards.

Powerful and prevalent though the public/private distinction has been historically, the boundaries between the public and private are never easily located. While "the private" can be identified with "the particular" in contrast to "the general", this definition does not in itself enable a precise boundary to be drawn round a territory of social life and labelled "private": as John Brewer points out, "some 'privates' are more particular than others".[73] Thus the concept of "the private" can be represented as a set of concentric circles, drawing in from the world of non-political social relationships towards the personal, intimate sphere of the family – which can appear as the ultimate domain of the private.

Feminist critiques of the public/private dichotomy have highlighted its nature as a gendered construct. The association of men with the world of public affairs and political power, and of women with the home, is as old as the public/private distinction itself.[74] Although ideas about the public and private have been recast in different historical periods, definitions of a "public sphere" have typically involved the exclusion from it of particular groups of persons on the basis of (among other criteria) gender. Conversely, definitions of a "private sphere" (that which is "not public") have consistently assigned women to that sphere alone. Men, by contrast, have been seen as belonging in both spheres in their different guises as members or heads of households and as public actors/citizens. For feminist theorists and historians, therefore, undertaking a critique of the public/private dichotomy has been an important way of exploring how different spheres of action for men and for women have been defined, enforced and challenged in the past and present.[75]

In the 1970s, American and British feminist historians were much struck by the extent to which bourgeois society in nineteenth-century America and Britain appeared to be structured by the concepts of a public and a private sphere where the public sphere represented the world "outside" and the private sphere the world "inside" the home.[76] While this association of masculine with public, feminine with private was nothing novel, so went the argument, the nineteenth century saw the notion of gendered public and private spheres being elaborated in more absolute and forceful terms than ever before by theorists who emphasized how such a separation of spheres was both natural and essential for the smooth functioning of society. However, for all the contemporary emphasis on the complementarity and equality in value of the two spheres, feminist analyses pointed out how the insistence upon separate public and private spheres actually served to uphold male power and perpetuate the subordination of women. It tended to shore up the hierarchy of power between the sexes at a time when liberal forces were attacking authoritarian governments and hierarchical social structures. In this context, where it appeared increasingly possible and likely that women might claim the newly formulated rights of the citizen – indeed, in the 1790s manifestos and treatises asserting the rights of women as citizens were appearing – political progressives in particular were under pressure to legitimate the exclusion of women from an active role in the public sphere.[77]

Feminist historians argued that the doctrine of separate spheres, whatever its origins, had a correlative in social reality to the extent that a growing number of middle-class women in the nineteenth century were able, or compelled, to withdraw from participation in manufacture and commerce, and to focus their activities more exclusively on child-rearing, the supervision of the household and sociability, mainly within a female network. Exploring this home-focused world of middle-class women's work and sociability, some historians stressed its restrictiveness, others discovered the female solidarity and intimacy that it could engender.[78]

During the 1980s and since, elements of this historical argument have been refined, elaborated, modified and attacked wholesale by feminists in the USA and UK. In particular, it has been stressed that the prescriptive literature of the period should not be confused with social reality, and that boundaries between a "male/public" and a "female/private" sphere were much less clear-cut in practice than theories and tracts proclaimed.[79] Since the late 1980s, there have been calls in some quarters to abandon altogether the notions of "separate spheres" and the public/private divide as overworked tropes that are too loose and unwieldy to illuminate the complex history of gender relations.[80]

However, while recognizing the difficulties involved, it would still seem that feminist historiography can gain from investigating how "spheres" and boundaries between public and private have been constructed, applied and challenged in the past. Certainly among historians working on women and gender relations in Germany since the eighteenth century, there appears so far little inclination to abandon this approach: for them, exploring the construction of "separate spheres" and the public/private dichotomy has been crucial.

Eve Rosenhaft has suggested that the fact the historiography on Germany has developed along these lines is no coincidence: it reflects an important dimension of historical reality.[81] In Germany the male monopoly of state power and of the political process – highlighted by the granting of universal male suffrage in the newly united German empire – was rigorously maintained until the advent of the Weimar Republic.[82] Marriage and family law in nineteenth-century Germany withheld from married women the full status of legal persons during an era when reforms were removing the legal disabilities of other disadvantaged groups.[83] However, the long-upheld exclusion of women from political life and the denial of civic equality was matched by a striking richness, from the early nineteenth century onwards, of women's participation in a "female sphere" of charitable and religious activism extending beyond the home into the community.[84] Parallels can be found between these developments and trends in other countries; and in Germany, as in other countries, the exclusion of women from political life did not go unchallenged. Nevertheless, there is, in Rosenhaft's view, a particular starkness about the way in which a separation of spheres evolved in nineteenth- and twentieth-century Germany. In Rosenhaft's words, "what is peculiar about German history in this respect is both the firmness of its boundaries and the extent of organic development within them".[85]

One major strand of this story has been the history of separate spheres ideology in the formation of German bourgeois society and political life in the nineteenth century. Historians have explored how ideas on the relationship between public and private life, between politics, work, marriage and the home shaped the beliefs and practices of the German middle classes.[86] Like historians of America and Britain, historians of Germany have focused on the late eighteenth and early nineteenth centuries as the era in which an ideology of "natural" gender polarity and correspondingly separate spheres of action for men and women was formulated – in part as a defensive concept against feared or actual social and political change.[87] Early modern society, as Heide Wunder points out in Chapter 2, had not been characterized by this dichotomy of public and private as separate spheres for men and women, derived from notions of natural *Geschlechtscharakter*. In examining how ideas of natural gender difference came to be so influential in the late eighteenth and early nineteenth centuries, historians have traced how an ideology of gender polarity and of separate but complementary male and female spheres was propagated in tracts, encyclopaedias and literary writings.[88] Gender inequality, now inscribed as the natural order, thus became one of the founding inequalities of German bourgeois society.[89]

More recently, attention has been focused explicitly on the concepts of the public and private (*Öffentlichkeit*, *Privatheit*, *das Öffentliche*, *das Private*) in German political and social thought and their relationship to the evolution of gender relations.[90] Other recent work has examined the boundaries between public and private as reflected in political and social movements and how – for instance in 1848 – supporters of the revolution deliberately transgressed them.[91] Dagmar Herzog in Chapter 4 examines how religious dissenting movements in the pre-revolutionary 1840s also challenged the exclusion of women from public life, on the grounds that the feminine strengths and virtues crucial to the home were equally crucial to the wider world of the congregation and community.

While the religious dissenters – on the grounds of their radical thinking on women's potential contribution to public life – have been celebrated in some accounts as early forerunners of feminism, Herzog highlights the contradictions and anxieties that characterized the dissenters' view of gender. While challenging the exclusion of women from public life, the dissenters continued to hold to the notion purveyed in the prescriptive literature of the time of the private sphere as the domain of intimacy, domestic harmony, emotional regeneration and freedom from outside interference. In emphasizing the intimacy and exclusivity of the marital bond and the inviolability of the marital home, the male dissenters were – Herzog argues – revealing their anxieties about wives being manipulated against their husbands' interests by "alien" forces (such as priests) outside the home. They thus continued to uphold a notion of the private sphere in which the subordination of women was inscribed.

The case of the religious dissenters' attitude to the privacy of the marital home, and their reluctance to contemplate any diminution of husbands' power over wives, raises the question of what notion of "privateness" prevailed in relation to the domestic sphere and whose interests it served. There was no unitary marital law in Germany before the codification of the civil law in the *Bürgerliches Gesetzbuch* of 1900, but a common denominator of the existing laws on marriage – including the *Code civil* – was the way in which they preserved the fiction that the interests of wives and children were identical with those of the male head of household.[92] Behind this façade, the authority of husbands and fathers was reinforced and conflicts of interest silenced. Many husbands abused that authority: cruelty cases in the divorce courts, such as those analyzed by Lynn Abrams in her contribution to this volume, represented only the visible part of a larger problem of domestic abuse.

Another strand of the story of gender and the public/private divide in German history has been the history of German feminism, with reference both to the ideology based on ideas of gender polarity that was characteristic of German feminism, and to the cultivation in practice by the German women's movement of a distinct sphere of female activism.[93] German nineteenth-century feminists, while avoiding arguments derived from "nature" or "biology", tended to base their claims for raising women's status and enhancing female influence in society on women's special capacities and qualities. They argued that if the values and skills cultivated within the private sphere by women in their capacity as carers and nurturers (and particularly in their role as mothers) were as important to social wellbeing as the prescriptive literature made them out to be, then women as the embodiment of those values should exert greater influence outside the home as well.[94] They thus sought to construct connections between the "private" and the "public", while retaining a positive view of the value of the private world of home, motherhood and family. By the end of the nineteenth century, the groups and organizations that constituted the growing German women's movement sought to implement this doctrine by engaging in moral and social reform campaigns at national and local level and through practical work in the field of social welfare, education and vocational training.[95] German feminists were not alone in cultivating the "maternal ethic": there were feminists in other countries too who adopted arguments for overcoming discrimination against women based on women's special qualities as well as arguments based on abstract principles of equal rights.[96] However, German feminists in the late nineteenth and early twentieth centuries, who were operating in a rapidly modernizing country where mass politics had been institutionalized but where women were systematically excluded from the political process, appear to have been particularly inclined to use the concept of "spiritual motherhood" or "organized motherhood" as the basis for their demands for social and political reform.

A third major focus for historians of gender relations in modern German history has been the era of the two world wars. The successive transformations of German political life initiated by the First World War and defeat threw received notions of a gendered public/private divide into flux without eradicating them.[97] At one level, the First World War tended to polarize the experience of men and women and their respective spheres of action. Richard Bessel has suggested that "[t]he First World War saw the development of two quite different but interdependent societies: the one a male society structured within the military; the other a civil society that consisted disproportionately of women".[98] In Chapter 6, Regina Schulte acknowledges that, in terms of contemporary representations of the war effort, the gendered dichotomy of the private and public spheres was writ large in the dichotomy of the home front (identified with women/civilians) and front line (identified with men/soldiers). Official propaganda, the press and even women's organizations purveyed stereotypical representations of complementary male and female heroism and self-sacrifice: such images emphasized the polarity, but at the same time the interdependence, of the masculine world of politics, war and death in action and the feminine world of childbearing, patient labour and silent renunciation.[99] However, as Schulte argues, the front nurses constituted a phenomenon that cut straight across such categorizations. They were a permanent anomaly, excluded both from the male brotherhood of the trenches and from the female-dominated world of the home front. In this situation, the nurses themselves tried to make sense of their experiences using the ideas about femininity and masculinity, family life, motherhood, public service and patriotic duty they had absorbed during their upbringing and training. Seeing themselves as the substitute sisters or mothers of the wounded soldiers, they tried to recreate the illusion of privacy, home comforts and a family atmosphere in the chaotic conditions of the field hospitals, and in doing so sought to harness the feminine skills and values associated with the private sphere to professional public service. Reconstructing the nurses' mental world through a close reading of their memoirs, Schulte shows how notions of the public and private informed, and were in turn shaped by, individual and collective experience.

The First World War images of the German soldier and the German mother, embodying public man and private woman and their respective complementary but separate spheres, also figured as a prominent theme in the propaganda of the Nazi regime. On the surface at least, the Nazi regime cultivated the conventional distinction between a male public and a female private sphere as part of its ostensible restoration of a supposedly natural and traditional division of labour between the sexes. In Goebbels' words: "Things pertaining to men must be left to men: these include politics and the ability of a nation to defend itself."[100] Certainly this thinking shaped and provided a rationale for the way in which the regime structured political authority. Breaking sharply with the principles and practices of the Weimar Republic, where women for the first time had had full political rights and had gained at least a foothold in party politics and government at national, *Land* and local level,[101] Nazi leaders reserved positions of political power for men. Nazi women co-operated in presenting the activities of the Nazi women's organizations, which were undeniably located within the public sphere, as being separate and distinct from those of men. These organizations thus constituted a distinctively female sphere that was presented as a natural extension of women's activities in the home.[102] As Claudia Schoppmann points out, Nazi policies towards homosexuality provide one illustration of the way the Nazi regime conceptualized the public sphere in terms of gender: male homosexuality was considered more of a threat than female homosexuality, and consequently persecuted more systematically, because homosexual men, in contrast to homosexual women, were regarded as being in a position to "corrupt" public life.

Despite the distinction upheld in Nazi-regime propaganda between the "small world" of woman and the "greater world" of man, the regime subverted such a distinction in fundamental ways.[103] This effort to undermine the separation of public and private spheres was hardly surprising: after all, such a distinction derived from a liberal world view that the National Socialists explicitly rejected. In 1936 an article in an SS journal proclaimed that:

> Last century there was the view that the body was the most fundamental private matter for each individual . . . Our view of the state rejects this view. Negative measures such as excluding the physically inferior from reproducing are not enough. We must create the conditions for the future, so that in times to come not only healthier people are born but also those who are born healthy live and look after themselves in such a way that they become the healthy parents of generations to come.[104]

Behind the façade of restoring "traditional" family life, the regime set out explicitly to impose public control over reproduction and, deploying levels of coercion unprecedented in Germany, embarked on a dual strategy of birth prevention and birth promotion. The family was to become not only a site of intimacy and emotional regeneration but also a modern unit of production, with healthy children as its products and motherhood as a task to be performed efficiently and rationally, under medical supervision, by those women deemed qualified to do it.[105] This immense project took the policing of the private sphere – for instance, behaviour relating to health and childcare, and sexual behaviour – to new lengths. One instance of this was the policing of homosexuals: as Claudia Schoppmann shows, while lesbians were not criminalized, they were, either as potential mothers to be "reclaimed" for reproductive duties, or as dangerous "asocials" to be removed from society, still targets for harassment and intimidation by the public authorities.

While the Nazi regime stressed motherhood as the highest form of "national service" to be performed by healthy, "Aryan" women, women were expected to perform a multiplicity of functions apart from the crucial task of biological reproduction. The regime sought to elicit the maximum level of performance out of every individual in the Third Reich regardless of sex or traditional "role": thus it not only allowed, but facilitated and promoted women's employment where it was deemed necessary in the economy and the state administration. As the economy boomed, ever-increasing numbers of women were drawn into manual and white-collar employment in industry and public bureaucracy and, particularly during the Second World War, into a proliferation of public activities, duties and "campaigns".[106]

Even where women were not mobilized for work outside the home, the regime sought ways to mobilize women within the home for the national effort, persuading housewives that their private world was indissolubly linked to the larger national destiny. As Kate Lacey shows in Chapter 9, radio propaganda to housewives functioned as a vehicle of the Nazi politicization and penetration of the private sphere. As a public medium that reached into private homes, the radio was potentially a powerful tool for bridging the divide between the public and private and persuading the housewife to respond to the regime's demands. Radio propaganda "from woman to woman" exalted the family and flattered the housewife by stressing her private power as a consumer to affect the life of the nation. It also had a larger, hidden agenda: by equating a woman's personal devotion to home and family with her dutiful performance of a national task, it sought to bind more closely to the regime those women whose lives were least susceptible to direct control by Nazi organizations and Nazified institutions. At the same time, Lacey argues, the very existence of women's programmes – with female presenters – served more general functions in relation to the listening public: such programmes anchored a female presence in a crucial public medium in such a way as to appease those who might resent women's exclusion from positions of real power. They also maintained the illusion of a cosy normality, which, Lacey argues, may have assisted the stabilization of the regime. This is a line of argument that recalls that of Claudia Koonz, who has suggested that without the illusion of normality which women who supported the regime helped to create (by promoting "traditional family life" and cultivating a "womanly" space within the public sphere), the regime would have less easily planned and carried out its policies of war and genocide.[107]

Despite the upheaval of wartime and the disruption to traditional gender roles that the immediate aftermath of war brought about, "normal" gender hierarchies and spheres of action were restored with remarkable speed in post-war Germany. Such a phenomenon was not unique to Germany, but Robert Moeller, who has analyzed this process in depth for the Western occupation zones and for the later Federal Republic, has suggested, "the salience of gender as a political category in postwar West Germany was particularly striking".[108] The re-affirmation of a clear distinction between the public and private spheres, together with the restoration of the male breadwinner/ female homemaker as the "natural" family norm, served to mark the

restabilization of a society traumatized by defeat and its consequences: the family seemed to represent one German institution that
had not been discredited by the National Socialist era. At the same
time, policies to protect motherhood and the family demonstrated the
"normality" of West German society compared to the alleged abnor-
mality of women's emancipation in the Soviet zone and later German
Democratic Republic.[109] While women's political and legal equality
were declared to be an important dimension of restoring democracy,
and embodied in the Basic Law of 1949, "family life", under the protection of the state – within which woman's role was still assumed to
be that of homemaker – was still considered by the mainstream West
German parties, above all by the CDU, as an essential ingredient of
freedom and democracy in the new Germany.[110] This was despite the
fact that the sex structure of the population would ensure that large
numbers of women in West Germany would remain single and childless, and that many mothers would not live in traditional families.[111]

Although less research has so far been undertaken on gender relations in the Soviet zone and later GDR than on West Germany, similar
trends towards a restoration of traditional home life following the
"exceptional" circumstances of wartime and post-war rubble-clearing
have been identified – albeit within a very different political context.[112]

Looking at both East and West, and focusing on the topic of household consumption, Katherine Pence explores in Chapter 10 the political and economic forces that shaped the private sphere of the
household in post-war Germany. Once again, German housewives
became the target of appeals to support the nation or the political
system in their capacity as rational consumers. The private household
and the housewife were also seen, as Pence shows, as having a major
economic role to play. Once the economy in the Western and the
Soviet zones had moved beyond the initial stages of basic recovery, in
particular after the currency reform of 1948, the role of the consumer
moved into the foreground of concern. Whether operating in the
social market economy or in the nascent planned economy of the
East, whether occupied full-time in the home or bearing the double
burden of waged work and housework, the housewife had to become
an educated and interested purchaser and processor of goods. Pence
argues that consumption as a marker of material welfare was an important element in the self-definition of the rival political cultures

emerging in West and East Germany. In shaping ideas about consumption, an important role was played by the notion of a private sphere of freedom and individual choice, of pleasure and recreation, in which women were to hold sway as compensation for their exclusion from power outside the home.

Conclusions

As the above discussion has suggested, an analysis of German history through the lens of gender may offer historians alternative perspectives on the traditional narrative. An examination of the construction and enforcement of gender roles from the sixteenth century to the present suggests a strong element of continuity in ways of speaking about gender and the means through which women and men were urged to fulfil these roles. At the same time, periods of crisis threw gender relations into flux: revolutions and reactions in political and intellectual life brought new ways of conceptualizing biological sexual difference and of carving out spheres of public and private action along the lines of gender.

The contributions to this volume show that gender is a useful conceptual category which, while uncovering the structures and ideologies influencing the position and experience of men and women and the power relations between them, need not conceal or play down the agency of individuals. The project of tracing the evolution of gender norms and gender relations is enlightening precisely because it has to explore the ways in which such models of behaviour were disseminated and accepted, or ignored and subverted, in the everyday lives of women and men.

Notes

1. See the bibliography on English-language works up to 1990: H. Cole, with the assistance of J. Caplan & H. Schissler, *The history of women in Germany from medieval times to the present: bibliography of English-language publications* (Reference guides of the German Historical Institute Washington, DC, no. 3) (Washington, DC: German Historical Institute, 1990).
2. See K. Canning, "Comment" on S. Rose, "Gender history/women's history: is feminist scholarship losing its critical edge?", *Journal of Women's History*

5, 1993, pp. 102–14; G. Bock, "Challenging dichotomies: perspectives on women's history", in *Writing women's history: international perspectives*, K. Offen, R. R. Pierson, J. Rendall (eds) (Bloomington, Indiana & Indianapolis: Indiana University Press, 1991), pp. 1–23; U. Frevert, *"Mann und Weib, und Weib und Mann": Geschlechter-Differenzen in der Moderne* (Munich: C. H. Beck, 1995), pp. 9–10.

3. J. W. Scott, *Gender and the politics of history* (New York: Columbia University Press, 1988), p. 42.

4. Studies of masculinity in German history are still relatively rare, but for some examples see: U. Frevert, *Men of honour* (Cambridge: Polity, 1995); K. Theweleit, *Male fantasies*, vol. 1: *Women, floods, bodies, history*; vol. 2: *Male bodies: psychoanalysing the white terror* (Cambridge: Polity, 1987 (vol. 1); 1989 (vol. 2)); G. Völger & K. von Welck (eds), *Männerbande, Männerbünde: zur Rolle des Mannes im Kulturvergleich*, [2 vols] (Cologne: Rautenstrauth-Joest-Museum, 1990); L. Roper, "Männlichkeit und männliche Ehre", in *Frauengeschichte – Geschlechtergeschichte*, K. Hausen & H. Wunder (eds) (Frankfurt am Main & New York: Campus, 1992), pp. 151–72; L. Roper, "Blood and codpieces: masculinity in the early modern German town", and "Stealing manhood: capitalism and magic in early modern Germany", both in L. Roper, *Oedipus and the devil: witchcraft, sexuality and religion in early modern Europe* (London & New York: Routledge, 1994), pp. 107–24, 125–44; M. E. Wiesner, "Guilds, male-bonding and women's work in early modern Germany", *Gender and History* 1, 1989, pp. 125–37; J. D. Steakley, "Iconography of a scandal: political cartoons and the Eulenburg affair in Wilhelmine Germany", in *Hidden from history: reclaiming the gay and lesbian past*, M. B. Duberman, M. Vicinus, G. Chauncey, jun. (eds) (London: Penguin, 1989), pp. 233–57; J. C. Fout, "Sexual politics in Wilhelmine Germany: the male gender crisis, moral purity, and homophobia", in *Forbidden history: the state, society, and the regulation of sexuality in modern Europe*, J. C. Fout (ed.) (Chicago & London: University of Chicago Press, 1992), pp. 259–92. As this book goes to press, two new titles have been announced: T. Kühne (ed.), *Männergeschichte – Geschlechtergeschichte: Männlichkeit im Wandel der Moderne* (Frankfurt am Main: Campus, 1996) and A.-C. Trepp, *Sanfte Männlichkeit und selbständige Weiblichkeit: Frauen und Männer im Hamburger Bürgertum zwischen 1770 und 1840* (Göttingen: Vandenhoeck & Ruprecht, 1996).

5. Eve Rosenhaft offers some suggestions in her essay, "Women, gender, and the limits of political history in the age of 'mass' politics", in *Elections, mass politics, and social change in modern Germany: new perspectives*, L. E. Jones & J. Retallack (eds) (Cambridge: Cambridge University Press, 1992), pp. 149–73.

6. M. E. Wiesner, *Women and gender in early modern Europe* (Cambridge: Cambridge University Press, 1993), p. 252.

7. *Ibid.*, p. 252.

8. See L. Roper, "Will and honor: sex, words and power in Augsburg criminal trials", *Radical History Review* 43, 1989, pp. 45–71.

9. C. Pateman, *The sexual contract* (Cambridge: Polity, 1994), p. 20.

10. J. M. Bennett, "Feminism and history", *Gender and History* 1, 1989, pp. 251–72. See also S. Walby, "From private to public patriarchy: the periodization of British history", *Women's Studies International Forum* 13, 1990, pp. 91–104.

11. A. Clark, "Comment", *Journal of Women's History* 5, 1993, pp. 115–20.

12. Roper, "Will and honor", p. 45.

13. The term patriarchy has come under sustained attack from many feminist historians, largely owing to the timeless and ahistorical nature of the concept. See Pateman, *The sexual contract*, esp. ch. 2.

14. Roper, "Will and honor", p. 47.

15. See C. Weedon, *Feminist practice and poststructuralist theory* (Oxford: Basil Blackwell, 1987), ch. 5.

16. Canning, "Comment", p. 105.

17. M. Foucault, *Discipline and punish: the birth of the prison* (Harmondsworth: Penguin, 1977); M. Foucault, *The history of sexuality: an introduction* (Harmondsworth: Penguin, 1978).

18. Foucault cited in L. McNay, *Foucault and feminism: power, gender and the self* (Cambridge: Polity, 1992), p. 39.

19. Scott, *Gender and the politics of history*, p. 6.

20. See Canning, "Comment". For a spirited critique of poststructuralist theory, see J. Hoff, "Gender as a postmodern category of paralysis", *Women's History Review* 3(2), 1994, pp. 149–68.

21. Clark, "Comment", p. 115.

22. *Ibid.* For Clark's extended analysis see A. Clark, *The struggle for the breeches: gender and the making of the British working class* (London: Rivers Oram Press, 1995).

23. Roper, *Oedipus and the devil*, pp. 37–9.

24. Wiesner, "Guilds, male-bonding and women's work".

25. See M. E. Wiesner, "Gender and the worlds of work", in *Germany: a new social and economic history,* vol. 1: *1450–1630*, B. Scribner (ed.) (London: Arnold, 1996), pp. 209–32; M. E. Wiesner, *Working women in Renaissance Germany* (New Brunswick, NJ: Rutgers University Press, 1986).

26. R. Scribner, "Reformation, Karneval and the world turned upside-down", *Social History* 3, 1978, pp. 303–29.

27. See S. D. Amussen, *An ordered society: gender and class in early modern England* (Oxford & New York: Basil Blackwell, 1988). On the relationship between gender, sex and reputation see L. Gowing, "Gender and the language of insult in early modern London", *History Workshop Journal* 35, 1993, pp. 1–21, and "Language, power and the law: women's slander litigation in early modern London", in *Women, crime and the courts in early modern England*, J. Kermode & G. Walker (eds) (London: UCL Press, 1994), pp. 26–47.

28. J. Wiltenburg, *Disorderly women and female power in the street literature of early modern England and Germany* (Charlottesville, Va. & London: University Press of Virginia, 1992), pp. 106–7.

29. *Ibid.*, p. 107.

30. For this point in relation to inter-war France, see M. L. Roberts, *Civilization without sexes: reconstructing gender in postwar France, 1917–1927* (Chicago: University of Chicago Press, 1994).

31. See L. Abrams, "Concubinage, cohabitation and the law: class and gender relations in nineteenth-century Germany", *Gender and History* 5, 1993, pp. 81–100; J. Schlumbohm, "'Wilde Ehen': Zusammenleben angesichts kirchlicher Sanktionen und staatlicher Sittenpolizei (Osnabrücker Land, c. 1790–1870)", in *Familie und Familienlosigkeit: Fallstudien aus Niedersachsen und Bremen vom 15. bis 20. Jahrhundert*, J. Schlumbohm (ed.) (Hanover: Hahnsche Buchhandlung, 1993), pp. 63–80.

32. On the gendering of the economic sphere see, for example, U. Nienhaus, *Vater Staat und seine Gehilfinnen: Die Politik mit der Frauenarbeit bei der deutschen Post (1864–1945)* (Frankfurt am Main: Campus, 1995); S. Schmitt, *Der Arbeiterinnenschutz im deutschen Kaiserreich: Zur Konstruktion der schutzbedürftigen Arbeiterin* (Stuttgart: J. B. Metzler, 1995). For a more discursive analysis see K. Canning, "Gender and the politics of class formation: rethinking German labor history", *American Historical Review* 97, 1992, pp. 736–68.

33. See R. J. Bessel, *Germany after the First World War* (Oxford: Clarendon Press, 1993), pp. 160–65.

34. Roper, *Oedipus and the devil*, p. 37.

35. Cf. A. Fletcher, *Gender, sex and subordination in England, 1500–1800* (New Haven, Connecticut & London: Yale University Press, 1995), which charts similar shifts in gender relations for England in the early modern period.

36. K. Canning, "Feminist history after the linguistic turn: historicizing discourse and experience", *Signs* 19, 1994, pp. 368–404, here pp. 385–6.

37. This is the approach adopted by Lyndal Roper in *Oedipus and the devil*: see p. 3.

38. Staatsarchiv Hamburg, Niedergericht 477: 22 November 1830.

39. T. Laqueur, *Making sex: body and gender from the Greeks to Freud* (Cambridge, Mass.: Harvard University Press, 1990), p. 135.

40. *Ibid.*, p. 134.

41. A. Rowlands, "To wear a virgin's wreath: gender and problems of conformity in early modern Germany", *European Review of History – Revue européenne d'Histoire* 1, 1994, pp. 227–32, here p. 232.

42. See L. Jordanova, *Sexual visions: images of gender in science and medicine between the eighteenth and the twentieth centuries* (London: Harvester Wheatsheaf, 1989), esp. ch. 3; and Fletcher, *Gender, sex and subordination*.

43. B. Duden, *The woman beneath the skin: a doctor's patients in eighteenth century Germany* (London & Cambridge, Mass.: Harvard University

Press, 1991), p. 6. The former approach which denies the historicity of bodily experience is exemplified by E. Shorter, *A history of women's bodies* (London: Penguin, 1984).

44. Laqueur, *Making sex*, ch. 3.

45. *Ibid.*, p. 25.

46. Rowlands, "To wear a virgin's wreath", p. 229. See also J. F. Harrington, *Reordering marriage and society in Reformation Germany* (Cambridge: Cambridge University Press, 1995) on the wearing of symbolic wreaths, masks and so on as punishment for adultery.

47. See L. Roper, "Exorcism and the theology of the body", in *Oedipus and the devil*, pp. 171–98.

48. See Wiesner, *Women and gender in early modern Europe*, pp. 41–81.

49. See Duden, *Woman beneath the skin*, pp. 7–26.

50. See R. J. Evans, "Gender and capital punishment in Germany from the 17th to the 19th century", paper presented at the German History Society Conference, Lancaster, UK, 1994. Also O. Ulbricht, "Infanticide in eighteenth-century Germany", in *The German underworld: deviants and outcasts in German history*, R. J. Evans (ed.) (London: Routledge, 1988), pp. 108–40; R. Schulte, *The village in court: arson, infanticide, and poaching in the court records of Upper Bavaria* (Cambridge: Cambridge University Press, 1994).

51. A. Rowlands, "'Inhuman and unnatural': infanticidal women in sixteenth- and seventeenth-century Germany", paper presented at Gender and Crime in Britain and Europe Conference, Roehampton Institute, London, 1995.

52. The process is described by Foucault as the "hysterization" of women's bodies. Foucault, *The history of sexuality*, p. 104.

53. Laqueur, *Making sex*, p. 150.

54. See O. Moscucci, *The science of woman: gynaecology and gender in England 1800–1929* (Cambridge: Cambridge University Press, 1990).

55. For a feminist critique of Foucault's notion of the body as a construction of discursive practice that arguably renders the body passive, see McNay, *Foucault and feminism*.

56. Duden, *Woman beneath the skin*, ch. 4.

57. See Moscucci, *The science of woman*; S. Jeffreys (ed.), *The sexuality debates* (London: Routledge & Kegan Paul, 1987).

58. See H. Wunder, "Überlegungen zum Wandel der Geschlechterbeziehungen im 15. und 16. Jahrhundert aus sozialgeschichtlicher Sicht", in *Wandel der Geschlechterbeziehungen zu Beginn der Neuzeit*, H. Wunder & C. Vanja (eds) (Frankfurt am Main: Suhrkamp, 1991), pp. 12–26.

59. See Wunder, "Überlegungen zum Wandel der Geschlechterbeziehungen"; Harrington, *Reordering marriage*, ch. 5; L. Roper, *The holy household: women and morals in Reformation Augsburg* (Oxford: Clarendon Press, 1989).

60. See C. Smart, "Disruptive bodies and unruly sex: the regulation of reproduction and sexuality in the nineteenth century", in *Regulating woman-*

hood: historical essays on marriage, motherhood and sexuality, C. Smart (ed.) (London: Routledge, 1992), pp. 7–32.

61. Abrams, "Concubinage, cohabitation and the law".
62. See L. Abrams, "Martyrs or matriarchs? Working-class women's experience of marriage in Germany before the First World War", Women's History Review 1, 1992, pp. 357–76.
63. This is argued in Foucault's Discipline and punish and The history of sexuality.
64. C. Usborne, The politics of the body in Weimar Germany: women's reproductive rights and duties (London: Macmillan and Ann Arbor, Mich.: University of Michigan Press, 1992); A. Grossmann, "The new woman and the rationalisation of sexuality in Weimar Germany", in Powers of desire: the politics of sexuality, A. Snitow, C. Stansell, S. Thompson (eds) (New York: Monthly Review Press, 1983), pp. 153–76. See also Canning, "Feminist history after the linguistic turn".
65. Usborne, The politics of the body.
66. See G. Bock, "Racism and sexism in Nazi Germany: motherhood, compulsory sterilisation and the state", Signs 8, 1983, pp. 400–21.
67. See A. Tröger, "German women's memories of World War II", in Behind the lines: gender and the two world wars, M. Higonnet et al. (eds) (New Haven, Connecticut & London: Yale University Press, 1987), pp. 285–99, esp. p. 293.
68. See A. Grossmann, Reforming sex: the German movement for birth control and abortion reform, 1920–1950 (New York & Oxford: Oxford University Press, 1995), ch. 8.
69. See Note 4 above for references on the history of masculinity in Germany. On masculinity in Britain and America, see for example J. A. Mangan & J. Walvin (eds), Manliness and morality: middle-class masculinity in Britain and America 1800–1940 (Manchester: Manchester University Press, 1987); and M. Roper & J. Tosh (eds), Manful assertions: masculinity in Britain since 1800 (London: Routledge, 1991).
70. "Preface", in Shifting the boundaries: transformation of the languages of public and private in the eighteenth century, D. Castiglione & L. Sharpe (eds) (Exeter: Exeter University Press, 1995), p. ix.
71. J. B. Elshtain, Public man, private woman: women in social and political thought (Oxford: Martin Robertson, 1981), pp. 19–54.
72. See the contributions to S. I. Benn & G. F. Gaus (eds), Public and private in social life (London: Croom Helm, 1983), esp. Benn & Gaus, "The liberal conception of the public and the private", pp. 31–65.
73. J. Brewer, "This, that and the other: public, social and private in the seventeenth and eighteenth centuries", in Shifting the boundaries, Castiglione & Sharpe (eds), pp. 1–21, here p. 9.
74. See L. Davidoff, "Regarding some old 'husbands' tales': public and private in feminist history", in L. Davidoff, Worlds between: historical perspectives on gender and class (Cambridge: Polity, 1995), pp. 227–76.

75. Elshtain, *Public man, private woman*; C. Pateman, "Feminist critiques of the public/private dichotomy", in *Public and private in social life*, Benn & Gaus (eds), pp. 281–303; L. Davidoff, "'Alte Hüte': Öffentlichkeit und Privatheit in der feministischen Geschichtsschreibung", *L'Homme: Zeitschrift für Feministische Geschichtswissenschaft* 4(2), 1993, pp. 7–36.

76. For an account of the historiography, see L. K. Kerber, "Separate spheres, female worlds, woman's place: the rhetoric of women's history", *Journal of American History* 75(1), 1988, pp. 9–39.

77. On the late-eighteenth-century debates on gender relations and the nature and rights of woman, see C. Honegger, *Die Ordnung der Geschlechter: Die Wissenschaften vom Menschen und das Weib, 1750–1850*, 2nd edn (Frankfurt am Main & New York: Campus, 1991), pp. 46–102. On the contradictions of Enlightenment thought on gender questions, see E. Rosenhaft, "Aufklärung und Geschlecht: Bürgerlichkeit, Weiblichkeit, Subjektivität", in *Rationale Beziehungen? Geschlechterverhältnisse im Rationalisierungsprozeß*, D. Reese et al. (eds) (Frankfurt am Main: Suhrkamp, 1993), pp. 19–37.

78. On female friendships, see for example C. Smith-Rosenberg, "The female world of love and ritual: relations between women in nineteenth-century America", in C. Smith-Rosenberg, *Disorderly conduct: visions of gender in Victorian America* (New York & Oxford: Oxford University Press, 1986), pp. 53–76.

79. Kerber, "Separate spheres", esp. pp. 27–8; A. Vickery, "Golden age to separate spheres? A review of the categories and chronology of English women's history", *Historical Journal* 36, 1993, pp. 383–414.

80. Kerber, "Separate spheres", p. 39; Vickery, "Golden age", pp. 411–12.

81. Rosenhaft, "Women, gender, and the limits of political history", p. 150.

82. On the campaign for women's political enfranchisement and on the granting of the suffrage following the November Revolution of 1918, see R. J. Evans, *The feminist movement in Germany 1894–1933* (London: Sage, 1976); B. Greven-Aschoff, *Die bürgerliche Frauenbewegung in Deutschland 1894–1933* (Göttingen: Vandenhoeck & Ruprecht, 1981); B. Clemens, *"Menschenrechte haben kein Geschlecht!": Zum Politikverständnis der bürgerlichen Frauenbewegung* (Pfaffenweiler: Centaurus, 1988).

83. U. Vogel, "Property rights and the status of women in Germany and England", in *Bourgeois society in nineteenth-century Europe*, J. Kocka & A. Mitchell (eds) (Oxford & Providence: Berg, 1993), pp. 241–69.

84. C. M. Prelinger, "Prelude to consciousness: Amalie Sieveking and the Female Association for the Care of the Poor and the Sick", in *German women in the nineteenth century: a social history*, J. C. Fout (ed.) (New York & London: Holmes & Meier, 1984), pp. 118–32; E. Meyer-Renschhausen, *Weibliche Kultur und soziale Arbeit: Eine Geschichte der Frauenbewegung am Beispiel Bremens 1810–1927* (Cologne & Vienna: Böhlau, 1989), pp. 44–56; A. Taylor Allen, *Feminism and motherhood in Germany, 1800–1914* (New Brunswick, NJ: Rutgers University Press, 1991).

85. Rosenhaft, "Women, gender, and the limits of political history", p. 150.
86. U. Frevert (ed.), *Bürgerinnen und Bürger: Geschlechterverhältnisse im 19. Jahrhundert* (Göttingen: Vandenhoeck & Ruprecht, 1988); Vogel, "Property rights and the status of women"; R. J. Evans, "Family and class in the Hamburg grand bourgeoisie 1815–1914", in *The German bourgeoisie: essays on the social history of the German middle class from the late eighteenth to the early twentieth century*, R. J. Evans & D. Blackbourn (eds) (London & New York: Routledge, 1991), pp. 115–39.
87. On the debate over rights for women in late-eighteenth-century Germany and on Theodor Gottlieb von Hippel as an advocate of women's rights, see Honegger, *Die Ordnung der Geschlechter*, pp. 46–93; on von Hippel, see also L. Sharpe, "Theodor Gottlieb von Hippel: argumentative strategies in the debate on the rights of women", in *Shifting the boundaries*, Castiglione & Sharpe (eds), pp. 89–104.
88. K. Hausen, "Die Polarisierung der 'Geschlechtscharaktere': eine Spiegelung der Dissoziation von Erwerbs- und Familienleben", in *Sozialgeschichte der Familie in der Neuzeit Europas: Neue Forschungen*, W. Conze (ed.) (Stuttgart: Klett-Cotta, 1976), pp. 363–93; English version: K. Hausen, "Family and role-division: the polarisation of sexual stereotypes in the nineteenth century – an aspect of the dissociation of work and family life", in *The German family: essays on the social history of the family in nineteenth- and twentieth-century Germany*, R. J. Evans & W. R. Lee (eds) (London: Croom Helm, 1981); U. Frevert, "Geschlecht – männlich/weiblich: zur Geschichte der Begriffe (1730–1990)", in Frevert, *"Mann und Weib, und Weib und Mann"*, pp. 13–60.
89. J. Kocka, "Vorwort", in *Bürgerinnen und Bürger*, Frevert (ed.), pp. 7–9; D. Herzog, "Liberalism, religious dissent, and women's rights: Louise Dittmar's writings from the 1840s", in *In search of a liberal Germany: studies in the history of German liberalism from 1789 to the present*, K. H. Jarausch & L. E. Jones (eds) (New York, Oxford, Munich: Berg, 1990), pp. 55–85.
90. K. Hausen, "Öffentlichkeit und Privatheit, gesellschaftspolitische Konstruktionen und die Geschichte der Geschlechterbeziehungen", in *Frauengeschichte – Geschlechtergeschichte*, Hausen & Wunder (eds), pp. 81–8.
91. C. Lipp, "Das Private im Öffentlichen: Geschlechterbeziehungen im symbolischen Diskurs der Revolution 1848–49", in *Frauengeschichte – Geschlechtergeschichte*, Hausen & Wunder (eds), pp. 99–116.
92. On the Prussian Civil Code of 1794 and its implications for women and gender relations, see U. Gerhard, *Verhältnisse und Verhinderungen: Frauenarbeit, Familie und Rechte der Frauen im 19. Jahrhundert. Mit Dokumenten* (Frankfurt am Main: Suhrkamp, 1981), pp. 154–89, and Vogel, "Property rights and the status of women", pp. 245–50; on the *Code civil* (not specifically in its application to Germany), see Vogel, "The fear of public disorder: marriage between revolution and reaction", in *Shifting the boundaries*, Castiglione & Sharpe (eds), pp. 71–88; on divorce law in nineteenth-

century Germany, see D. Blasius, "Bürgerliche Rechtsgleichheit und die Ungleichheit der Geschlechter", in *Bürgerinnen und Bürger*, Frevert (ed.), pp. 67–84, esp. pp. 75–81.

93. On the history of German feminism in the nineteenth and early twentieth centuries, see Evans, *The feminist movement in Germany*; Greven-Aschoff, *Die bürgerliche Frauenbewegung in Deutschland*; Meyer-Renschhausen, *Weibliche Kultur und soziale Arbeit*; Allen, *Feminism and motherhood*; Clemens, *"Menschenrechte haben kein Geschlecht!"*; H.-U. Bussemer, *Frauenemanzipation und Bildungsbürgertum: Sozialgeschichte der Frauenbewegung in der Reichsgründungszeit* (Weinheim & Basel: Beltz, 1985); I. Stoehr, *Emanzipation zum Staat? Der Allgemeine Deutsche Frauenverein – Deutscher Staatsbürgerinnenverband (1893–1933)* (Pfaffenweiler: Centaurus, 1990).

94. For a sympathetic exploration of this thinking and its consequences, see Allen, *Feminism and motherhood*.

95. On the campaigns and practical projects of the nineteenth- and twentieth-century German women's movement, see Evans, *The feminist movement in Germany*; Meyer-Renschhausen, *Weibliche Kultur und soziale Arbeit*; Stoehr, *Emanzipation zum Staat?*; I. Stoehr, "Housework and motherhood: debates and policies in the women's movement in Imperial Germany and the Weimar Republic", in *Maternity and gender policies: women and the rise of the European welfare states, 1880s–1950s*, G. Bock & P. Thane (eds) (London & New York: Routledge, 1991), pp. 213–32; Allen, *Feminism and motherhood* (esp. on kindergartens); J. C. Albisetti, *Schooling German girls and women: secondary and higher education in the nineteenth century* (Princeton, NJ: Princeton University Press, 1988); C. Sachße, "Social mothers: the bourgeois women's movement and German welfare-state formation, 1890–1929", in *Mothers of a new world: maternalist politics and the origins of welfare states*, S. Koven & S. Michel (eds) (New York & London: Routledge, 1993), pp. 136–58; C. Sachße, *Mütterlichkeit als Beruf: Sozialarbeit, Sozialreform und Frauenbewegung, 1871–1929* (Frankfurt am Main: Suhrkamp, 1986); Y. S. Hong, "Femininity as a vocation: gender and class conflict in the professionalization of German social work", in *German professions, 1800–1950*, G. Cocks & K. H. Jarausch (eds) (New York & Oxford: Oxford University Press, 1990), pp. 232–51; G. Czarnowski & E. Meyer-Renschhausen, "Geschlechterdualismen in der Wohlfahrtspflege: 'Soziale Mütterlichkeit' zwischen Professionalisierung und Medikalisierung, Deutschland 1890–1930", *L'Homme: Zeitschrift für Feministische Geschichtswissenschaft* 5(2), 1994, pp. 121–40.

96. See K. Offen, "Defining feminism: a comparative historical approach", *Signs* 14, 1988, pp. 119–57.

97. On gender relations generally during the First World War, see Higonnet et al. (eds). *Behind the lines*. On Germany, see the literature cited in Regina Schulte's contribution (Ch. 6).

98. Bessel, *Germany after the First World War*, p. 10.

99. On pronatalism, see C. Usborne, "'Pregnancy is the woman's active service': pronatalism in Germany during the First World War", in *The upheaval of war: family, work and welfare in Europe, 1914–1918*, R. Wall & J. Winter (eds) (Cambridge: Cambridge University Press, 1988), pp. 192–236. On Protestant women's organizations during wartime, see U. Baumann, *Protestantismus und Frauenemanzipation in Deutschland 1850 bis 1920* (Frankfurt am Main & New York: Campus, 1992), pp. 229–44. On the Bund Deutscher Frauenvereine during the war, see Evans, *The feminist movement in Germany*, ch. 7.

100. Quoted by Ute Frevert, *Women in German history*, p. 208.

101. On women in Weimar politics, see H. Boak, "Women in Weimar Germany: the Frauenfrage and the female vote", in *Social change and political development in Weimar Germany*, R. Bessel & E. J. Feuchtwanger (eds) (London: Croom Helm, 1981), pp. 155–73; J. Stephenson, *Women in Nazi society* (London: Croom Helm, 1975), p. 16; R. Bridenthal & C. Koonz, "Beyond Kinder, Küche, Kirche: Weimar women in politics and work", in *When biology became destiny: women in Weimar and Nazi Germany*, R. Bridenthal, A. Grossmann, M. Kaplan (eds) (New York: Monthly Review Press, 1984), pp. 33–65, esp. pp. 35–44.

102. On Nazi women's organizations, see J. Stephenson, *The Nazi organisation of women* (London: Croom Helm, 1981); C. Koonz, *Mothers in the fatherland: women, the family and Nazi politics* (London: Jonathan Cape, 1987).

103. E. Rosenhaft, "Women in modern Germany", in *Modern Germany reconsidered 1870–1945*, G. Martel (ed.) (London: Routledge, 1992), pp. 140–58, here p. 146.

104. Quoted in L. Crips, "Modeschöpfung und Frauenbild am Beispiel von zwei nationalsozialistischen Zeitschriften: Deutsche Mutter versus Dame von Welt", in *Frauen und Faschismus in Europa: Der faschistische Körper*, L. Siegele-Wenschkewitz & G. Stuchlik (eds) (Pfaffenweiler: Centaurus, 1990), pp. 228–35, here p. 229.

105. G. Bock, *Zwangssterilisation im Nationalsozialismus: Studien zur Rassenpolitik und Frauenpolitik* (Opladen: Westdeutscher Verlag, 1986); G. Bock, "Antinatalism, maternity and paternity in National Socialist racism", in *Maternity and gender policies*, Bock & Thane (eds), pp. 233–55; G. Czarnowski, *Das kontrollierte Paar: Ehe- und Sexualpolitik im Nationalsozialismus* (Weinheim: Deutscher Studienverlag, 1991).

106. On women's employment in Nazi Germany, see D. Winkler, *Frauenarbeit im Dritten Reich* (Hamburg: Hoffmann & Campe, 1977); T. Mason, "Women in Germany, 1925–1940: family, welfare and work," in *Nazism, Fascism and the working class: essays by Tim Mason*, J. Caplan (ed.) (Cambridge: Cambridge University Press, 1995), pp. 131–211. For a useful discussion of the literature, see Rosenhaft, "Women in modern Germany", pp. 142–6. On women during the Second World War, see Stephenson, *The Nazi organization of women*, ch. 5, and L. J. Rupp, "'I don't call that

Volksgemeinschaft': women, class, and war in Nazi Germany", in *Women, war and revolution*, C. R. Berkin & C. M. Lovett (eds) (New York & London: Holmes & Meier, 1980), pp. 37–53.

107. Koonz, *Mothers in the fatherland*, p. 389.

108. R. G. Moeller, *Protecting motherhood: women and the family in the politics of postwar West Germany* (Berkeley, New York, Los Angeles, London: University of California Press, 1993), p. 2.

109. Moeller, *Protecting motherhood*, p. 6; M. Höhn, "Frau im Haus und Girl im *Spiegel*: discourse on women in the interregnum period of 1945–1949 and the question of German identity", *Central European History* **26**(1), 1993, pp. 57–90, here p. 60.

110. On the Basic Law, see Moeller, *Protecting motherhood*, ch. 2.

111. On the situation of single women, see S. Meyer & E. Schulze, "Von Wirtschaftswunder keine Spur", in *Perlonzeit: Wie die Frauen ihr Wirtschaftswunder erlebten*, A. Delille & A. Grohn (eds) (Berlin: Elefanten Press, 1985), pp. 92–9.

112. I. Merkel, ". . . und Du, Frau an der Werkbank": Die DDR in den 50er Jahren (Berlin: Elefanten Press, 1990), pp. 61–2.

Chapter Two

Gender norms and their enforcement in early modern Germany

Heide Wunder

The way men and women relate to one another is central to social organization and the distribution of power. The notion of "gender" encompasses the differences and similarities between men and women and also comprises norms marking the boundaries between the sexes by defining what is male/masculine and female/feminine. Neither the body itself nor "perceived differences between the sexes",[1] be they physical or mental, determine once and for all which social roles and symbolic representations are ascribed to men and women. Which meaning is attributed to the male or female body, and how "man" and "woman" are defined, depend on the various historical and cultural settings.[2] While the difference male–female is universal, gender norms are not, they can only be identified and analyzed by reference to the specific system of values they affirm and sustain.

I want to explore some of the issues involved in analyzing gender norms and their enforcement by looking at the early modern period. In the first section, the problem of how to identify gender norms is considered, which entails reminding ourselves of some aspects of the political, social and cultural structures of early modern Germany. The second section discusses the production of gender norms during the Reformation, and the third section reflects upon their "enforcement".

Identifying gender norms

Early modern society was structured not only by social, but also by legal and political inequality. Social estates (*Stände*) were ranked in a hierarchy and only those at the top were able to participate in government (*Herrschaft*). The "modern state" as a centralized institution was only in its infancy, and a great number of secular as well as ecclesiastical authorities were competing for power in the Holy Roman Empire. On the other hand secular authority still depended on spiritual authority – administered by the churches – in its attempt to establish an "ordered society".[3] Social order was imagined as having been created by God himself, and therefore was a value central to early modern society.[4] To ensure it, ordinances (*Polizeyordnungen*)[5] were issued in great numbers that regulated many aspects of economic and social life, while church ordinances (*Kirchenordnungen*) prescribed morals. Historians have duly taken account of this social and moral policing in their analysis of the emerging modern state and bourgeois society. But mostly they have not regarded gender norms as worth including in their analysis of norms, just as they have not regarded "gender" as a useful tool for analyzing the distribution and exercise of power. Victims of their own bourgeois ideas about women and the family, historians have interpreted gender relations as part of the private sphere, which to them has no place in the history of society.[6] From this perspective women seem to be part of the natural order firmly established and unchanging since "Adam and Eve",[7] while norms for men are discussed in terms of progress in the history of mankind.

Notwithstanding the impact of the emergence of the modern state and the rise of capitalism, the call for order and the insistence on social stability in early modern society has been interpreted by some historians as being typical for pre-industrial "static" society. It seems, though, that it was precisely the dynamics in early modern society highlighted by urban conflicts since the late Middle Ages and by the German Peasants' War (1524–6) which called for a new system of policing society. Other historians have pointed to religious and cultural changes right at the beginning of the early modern period: humanists developed new standards of humanity, Protestant reformers read Holy Scripture afresh in order to build a truly Christian society, the sciences acquired new knowledge about the world, and artists began to discover the human body as a new subject. Gender and gender relations were explicitly discussed in these attempts at newly envisioning the world and Christian society, but they have been neglected by the modern generalizing approaches of social and political history mentioned above. The abundance of sources debating attitudes to gender and gender relations since the fifteenth century testifies to the centrality of the values incorporated in these relations in structuring society.

Following the invention of printing, learned discourses and controversies were published in quantities previously unknown, making available to us the vast territory of contested ground.[8] The arguments about gender and gender relations put forward in prescriptive literature such as theological treatises and legal texts, conduct books, educational tracts, prayer-books, devotional books and fiction appear to be rather inconsistent or even contradictory: such diversity poses problems of interpretation. This initial impression of confusion can, however, be made sense of if we take account of the different genres of text production, with their specific topics and logics: *Fastnachtspiele* (carnival plays) and funeral sermons differ in the way they treat matrimony; again, education manuals, which were written in order to produce a model woman[9] and a model man, differ from *Ehebücher* (marriage manuals), which were devised to promote matrimony. Different aspects of gender relations were treated in different types of literary genres. It is also essential to remember that early modern rhetoric was still firmly rooted in the classical and scholastic tradition, favouring the dialogue as the form to present one's arguments: in consequence, no single argument can be isolated to verify a viewpoint, but the whole debate has to be analyzed, as is demonstrated by the famous *querelle des femmes*.[10]

Nevertheless, the diversity of views on gender and gender relations is not solely to be explained by the literary aspect of written sources. It also points to conceptual differences, for instance between theological and secular positions, and to changes over time. Therefore we have to consider several discourses going on simultaneously and also how they were interconnected. Fundamental, though, to the understanding of all discourses about gender relations is Christian anthropology. This, however, was not as unequivocal as we have been made to believe: there are two versions of Genesis telling two different stories about the creation of Adam and Eve and thus testifying to the *querelle des femmes* in biblical times. In Genesis 2:23 ff. God created Adam as his image, while Eve was created out of Adam and therefore did not have the same likeness to God as Adam. In Genesis 1:27 Adam and Eve together had been created as God's image and thus both were similar to God and equals to one another in this respect.[11] Which version of Genesis was preferred made a great difference to the construction of gender, as it decided whether women were acknowledged as men's consorts (*Gefährtinnen*) or merely as their assistants (*Gehilfinnen*).[12] The dominant version was Genesis 2, but Genesis 1 could nevertheless not be totally suppressed. It was always at hand, whenever gender relations were debated.

Thus notions of difference and similarity, equality and inequality of the sexes existed side by side. How, then, did gender norms have to be constructed in order to conform with these notions? Hans Sachs (1494–1576), shoemaker and popular poet from Nuremberg, shall be our guide. In one of his famous *Fastnacht* plays he defined "piety" (*frumkeit*) as follows:

> Piety is obedient and humble,
> subservient, fair, true and gracious,
> peaceful, friendly, mild and communal,
> honest, sincere and demure,
> silent, truthful, discreet, undemanding,
> modest, soft tempered, composed,
> moderate and well disciplined at all times.[13]

Whom was Sachs addressing? The modern reader's answer will be: women, of course, because piety is central to the bourgeois notion of femininity, and because all the explanations Sachs used to define *frumkeit* are "passive" virtues that are attributed to women. Yet, on closer examination, it turns out that piety here is spelled out in terms of civic virtues (*Bürgertugenden*),[14] and that Sachs was addressing a male urban public in Nuremberg during the Reformation period. Lyndal Roper has shown for Augsburg how anxious magistrates were to civilize urban men, both married and unmarried,[15] and there are many more examples demonstrating that savage and cruel behaviour by men was not the exception but the rule.

In sixteenth-century Germany, piety (*frumkeit*) did not belong amongst those virtues particular to the female sex alone. It was a complex pattern of virtues, secular as well as spiritual, shared by men and women.[16] Yet it was gendered at the same time: it acquired a specific meaning when applied to men or women, as can be shown by one aspect of *frumkeit*: obedience. Obedience was the wife's duty towards her husband, but it also characterized the relationship between men as citizens and magistrates as city fathers. Thus, men as citizens played the female role, while as heads of their household (*Hausvater*) they played the male role. Nevertheless, although dependence was identified as female and independence as male, women and men can be found holding both positions.

Obviously, "obedience" was a general value in early modern society. It was prescribed for children in their relationship with parents and elders, and as a gender norm for women in general, while for men it was demanded in their relationship with public authorities. As the expression of loyalty, obedience figured as a cardinal virtue, because it legitimized every authority, be it in the household,[17] in the community or in the larger polity. It guaranteed social coherence, which in early modern society could not yet be achieved by transpersonal means. Obedience, then, has to be evaluated as part of a system of reciprocal obligations connecting social spheres.

The modern dichotomy of public and private as separate spheres for men and women according to their gender characteristics cannot be found in early modern society.[18] There was no catalogue of virtues and their corresponding norms specific either to men or to women. Instead "man" and "woman" were defined in relation to one another in terms of comparative differences as "stronger" and "weaker".[19] This was an asymmetrical relationship that placed men at the top of the social and political hierarchy. But this hierarchy was not based on dichotomies and not constructed as binary:[20] it depended on the delicate balance of mutual obligations and reciprocity. Therefore, I suggest, gender norms affirming social inequality instead of spiritual similarity had to be erected and enforced.

The production of gender norms during the Reformation

The hypothesis that new gender norms were created in the early modern period as compared to the Middle Ages is based on assumptions about the impact of Protestantism, which was intimately interwoven with the emergence of the modern state.[21] At first sight, though, Reformation disputes and juridical controversies do not seem to offer anything new. Theologians continued to subordinate women in general to men in general, basing their argument on Genesis 2. Jurists – true to their clerical tradition – did the same when arguing that "female weakness" disqualified women from being the equals of men: being weaker than men they had to be protected, and when they were found guilty of criminal deeds they were not punished as severely as men, as they were not held fully responsible because of their "imbecility" (*Torheit*).[22] But when we look at Protestant moral codes the change in values is obvious. Matrimony, which during the Middle Ages had only been a minor institution as compared with the monastical way of life, was moved right into the centre of the new concept of true Christian life. It was held that living in matrimony, in contrast to an "unnatural" Catholic virginity that violated human nature, was truly "chaste". But, as the relationship of men and women in matrimony was supposed to be the "natural" condition of all adults, as instituted by God himself, it was also the primary source of order in society and the model for godly rule.[23] Thus, gender relations in matrimony based on the subordination of women were of enormous import to a society ordered by inequality because they made social and political hierarchy appear natural and godly.

The political implications of matrimony help to explain why it was so important to establish gender norms that clearly marked the boundaries between men and women and why they were upheld at any price. If society was based on matrimony, all adult members of society had to be either men or women, identifiable as such at first sight by behaviour and dress. The transgression of these limits by changing clothes was punished by death – except during carnival.[24] Public order seemed threatened more by transvestism than by adultery and fornication, which in general were not punished as severely. Even matrimony itself would not be upheld at any price, if it did not function as a model of godly order. Divorce was possible, though only as the *ultima ratio* of a disorderly marriage.[25]

In Protestant territories matrimony was institutionalized as the fundamental order of Christian society, and Catholic territories, despite the continuity of celibate priesthood and monastic institutions, followed their example after the Council of Trent. But who had invented the new concept of matrimony? Was it, as it may seem, the creation of the theologians or the jurists? In fact, the social origins of the concept reach further back in time and can be traced to the guilds. In their efforts during the fifteenth century to limit access to the craft, the guilds had developed a new concept of matrimony as a social strategy. They had made it a condition for all who wanted to be trained in the craft that they be born of legally married parents, and they even had made this condition a point of honour. As craftsmen were among the prominent promoters of the Reformation, it seems natural that their moral concepts found their way into the Protestant programme.[26] Yet the social origins of this dominating model of gender relations are by no means limited to the guilds, which represented the old order in the rapidly changing society of the early modern period. The model was of equal importance to the new learned elites of the emerging modern state. While Italian humanists had debated whether it was better to marry or not,[27] German humanists had already favoured matrimony, which they interpreted as a learned partnership.[28] After Luther had declared monastic life to be contrary to God's commandments, matrimony was debated once again, but this time its focus was on *Priesterehe* (marriage of priests), as the future status of Lutheran clergymen was at stake.[29] Coming from a clerical tradition, the notion of "true chastity" in matrimony surely helped to persuade Lutheran pastors. The Protestant model of matrimony was also adopted by other newcomers to the social system: the learned elites, who also had a clerical background, adjusted it to their situation in order to establish themselves in secular society. For matrimony had since the early Middle Ages been of great importance for freemen and nobles and since the beginning of the late Middle Ages for citizens and peasants as well.

Although they belonged to different social spheres, the crafts and the new learned elites both favoured a normative system known as *das ganze Haus*.[30] It has been interpreted by historians as a description of social reality, but it was in fact a construct interpreting social reality. Besides being a model of asymmetrical reciprocal relations incorporating also "economic virtues" such as orderliness, industry and economizing, this construct generated gender norms in a way specific for early modern society. The notion of estate (*Stand*) structured society as a whole, but also smaller social units, such as the community and the household. At the top of the household were housefather and housemother – "master" and "mistress". Their children were closer to them than male and female servants although these held the same legal status as children in respect to the household's authorities. The differences between these household positions emerge most clearly when we look at the terminology: father[31] and mother for master and mistress, daughter and son for their children, while maid and servant were often termed *Mensch* and *Kerl*.[32] These terms not only indicate the fact that servants were strangers, but also that the norms relating to them differed from those expected of their superiors. Gender meant something different to a mistress than it meant to a maid, and the same was true with master and male servant. While children held the status of future masters and mistresses, the servants were more or less dependent, and it was uncertain whether they could change it to independence – as a rule by marriage. Master and mistress were the ideal picture of manhood and womanhood, while male and female servants did not live in legally legitimized sexual relationships and therefore were regarded as a potential danger to public order. In this respect, too, master and mistress were responsible for their servants: they had to watch over public morals in their house and were even empowered to discipline transgressors.[33] In consequence, gender meant different things depending on the stage in one's life (*Lebensalter*) and in the family cycle, with gender norms varying correspondingly. True manhood and womanhood were only achieved by independent householders, but this status was diminished if one was widowed or lost one's property. The inequality of gender norms within the household, of course, strengthened once again the servants' wish to attain the status of married people.[34]

In spite of this complex system of norms relating to one's status in society, general gender norms existed. They were always referred to when a person had to be proven to be a proper man or a proper woman, for instance in the case of conflicts. They were of great importance when male honour and female honour were at stake,[35] as for example in trials at matrimonial courts[36] or in witch-trials.[37]

These findings about gender norms and their social production in early modern Germany also make visible new aspects of their enforcement. As gender norms were not only promulgated by a disciplining authority (*Obrigkeit*), but also by social groups such as the craftsmen and the new learned elites, current notions about their enforcement have to be reconsidered and re-evaluated.

The enforcement of gender norms

The enforcement of norms in early modern society has been perceived as a process initiated "from above": by "the state" assisted by "the Church".[38] Drawing on concepts of the absolutist state as a quasi-omnipotent agent, notions of institutional enforcement by courts of law, public punishment and imprisonment still dominate. While this concept is based on the dichotomy of the enlightened bureaucratic state versus the mass of ignorant and stubborn subjects, we have been taught by more recent studies in social history to recognize that early modern society was a complex system of social groups[39] that also made use of gender norms and gender relations to distinguish themselves from one another. Thus the learned elites were not just instruments of "the state" or of abstract political aims, but a social formation in their own right and with their own set of values, which were only partly identical with those of the state or other social groups. A striking example for specific gender norms is provided by sixteenth-century prostitutes. Whenever prostitutes got to know that a woman was offering her services secretly, they arranged her coming-out and forced her to enter the whorehouse. Thus prostitutes tried to eliminate cheaper competitors, but at the same time they accomplished the magistrate's concept of order by clearly separating prostitutes from "honest women".[40] Another example with women again figuring as enforcers of gender norms comes from seventeenth-century Hesse.

A scandal came to the attention of the Hessian landgrave's counsellors in Kassel. In the nearby village of Breitenbach women had formally set up a court of law, in order to sanction a couple because the wife had beaten the man and had won the battle. Marital order had been damaged by this turning the world upside down and had to be restored by the women's jurisdiction, the consequence of which was the uncovering of the roof of the couple's house.[41] What seems important here is that among popular forms of enforcing "morality", the marital order was the moral field that had to be defended by married women themselves as a self-regulating system. What was at stake for them? Obviously the delicate balance of power based on asymmetrical reciprocal relationships between husband and wife had been disturbed and therefore had to be restored if married women were to retain their status as mistress of the house.

The "enforcement" of norms thus appears in a new light. There was always some social group that had already identified with these norms and that became an agent in propagating them. Major problems arose when normative standards originating in one social stratum were made obligatory for all orders of Christian society. I suggest that it was this problem that has coloured our perception of the enforcement of gender norms. While in the Middle Ages matrimonial courts had been part of ecclesiastical jurisdiction,[42] matrimony and gender relations for reasons already discussed above now became of fundamental interest to secular Protestant authorities. New criminal courts, to execute the new legislation on gender relations, for instance relating to fornication,[43] were installed by magistrates and territorial lords. Criminal courts of law, secular or ecclesiastical, were indeed fundamental in demonstrating the authorities' will to enforce their rules, and they were equally important in enforcing gender norms as norms, because behaving according to general gender norms was essential to establishing one's standing in the court.[44] This was of eminent importance in trials for fornication. In this respect enforcement functioned less through threatened or actual punishment than through a process in which the accused person anticipated the judge's stereotyped perceptions of gender roles. But, of course, the point of honour touched by spiritual or corporeal penalties performed in public put the persons found guilty under enormous pressure.

The efforts of church and state during the early modern period to establish Christian society with its new standards of gender relations are well documented. Their records have been the main source for studies in the enforcement of gender norms and their differing relevance for women and men. But besides courts of justice and their administrative context there was a great variety of strategies and many agents to enforce norms, as urban magistrates and territorial lords were very well aware of the limits of their own executive apparatus to implement new norms.

One strategy was to incorporate all those communal institutions and their officers – including midwives[45] – which controlled local societies:[46] local community institutions (secular and spiritual), corporations (e.g. guilds) and the household. Yet not all local institutions were included in the bureaucratic system: for instance, youth groups holding an important position in controlling marriage strategies were left out, thus indicating that this field – in contrast to adultery – was of no interest to the authorities.[47]

In addition, great attempts at inculcating norms into the population were made by using popular media of indoctrination and disciplining (*Zucht, Erziehung*), for example books on education[48] and housekeeping[49] or religious instruction in the community. Catechizing was very important for diffusing gender norms, but preaching must have been an even more powerful medium to transfer messages. Preachers such as the famous *Barfüßer-Augustiner* Abraham a Santa Clara (1644–1709), whose sermons were also printed, enjoyed enormous popularity in Graz and Vienna.[50] In Protestant countries, funeral sermons propagated models of Christian life for women and men.[51] A woman in the imperial city of Schwäbisch Hall is reported to have listened to more than 1,000 funeral sermons.[52] And pious Catholics such as Maria Elisabeth Stampferin (1638–1700) from Styria enjoyed having the chance to attend Mass and sermons several times a day during her stay at Leoben.[53]

But not all Christians attended church of their own free will. Attendance was controlled by the church elders and absence was subject to sanctions. What could be enforced, however, was physical but not spiritual attendance, and therefore "church-sleep" was widespread.[54]

Protestant and Catholic clergy were very well aware of this problem. It was the Jesuits who developed a new concept of *Seelsorge* in order to reach people and help them cope with their daily troubles.[55] They also engaged in writing popular literature that was spiritual and entertaining at the same time. Friedrich von Spee, known for his opposition to witch-trials, wrote a *Tugendbuch* (book of virtues) for the pious women of St Ursula's Society at Cologne, which the women also used, I am sure, in their profession as teachers in elementary schools.[56] But the Jesuits were even more down to earth. They invented tales that became part of popular tradition and are known to us as fairy-tales. In *König Drosselbart*, a proud princess arrogantly rejects several suitors, but is subsequently humbled and ends up glad to be married to a prince she had made fun of.[57]

Gender norms were not only propagated by literature, but also by pictures. The broadsheet of the "Christian housemaid" (*christliche Hausmagd*), widespread in Protestant and Catholic regions, illustrated the maid's humble work in analogy to the Passion of Christ.[58] On the one hand the maid's work was elevated above its misery, but on the other hand it stressed submissiveness and obedience as becoming to women. It is not by accident that the Catholic Church also created new saints around 1700, for example Notburga as a saint for female servants. Moreover, it has been pointed out recently that images in popular literature were employed to propagate women's subordination.[59]

Were these efforts successful? From the perspective of our modern experience, we may be too inclined to believe in the effectiveness of "indoctrination" and controlling institutions. But the endless repetitions of gender norms throughout the early modern period make it doubtful whether authorities really were so successful in their attempts at regulating gender relations according to their ideas. What did take place, though, during the eighteenth century was the decriminalization of illegal sexual relationships, pointing to new strategies for guaranteeing social order.

What hindered the general enforcement of gender norms? Lack of local control, competition between conflicting gender norms, and the gap between general norms and the social practice of different social strata can all be identified as obstacles to effective enforcement. Nevertheless, gender norms organized gender relations in a very practical way for every woman and every man, as they were manifested in legal inequality between the sexes. Inequality was spelled out in different rights of possession, political rights and access to work. It privileged men in their various "estates" compared with women of the same age and social group. Women were not without rights, but they were not equals.[60] Well aware of their situation, women tried to change it by contesting the very roots of inequality in the *querelle des femmes*, but only their intellectual faculties were recognized as equal to those of men.[61] Nevertheless, it was precisely in the field of learning that the normativity of gender norms functioned best in separating men and women by excluding women altogether from universities and thereby excluding them also from holding public office in the emerging modern states. In consequence von Hippel (1741–96), impressed by the French Revolution, claimed the right of higher public education for women in order to open up new professional prospects to them, ending their economic dependency. Yet it was not this revolutionary claim for equal opportunities for men and women that was successful, but Rousseau's Sophie and the new concept of *Geschlechtscharakter*.

In modern democratic societies legal and political equality of women and men has been achieved. Yet gender stereotypes are still prevalent in legal practices when conflicting interests of men and women are at stake, and they continue to structure the life careers of men and women. There is still a strong tendency in society to insist on sexual difference as the first instance of inequality. That is what makes it so easy to deal with urgent social problems by relying on familiar distinctions and treating men and women differently.

Notes

1. J. W. Scott, "Gender: a useful category of historical analysis", *American Historical Review* **91**, 1986, p. 1067.
2. C. Eifert et al. (eds), *Was sind Männer, was sind Frauen? Geschlechterkonstruktionen im historischen Wandel* (Frankfurt am Main: Suhrkamp, 1996).
3. S. D. Amussen, *An ordered society: gender and class in early modern England* (Oxford: Basil Blackwell, 1988).
4. C. Fasolt, "Visions of order in the canonists and civilians", in *Handbook of European history 1400–1600: Late Middle Ages, Renaissance and Reformation*, vol. 2: *Visions, programs and outcomes*, T. A. Brady, jun., H. A. Oberman, J. D. Tracy (eds) (Leiden, New York, Cologne: Brill, 1995), pp. 31–59.
5. H. Maier, *Die ältere deutsche Staats- und Verwaltungslehre*, 2nd edn (Munich: C. H. Beck, 1980); M. Stolleis, *Geschichte des öffentlichen Rechts in Deutschland*, vol. 1 (Munich: C. H. Beck, 1988).
6. H.-U. Wehler, *Deutsche Gesellschaftsgeschichte*, vol. 1 (Munich: C. H. Beck, 1987), p. 10.
7. M. E. Müller, "Naturwesen Mann: Zur Dialektik von Herrschaft und Knechtschaft in Ehelehren der Frühen Neuzeit", in *Wandel der Geschlechterbeziehungen zu Beginn der Neuzeit*, H. Wunder & C. Vanja (eds) (Frankfurt am Main: Suhrkamp, 1991), pp. 43–68.
8. M. E. Wiesner, *Women and gender in early modern Europe* (Cambridge: Cambridge University Press, 1993), pp. 9–25.
9. S. W. Hull, *Chaste, silent and obedient: English books for women* (San Marino: Huntington Library, 1982); for Germany: C. N. Moore, "Mein Kindt, nimm diß in acht", *Pietismus und Neuzeit* 6, 1980, pp. 164–85; C. N. Moore, "Die adelige Mutter als Erzieherin: Erbauungsliteratur adeliger Mütter für ihre Kinder", in *Europäische Hofkultur im 16. und 17. Jahrhundert*, A. Buck et al. (eds), vol. 3 (Hamburg: Hauswedell, 1981), pp. 505–10; C. N. Moore, "Mädchenlektüre im 17. Jahrhundert", in *Literatur und Volk im 17. Jahrhundert: Probleme populärer Kultur in Deutschland*, W. Brückner et al. (eds), pt 2 (Wiesbaden: Harrassowitz, 1985), pp. 489–97; C. N. Moore, *The maiden's mirror: reading material for German girls in the sixteenth and seventeenth centuries* (Wiesbaden: Harrassowitz, 1987); C. Ulbrich, "Unartige Weiber: Präsenz und Renitenz von Frauen im frühneuzeitlichen Deutschland", in *Arbeit, Frömmigkeit und Eigensinn*, R. van Dülmen (ed.) (Frankfurt am Main: Fischer, 1990), pp. 13–42.
10. E. Gössmann, "Anthropologie und soziale Stellung der Frau nach Summen

und Sentenzenkommentaren des 13. Jahrhunderts", *Miscellania Medievalia* 12, 1979, pp. 281–97; E. Gössmann (ed.), *Ob die Weyber Menschen seyn, oder nicht?* (Munich: iudicium, 1988).

11. H. Schüngel-Straumann, *Die Frau am Anfang: Eva und die Folgen* (Freiburg im Breisgau: Herder, 1989).

12. L. Schorn-Schütte, " 'Gefährtin' und 'Mitregentin'. Zur Sozialgeschichte der evangelischen Pfarrfrau in der Frühen Neuzeit", in *Wandel der Geschlechterbeziehungen zu Beginn der Neuzeit*, H. Wunder & C. Vanja (eds) (Frankfurt am Main: Suhrkamp, 1991), pp. 109–53.

13. Frümkeit ist ghorsam und demütig,
    Diensthafft, holdtselig, trew und gütig,
    Friedtlich, freundtlich, milt und mitsam,
    Redtlich, auffrichtig und sitsam,
    Stil, warhafft, verschwiegen, genügsam,
    Bescheiden, senfftmütig, gerügsam,
    Messig und züchtig all zeyt.
    Cited in B. Könneker, "Die Ehemoral in den Fastnachtsspielen von Hans Sachs", in *Hans Sachs und Nürnberg*, H. Brunner et al. (eds) (Nuremberg: Verein für Geschichte der Stadt Nürnberg, 1976), pp. 219–44, here p. 235 – I want to thank Lyndal Roper for the translation.

14. P. Münch (ed.), *Ordnung, Fleiß und Sparsamkeit: Texte und Dokumente zur Entstehung der "bürgerlichen Tugenden"* (Munich: dtv, 1984); P. Münch, "Parsimonia summum est vectigal – Sparen ist ein ryche gült: Sparsamkeit als Haus-, Frauen- und Bürgertugend", in *Ethische Perspektiven: "Wandel der Tugenden"*, H.-J. Braun (ed.) (Zurich: Chronos, 1989), pp. 169–87.

15. L. Roper, "Will and honour: sex, words and power in Reformation Augsburg", in L. Roper, *Oedipus and the devil: witchcraft, sexuality and religion in early modern Europe* (London & New York: Routledge, 1994), pp. 53–78; L. Roper, "Blood and codpieces: masculinity in the early modern German town", in Roper, *Oedipus and the devil*, pp. 107–24; L. Roper, "Drinking, whoring and gorging: brutish discipline and the formation of Protestant identity", in Roper, *Oedipus and the devil*, pp. 145–67.

16. H. Wunder, "Von der 'frumkeit' zur Frömmigkeit: Ein Beitrag zur Genese bürgerlicher Weiblichkeit (15.–17. Jahrhundert)", in *Weiblichkeit in geschichtlicher Perspektive: Fallstudien und Reflexionen zu Grundproblemen der historischen Frauenforschung*, U. Becher & J. Rüsen (eds) (Frankfurt am Main: Suhrkamp, 1988), pp. 174–88.

17. M. Weber, *Wirtschaft und Gesellschaft: Grundriss der verstehenden Soziologie*, ed. J. Winckelmann, 5th edn (Tübingen: Mohr, 1976), p. 122; P. Münch (ed.), *Ordnung, Fleiß und Sparsamkeit*, Einleitung.

18. K. Hausen, "Die Polarisierung der 'Geschlechtscharaktere' ", in *Sozialgeschichte der Familie in der Neuzeit Europas: Neue Forschungen*, W. Conze (ed.) (Stuttgart: Klett-Cotta, 1976), pp. 363–93.

19. Also the differences between male and female body were interpreted as gradual. B. Duden, *The woman beneath the skin: a doctor's patients in*

eighteenth century Germany (London & Cambridge, Mass.: Harvard University Press, 1991); T. Laqueur, *Making sex: body and gender from the Greeks to Freud* (Cambridge, Mass.: Harvard University Press, 1990).

20. K. Fietze, *Spiegel der Vernunft: Theorien zum Menschsein der Frau in der Anthropologie des 15. Jahrhunderts* (Paderborn, Munich, Vienna, Zurich: Schöningh, 1991); G. Bock, "Challenging dichotomies: perspectives on women's history", in *Writing women's history: international perspectives*, K. Offen, R. R. Pierson, J. Rendall (eds) (Bloomington, Indiana & Indianapolis: Indiana University Press, 1991), pp. 1–23, here p. 6.

21. N. Z. Davis, " 'Women's history' in transition: the European case", *Feminist Studies* 3, 1975/76, pp. 83–103; L. Roper, *The holy household: women and morals in Reformation Augsburg* (Oxford: Clarendon Press, 1989).

22. E. Koch, *Maior dignitas est in sexu virili: Das weibliche Geschlecht im Normensystem des 16. Jahrhunderts* (Frankfurt am Main: Klostermann, 1991); Wiesner, *Women and gender*, pp. 30–35.

23. Roper, *The holy household*.

24. H. Wunder, "Geschlechtsidentitäten: Frauen und Männer im späten Mittelalter und am Beginn der Neuzeit", in *Frauengeschichte – Geschlechtergeschichte*, K. Hausen & H. Wunder (eds) (Frankfurt am Main & New York: Campus, 1992), pp. 131–6; K. Simon-Muscheid, "Geschlecht, Identität und soziale Rolle: Weiblicher Transvestismus vor Gericht, 15./16. Jahrhundert", in *Weiblich – männlich. Geschlechterverhältnisse in der Schweiz: Rechtsprechung, Diskurs, Praktiken. Féminin – masculin. Rapports sociaux de sexes en Suisse: législation, discours, pratiques*, R. Jaun & B. Studer (eds) (Zurich: Chronos, 1995), pp. 45–57; R. Dekker & L. C. van de Pohl, *The tradition of female transvestism in early modern Europe*, trans. J. Marcure & L. C. van de Pohl (London: Macmillan, 1989); M. Lindemann, "Jungfer Heinrich: Transvestitin, Bigamistin, Lesbierin, Diebin, Mörderin", in *Von Huren und Rabenmüttern: Weibliche Kriminalität in der Frühen Neuzeit*, O. Ulbricht (ed.) (Cologne, Weimar, Vienna: Böhlau, 1995), pp. 259–79.

25. T. M. Safley, *Let no man put asunder. The control of marriage in the German southwest: a comparative study, 1550–1600* (Kirksville, Mo.: Sixteenth Century Journal Publishers, 1984).

26. B. Schuster, *Die freien Frauen: Dirnen und Frauenhäuser im 15. und 16. Jahrhundert* (Frankfurt am Main & New York: Campus, 1995); L. Roper, "Discipline and respectability: prostitution and the Reformation in Augsburg", *History Workshop Journal* 19, 1985, pp. 3–28.

27. C. Jordan, *Renaissance feminism: literary texts and political models* (Ithaca, New York & London: Cornell University Press, 1990); I. Maclean, *The Renaissance notion of woman: a study in the fortunes of scholasticism and medical science in European intellectual life*, repr. (Cambridge: Cambridge University Press, 1985); S. Heißler & P. Blastenbrei, *Frauen in der italienischen Renaissance: Heilige – Kriegerinnen – Opfer* (Pfaffenweiler: Centaurus, 1990).

28. U. Hess, "Lateinischer Dialog und gelehrte Partnerschaft: Frauen als humanistische Leitbilder in Deutschland (1500–1550)", in *Deutsche Literatur von Frauen*, G. Brinker-Gabler (ed.), vol. 1 (Munich: C. H. Beck, 1988), pp. 113–48.

29. B. Moeller, "Die Brautwerbung Martin Bucers für Wolfgang Capito: Zur Sozialgeschichte des evangelischen Pfarrerstandes", in *Philologie als Kulturwissenschaft. Studien zur Literatur und Geschichte des Mittelalters: Festschrift für K. Stackmann zum 65. Geburtstag*, L. Grenzmann (ed.) (Göttingen: Vandenhoeck & Ruprecht, 1987), pp. 306–25.

30. O. Brunner, "Das ganze Haus und die alteuropäische Ökonomik", in O. Brunner, *Neue Wege der Sozialgeschichte* (Göttingen: Vandenhoeck & Ruprecht, 1956), pp. 33–61; C. Opitz, "Neue Wege der Sozialgeschichte? Ein kritischer Blick auf Otto Brunners Konzept des 'ganzen Hauses'", *Geschichte und Gesellschaft* 20, 1994, pp. 88–98; V. Groebner, "Außer Haus: Otto Brunner und die 'alteuropäische Ökonomik'", *Geschichte in Wissenschaft und Unterricht* 46, 1995, pp. 69–80; W. Troßbach, "Das 'ganze Haus' – Basiskategorie für das Verständnis der ländlichen Gesellschaft in der Frühen Neuzeit?", *Blätter für deutsche Landesgeschichte* 129, 1993, pp. 277–314; Schorn-Schütte, " 'Gefährtin' und 'Mitregentin' "; Münch (ed.), *Ordnung, Fleiß und Sparsamkeit*.

31. P. Münch, "Die Obrigkeit im Vaterstand – Zu Definition und Kritik des 'Landesvaters' während der Frühen Neuzeit", *Daphnis* 11, 1982, pp. 16–40.

32. U. Gleixner, *"Das Mensch" und "der Kerl": Die Konstruktion von Geschlecht in Unzuchtsverfahren der Frühen Neuzeit (1700–1760)* (Frankfurt am Main & New York: Campus, 1994).

33. This has mostly been interpreted as a proof of the close relationship between householders and the state, but has also been contested by Amussen, *An ordered society*, p. 47.

34. R. Dürr, *Mägde in der Stadt: Das Beispiel Schwäbisch Hall in der Frühen Neuzeit* (Frankfurt am Main & New York: Campus, 1995); G. Frühsorge (ed.), *Gesinde im 18. Jahrhundert* (Hamburg: Meiner, 1995).

35. K. Schreiner & G. Schwerhoff (eds), *Verletzte Ehre: Ehrkonflikte in Gesellschaften des Mittelalters und der Frühen Neuzeit* (Cologne, Weimar, Vienna: Böhlau, 1995).

36. S. Burghartz, "Ehen vor Gericht: Die Basler Ehegerichtsprotokolle im 16. Jahrhundert", in *Eine Stadt der Frauen*, H. Wunder (ed.) together with S. Burghartz, D. Rippmann, K. Simon-Muscheid (Basel & Frankfurt am Main: Helbing & Lichtenhahn, 1995), pp. 167–214.

37. I. Ahrendt-Schulte, *Weise Frauen – böse Weiber: Die Geschichte der Hexen in der Frühen Neuzeit* (Freiburg, Basel, Vienna: Herder, 1994), pp. 120 ff.; I. Ahrendt-Schulte, "Schadenzauber und Konflikte: Sozialgeschichte von Frauen im Spiegel der Hexenprozesse des 16. Jahrhunderts in der Grafschaft Lippe", in *Wandel der Geschlechterbeziehungen*, Wunder & Vanja (eds), pp. 198–228.

38. G. Oestreich, "Strukturprobleme des europäischen Absolutismus", *Vier-*

teljahresschrift für Sozial- und Wirtschaftsgeschichte 55, 1968, pp. 329–47.

39. M. Dinges, "Frühneuzeitliche Armenfürsorge als Sozialdisziplinierung: Probleme mit einem Konzept", *Geschichte und Gesellschaft* 17, 1991, pp. 5–29.

40. Schuster, *Die freien Frauen: Dirnen und Frauenhäuser*, p. 183.

41. C. Vanja, " 'Verkehrte Welt': Das Weibergericht zu Breitenbach, einem hessischen Dorf des 17. Jahrhunderts", *Journal für Geschichte* 5, 1986, pp. 22–9.

42. R. Weigand, "Zur mittelalterlichen kirchlichen Ehegerichtsbarkeit", *Zeitschrift für Rechtsgeschichte, Kanonistische Abteilung* 67, 1981, pp. 213–47.

43. Roper, "Will and honour".

44. Gleixner, *"Das Mensch" und "der Kerl"*.

45. M. E. Wiesner, "The midwives of south Germany and the public/private dichotomy", in *The art of midwifery: early modern midwives in Europe*, H. Marland (ed.) (London & New York: Routledge, 1993), pp. 77–94; U. Gleixner, "Die 'Gute' und die 'Böse': Hebammen als Amtsfrauen auf dem Land (Altmark/Brandenburg, 18. Jahrhundert)", in *"Weiber", "Menscher", "Frauenzimmer": Frauen in der ländlichen Gesellschaft 1500–1800*, H. Wunder & C. Vanja (eds) (forthcoming).

46. K.-S. Kramer, *Grundriß einer rechtlichen Volkskunde* (Göttingen: Schwartz, 1974); H. Wunder, *Die bäuerliche Gemeinde in Deutschland* (Göttingen: Vandenhoeck & Ruprecht, 1986).

47. H. Wunder, *"Er ist die Sonn', sie ist der Mond": Frauen in der Frühen Neuzeit* (Munich: C. H. Beck, 1992), p. 229.

48. Hull, *Chaste, silent and obedient*.

49. O. Brunner, "Das ganze Haus".

50. U. Herzog, *Geistliche Wohlredenheit: Die katholische Barockpredigt* (Munich: C. H. Beck, 1991); E. Moser-Rath, *Predigtmärlein der Barockzeit* (Berlin: de Gruyter, 1964).

51. R. Lenz (ed.), *Leichenpredigten als Quelle historischer Wissenschaften*, vol. 1 (Cologne & Vienna: Böhlau, 1975), vols 2 and 3 (Marburg a.d. Lahn: Schwarz, 1979 and 1984 respectively); H. Wunder, "Frauen in den Leichenpredigten des 16. und 17. Jahrhunderts", in *Leichenpredigten als Quelle historischer Wissenschaften*, Lenz (ed.), vol. 3, pp. 57–68; I. E. Kloke, "Die gesellschaftliche Situation der Frauen in der Frühen Neuzeit im Spiegel der Leichenpredigten", in *Die Familie als sozialer und historischer Verband: Untersuchungen zum Spätmittelalter und zur Frühen Neuzeit*, P.-J. Schuler (ed.) (Sigmaringen: Thorbecke, 1987), pp. 147–63.

52. G. Wunder, *Die Bürger von Hall: Sozialgeschichte einer Reichsstadt 1216–1802* (Sigmaringen: Thorbecke, 1980), p. 173.

53. G. Hackl (ed.), *Das Hausbüchl der Stampferin, einer geborenen Dellatorin, Radmeisterin zu Vordernberg* (Graz: Leuschner & Lubensky, 1928).

54. Herzog, *Geistliche Wohlredenheit*, pp. 22–8, Exkurs: Predigtschlaf; E. Moser-Rath, *Dem Kirchenvolk die Leviten gelesen . . .* (Stuttgart: Metzler, 1991), pp. 19, 176 ff.

55. B. Duhr, *Geschichte der Jesuiten in den Ländern deutscher Zunge*, [4 vols] (Freiburg im Breisgau, 1907–28).

56. A. Conrad, *Zwischen Kloster und Welt: Ursulinen und Jesuitinnen in der katholischen Reformbewegung des 16./17. Jahrhunderts* (Mainz: Philipp von Zabern, 1991).

57. D.-R. Moser, "Exempel – Paraphrase – Märchen: Zum Gattungswandel christlicher Volkserzählungen im 17. und 18. Jahrhundert am Beispiel einiger 'Kinder- und Hausmärchen' der Brüder Grimm", in *Sozialer und kultureller Wandel in der ländlichen Welt des 18. Jahrhunderts*, E. Hinrichs & G. Wiegelmann (eds) (Wolfenbüttel: Herzog August Bibliothek, 1982), pp. 117–48.

58. A. Spamer, *Bilderbogen von der "Geistlichen Hausmagd": Ein Beitrag zur Geschichte des religiösen Bilderbogens und der Erbauungsliteratur im populären Verlagswesen Mitteleuropas* (Göttingen: Schwartz, 1970); W. Brückner, "Neues zur 'Geistlichen Hausmagd'", *Volkskunst* 2, 1981, pp. 71–78.

59. J. Wiltenburg, *Disorderly women and female power in the street literature of early modern England and Germany* (Charlottesville, Va. & London: University Press of Virginia, 1992).

60. M. E. Wiesner, "Frail, weak and helpless: women's legal position in theory and reality", in *Regnum, religio et ratio: essays presented to R. M. Kingdon*, J. Friedman (ed.) (Kirksville, Mo.: Sixteenth Century Journal Publishers, 1987), pp. 161–9.

61. E. Gössmann (ed.), *Das wohlgelahrte Frauenzimmer* (Munich: iudicium, 1984); E. Gössmann (ed.), *Eva Gottes Meisterwerk* (Munich: iudicium, 1985); E. Gössmann (ed.), *Kennt der Geist kein Geschlecht?* (Munich: iudicium, 1994); L. Steinbrügge, *Das moralische Geschlecht: Theorien und literarische Entwürfe über die Natur der Frau in der französischen Aufklärung* (Weinheim: Beltz, 1987).

Chapter Three

✎

The public body: policing abortion in early modern Germany

Ulinka Rublack

In the spring of 1688, a 27-year-old Constance maidservant named Elsbetha Eggenmann fell sick. Her belly had swollen up "like a sponge", and then contracted again. She was unsure whether this was caused by a pregnancy or by a wandering uterus, but since that year she had had intercourse ten times or so with different men, all using *coitus interruptus*, she decided to send a urine sample to Master Däubler, the former executioner. Examining it, he delivered his opinion that Elsbetha was suffering from dropsy: her stomach was full of "mucus" that needed to be expelled. Däubler's wife also examined the urine. She advised Elsbetha to buy from the pharmacy "three types of ash" that she herself had once successfully used against a "growth". Elsbetha did so, and put the remedy into cloth to soak it in red wine. After drinking a litre of the mixture little changed, so she consulted a woman who prescribed herbs. These too failed to help. By now, her master and mistress thought her illness suspicious: her "whole body" was swollen and she could work only at the spinning-wheel. A doctor now analyzed her urine and recommended a "purgative" drink. Later he prescribed a potion against dropsy and pills for her headaches. After consuming these, Elsbetha woke up at night, her belly "bursting". She miscarried soon afterwards.[1]

What does Elsbetha's story tell us about early modern attitudes to the termination of pregnancies? In the past fifteen years or so, historians have investigated herbal texts, medical tracts, diaries and (occasionally) court records in order to identify the abortifacients known from antiquity to modern times.[2] Past theological, legal, medical and political debates about abortion have been examined,[3] and the termination of pregnancies has been analyzed in the context of early

57

modern birth control practices.[4] The present chapter is also concerned with why and how women terminated pregnancies, how they
described their condition and interacted with doctors and healers. But
its main concern is with how men and women *felt* about the termination of pregnancies during this period and how pregnancies came
to be policed in the public domain. The answer challenges what has
become almost an orthodoxy in much gender-historical writing:
namely that for most of this period a subversive and exclusively
female culture, partly dependent on midwives' participation, established women's autonomy over reproductive processes – an autonomy that obstetric scientists and male midwives are supposed then to
have extinguished during the eighteenth century.[5] I argue that this
view vastly underestimates the controls to which illegitimately pregnant women attempting an abortion were subjected from the sixteenth century onwards. Far from helping them, female midwives had
themselves become chief agents in the control of women who practised "deviant" sexuality and motherhood, while the notion that
knowledge about contraception and abortion was exchanged within
a "separate female sexual culture" implies a homogeneity of attitudes
and a solidarity among women that is hard to verify and ignores
potential conflicting feelings about fertility and motherhood.[6]
Elsbetha's case demonstrates a further point: the ways in which pregnancies could be terminated in the early modern period needs to be
understood with reference to contemporary ways of diagnosing pregnancy.[7] Women frequently missed their period. This was generally
considered to be a serious condition that did not necessarily, however,
point to pregnancy. The symptoms for a pregnancy were very similar
to illnesses like dropsy, growths and the assumed stagnation of the
blood. "Clogged", unmenstruated blood was understood to be
impure, blocking the bodily functions and impeding the circulation
of inner fluids; the "purging" remedies needed to restore the "flow"
consisted of herbs that were also used to induce abortions. This overlap explains why knowledge about abortifacients could be transmitted quite openly in the early modern period and was shared by men
and women.[8]

To pursue these issues, the first part of this chapter draws on 62
cases involving charges of attempted abortion brought before southwest German courts between 1515 and 1690. In Germany, aborting
a "living" child had been made a capital crime in 1532, while the

punishment for aborting an un-souled embryo was discretionary. The expression "living child" was deliberately imprecise, but it referred legally either to the moment when a foetus acquired a soul or to its quickening during the fourth month of pregnancy. For aborting a "living child" the imperial law code of Charles V prescribed decapitation for men and death by drowning (or other forms of death) for women.[9] However, since abortion was difficult to detect, and because it was virtually impossible to prove that a woman had knowingly intended to terminate her pregnancy, very few women were accused of abortion as a major crime. For this reason most material about abortion used in this chapter is drawn from infanticide trials, in which allegations about abortion often featured.

Such material inevitably focused on women who were single, mobile and from poorer sections of society. For insights into married women's attitudes to fertility and its control, the second part of this chapter tells the extraordinary story of a village woman who claimed to have given birth to eight frogs in 1715. The parson, midwife and civic doctor believed her, while others in the village community were so convinced that she had harmed a child that they insisted on an investigation. The fact that the doctor's "professional" diagnosis failed to overrule the community's own observations of her behaviour and symptoms indicates how a pregnant woman's body could become a matter of public concern. Through understanding and help, communities might protect pregnant women and unborn children from shocks, violence and harm.[10] But by the same token, through close observation and interrogation, they controlled mothers suspected of wrongdoing or evil.

The uncertainty of diagnosis

In the early modern period most women believed that a child acquired life when it "quickened" and the mother felt its movements.[11] Of course many earlier signs were understood to indicate a pregnancy: the loss of periods, a swelling belly, vomiting, loss of appetite, tiredness, moodiness, swollen breasts, and whitish urine with a hint of blue in it. But even Christoph Völter, the author of the first handbook for Württemberg midwives that listed all these indicators, had to admit in 1664 that these signs were difficult to discern in most women before the child quickened.[12] Dropsy in young people was easily misdiagnosed as a pregnancy and vice versa.[13] Also, if nature had been "confused" after conception, a "mole" (*mola* or *Mondkalb*) might develop. Then a woman would show the symptoms of pregnancy until her belly firmed up in the third or fourth month and the "mole" was emitted as a "flow of blood".[14] It was due to such uncertainties, Völter lamented, that "honourable virgins" were sometimes suspected of "losing their honour", while "lewd" pregnant "wenches" successfully pretended they were only ill.[15] Six years earlier, the deliberate hiding of a pregnancy had been made a criminal offence in Württemberg, despite the fact that the charge could not be proven.[16] The statute was a largely symbolic affirmation that the state was determined to intervene in matters of fertility control, a question all the more pressing after the population decline during the Thirty Years War. Diagnosis continued to be problematic throughout the eighteenth century, however, a period when illegitimate pregnancies rose dramatically. In 1788 the Tübingen physician Wilhelm Ploucquet could only fantasize about instituting monthly public baths for all single women between the ages of 14 and 48 to investigate the shapes of their bodies and "detect pregnancies".[17] Even by the late nineteenth century it was still difficult to diagnose a pregnancy safely before quickening.[18]

Court records had therefore consistently to engage with women's subjective interpretations of physical symptoms and their causes. In 1680, for example, a mother in Erdmannshausen near Marbach denied that her daughter Barbara had kept her pregnancy secret. She had admittedly worried that Barbara's belly was "clogged up" and that she might "die from it, like Kappen's daughter", but it was far from clear that she might be pregnant. Barbara had not had her period for four years. Moreover, after the mayor's son had raped her, her belly had swelled up, but her breasts had not. And when the mayor's wife had examined her belly, she did not think Barbara was pregnant. It was only to bring the stagnant blood back into flow that Barbara and her mother had gathered purgative herbs in the forest. These caused Barbara suddenly to give birth to a child, which soon died.[19] Similarly, when Anna Maria Hamberger had missed her period in 1673, she took a herb called penny royal because she felt something "tearing" in her back rather than in her belly. Her mistress bought crushed laurel in the pharmacy, mixed it with another herb, and gave the mixture to Anna, once with water, once with saffron and wine.

"All this", they emphasized, had been done "to provoke her month-lies" (*weibliche Zeit*).[20]

When seeking advice from mistresses, friends or healers, very few women confessed to having had intercourse. Fornication was a punishable crime; moreover, they knew that they were extremely likely to be refused treatment. Women who were able to send a member of their family would commonly even prefer not to see the healers themselves. Thus, in 1683, Regina Kapphan sent her father from Rutesheim to the district town of Leonberg to get melissa water from a barber's widow. He told her that his daughter suffered from a stagnant blood flow and needed a purge. The widow's male apprentice gave him herbs that Regina had to take for eight weeks, and some time later, as her parents were eating, Regina suddenly felt it "purging" and could hardly hold her water. She was delivered of a dead foetus.[21]

We take it for granted today that doctors can, as it were, see inside us or use reliable tests to establish objective physiological facts. We are increasingly inclined to define as "real" what can technically be made visible rather than what we feel. Only a century ago, as Ellen Ross writes of London working-class women, "pregnancies *happened* to a woman; the mothers were conscious mainly of getting fat and of eventually feeling foetal movements". Now, pregnancy is defined "as something a women *does*, a project that requires careful attention to diet, exercise, and the use of medicine, drugs and cigarettes",[22] forcing women to internalize the message that it is their duty to provide a stable foetal environment. So Elsbetha, Anna Maria and Regina's stories remind us how bodily experiences like pregnancy have been constructed along with definitions of unborn life itself.

Abortifacients and healers

Thanks to prevalent anxieties about stagnant blood flows, early modern knowledge about purging remedies was abundant. Furthermore, midwives needed abortifacients in order to expel stillborn babies from their mothers' wombs. Similar potions were used in veterinary medicine: in 1667 one surgeon judged the herbs taken by a woman strong enough to "drive a filly from a horse",[23] and in 1666, a shepherd reported that he had been asked to prescribe a remedy for a horse, not for a woman.[24] Small doses of mild abortifacients were also

61

used to restore a woman's period or expel what was believed to be a growth. There was a wide variety of herbs to choose from. During the fifteenth and sixteenth centuries, scholarly interest in the medical writings of Dioskurides and Galen led to a rediscovery of many ancient abortifacients.[25] Two well-known sixteenth-century German herbals each described some 30 abortifacients, along with different methods of applying them.[26] In our sample, women mentioned 23 herbs and essences that they knew themselves or had been given by others.[27] Laurel, penny royal, *Haselwurz* and savin topped the list. Herbs were usually taken in potions, but unspecified "powders" were taken in eight instances and pills in six. In seven cases external treatments were used: foot baths, hot baths and roots applied to body parts.[28]

Knowledge about the preparation of purging drinks was part of oral folk knowledge, and it concerned issues much graver than cures for colds and flu. There was street-talk about the remedies traded on markets and advice about the seasonal herbs available in forests. Although both men and women knew about the use of herbs, it was a female domestic duty to crush, mix, soak and boil them. In a proper household, a wife had her own stock of recipes for illnesses. Her care often extended to maidservants, to save them spending money on doctors and pharmacists. Widows, too, might offer time and skills: in 1600, a Constance woman, after visiting the doctor, was given rosemary, laurel, rhubarb and penny royal soaked in wine by "Hansen Mayer's mother" who lived down the street.[29] Self-help was ubiquitous. Many plants like sennet could be found in cemeteries, forests and fields. In 1667, Margaretha Schmollinger's lover showed her some purging herbs as they walked to a nearby village. When she became pregnant he brought them to her and told her to bind her belly.[30] Gardens were a further source. In 1680 a Hall maidservant took savin from "Evely the herbalist's garden";[31] in 1597, Anna Dischler took savin "from the painter's wife's garden in the *Neue Gasse*" and bought *Haselwurz* at the *Tiergarten*.[32] Others tried household remedies.[33] Those who had money to spend and did not mind buying purgatives in public bought herbs and powders from doctors, healers, pharmacists, and sellers of herbs and roots.

Women also had to know how to make their mixtures effective while avoiding risks to their health. Strong potions caused pain. Margaretha Frank described how her mouth and nostrils had bled.[34]

Women feared not only such discomforts. Even more alarming were the physical and social difficulties that ensued if the pregnancy was not terminated early enough. Elisabeth Maurer in Schorndorf had an adulterous affair in 1668, which she tried to keep secret from her husband, a grave-digger. Her mother prepared her a mixture that made Elisabeth vomit five times. It felt as if her "heart" was being "pushed away", but at least the movements in her belly diminished. Nonetheless, rumours spread that she might be hiding a pregnancy, so her mother urged her to remain lying "in her blood" (*Geblüth*) after the birth so that the midwife and other women would assume that she had suffered a normal miscarriage.[35]

If a woman's condition seemed too serious or persistent to be treated domestically, or if she wanted to keep it secret from her employer, or could not contact the child's father or her family, she would typically resort to doctors and healers. Their wide range of proficiency and the fact that even maidservants sought advice from them shows how pluralistic the world of early modern medicine was.[36] Those who had to watch their savings tended to consult less expensive healers first, and trained doctors only as a last resort. A case in point is that of Anna Martha Laistler, a 26-year-old maidservant impregnated and then deserted by a baker's apprentice in 1665 after, falsely, he had promised marriage. Anna moved to Stuttgart, where, she hoped, people would be less suspicious of her belly. Consulting a herb-seller in an inn and explaining that her blood flow was stagnant, she was sold a little basket of herbs. Her pain continuing, however, Anna went to see a Doktor Müller. He felt her belly, told her it was hard, which pointed to a growth rather than a pregnancy. He sent her off with 17 pills to be taken at once. Anna took lower doses than he advised – a common alteration – presumably to avoid the strong physical effects of abortifacients. The trouble was that such dilution might prolong pregnancies and increase the risk of prosecution. During the next months, "no food stayed inside" Anna; this she wrote to her mother, who then sent her a powder bought from the barber in Sulz. None of these remedies was strong enough to expel the child from her body.[37]

Cases like these suggest that the diagnostic means by which healers and common people sought to detect pregnancies were largely identical (except perhaps for the diagnosis of urine, which, however, did not give very reliable results). Healers never examined the woman's naked body. They usually touched her belly underneath her shirt to see how hard it was. Women did the same to each other, and they also checked suspects' breasts (which no man did). Generally, healers had to rely on a woman's account of her symptoms. The diagnostic process was strongly self-referential. One function of a consultation was therefore for women to have their own diagnosis professionalized; they appropriated the diagnostic process to stabilize a constructed illness narrative that, rather than being a mere "tactic", very often had become real for them.

The transmission of knowledge about abortifacients

Single women's use of illness narratives to control reproductive processes was under increasing threat. Doctors, healers and pharmacists became increasingly cautious in their dealings with single women who had lost their "flow". When Anna Dietschler went to the Constance midwife in 1597 to complain that her mother (uterus) was wandering about in her body, and to ask her for the "mother-herb" that she had given another woman, the midwife drily replied, "no, because you must be pregnant".[38] Women were commonly sold or given remedies too weak to terminate a pregnancy. They might even be reported to the authorities if they returned asking for stronger potions.[39] Male and female healers did not follow different policies. Take the case of Maria Hippenmayer, a Constance healer. Called to prescribe a purge to a single woman in 1697, she explained that she prescribed remedies only to "provoke the monthlies" for lying-in women, mature wives or widows who assured her that they "had not borne children for a long time".[40] Other healers dispensed herbs to single women only reluctantly, or they might refuse treatment in particular cases. The former Constance executioner Däubler, for example, who wrongly diagnosed Elsbetha as suffering from dropsy, was by no means an irresponsible quack. In 1669 he told one maidservant bluntly that she was pregnant and should not take any remedies.[41] A barber's widow assured the court in 1683 that she had prescribed to one single woman (whose father had personally assured her that his daughter was not pregnant) only the herbs she commonly gave her husband, or to women "who had missed their monthlies".[42] In 1699 the executioner in the Württemberg town of Bottwar sold a powder to a maidservant with the warning that she should not take it if she was pregnant. Even so, she took three different abortifacients, and marks on the baby's corpse were later accepted in court as proof that she had banged her belly with stones or knocked it against tables. Fathered by a soldier, the child would have been taunted as a bastard had it lived, and his mother would have been defamed as a soldier's whore. Instead she was beheaded for infanticide – presumably by the Bottwar executioner who had given her the powder and a warning.[43]

Of course there are contrary examples in which professional or private help was given. The books of recognizances in the Protestant imperial city of Hall contain three cases of women who helped maidservants or wives to terminate pregnancies. In 1566, a married woman was banished because she had "stirred, steamed, and given" several abortifacient drinks for a pregnant woman.[44] In 1600, a widow from a village in the territory was banished because she sold roots and drinks for abortions.[45] And in 1680, a married resident gave a maidservant an *expulsiorum* of melissa and savin, recommending her also to take three small doses of fine sage in the morning; this she took herself when "big with a child".[46] In such giving of advice we therefore encounter gender-specific *cultural practices* among some women rather than gender-specific *cultures*, based on different norms and attitudes about birth control among all women. It is interesting to note that prostitutes do not seem to have played any significant role in the transmission of contraceptive knowledge, which testifies to their social stigmatization after the closure of all civic brothels during the sixteenth century.[47] Only once, in 1574, do we hear of a Memmingen prostitute, Agatha Menzler, teaching her daughter the tricks of the trade, instructing her "how to deal with men"; "should she become pregnant . . . she should put her feet into a foot-bath with mercury".[48] Like Menzler, several mothers were prosecuted for helping their daughters to abort. In 1669, a village woman prepared a drink of herbs and laurel for her daughter,[49] and in 1690 Katharina Ruotweiß, a married woman suspected of being impregnated by a soldier, went several times to pick five different herbs near Höffigheim, to which her mother added savin, *Haselwurz* and shredded horseradish.[50]

Views about the legitimacy of abortion varied according to the circumstances of the case. In 1681, a Hall barber helped his stepdaughter to terminate a pregnancy after she had been raped in vengeance by a wandering apprentice he had refused to employ.[51] Similarly, a maidservant who told a woman that she had been abused and impregnated by a cleric, was sympathetically heard, and told to take a certain "drink".[52] A fellow maidservant told Anna Dietschler openly that when she herself had been single and pregnant, she had taken *Haselwurz* to abort, although without effect: she had to marry instead.[53] Married men, or soldiers who were not allowed to marry, or apprentices or journeymen who were not ready to marry the women they had impregnated, or monks and Catholic clerics, often had a strong interest in preventing the birth of an illegitimate child and exchanged knowledge about abortifacients.[54] When in 1660, for example, Johann Schreiber of Constance had impregnated his maidservant, Anna, a male friend advised him to buy "gallow roots" from a Lindau man.[55]

In other cases, it is difficult to decide whether or not women or men consciously gave advice about abortifacients. In 1690 a single woman successfully asked a Constance woman for a remedy tellingly called "child's balm",[56] and in 1699 Anna Sailer asked an old widow for "savin-tree water" and was given a cow's horn full of it.[57] Savin was by then widely known as a "shameful herb",[58] but it, too, had its good and its bad uses. It was, for example, a standard ingredient in dietary medicine. Anna Weckerin's cookbook in 1598 recommended purges for the sick to be made from plums, raisins, cinnamon, ginger, and as many savin-leaves as a doctor recommended; this "purged powerfully, without weakening" patients.[59] Domestic advice about purging herbs might increasingly have been combined with warnings, even though this might have adverse effects. One summer evening in 1665, for example, a maidservant and her mistress were walking home from the fields when the mistress pointed out red penny royal. She explained that "this was a good herb for a woman whose period did not come properly". Then she added, with a reference to the Thirty Years War, that "before the terrible invasion of 1634 a local maidservant had abused the herb and with it had expelled a child from herself".[60] The maidservant had been harassed by the mistress's son, so this might have been a coded message how to terminate a possible pregnancy. Sure enough, when the maidservant became pregnant, she resorted to a drink of red penny royal. On the other hand, this was probably how any young woman would be instructed in the use and abuse of any herb. Moreover, the fact that someone could recall the story of an abortion from over thirty years earlier shows how rare these crimes were.

The control of sexuality and fertility

So far we have seen that attitudes towards the termination of pregnancies were crucially determined by the timing of such attempts. Although many people might have morally objected to a termination even before quickening, as long as the woman did not appear to be pregnant and the foetus looked like a "discharge" few would take much notice of it. An abortion could not always be achieved before quickening, however, and continued attempts to abort often did become visible. Most men and women clearly regarded this as the murder of a "living child", ensouled by God. Deliberate support for such women was most likely to come from their family, and hence it was largely unavailable for mobile women, who had to trust to healers – a trust increasingly denied to them. Moreover, as many places published new laws against fornication, infanticide or hiding pregnancies, and as public sentences for those crimes in turn became more common, people began to regard single women from outside their community as a "problem group" who almost inevitably would commit such crimes. Pre-marital sex itself was not frowned upon and it was widely practised. When both partners were local and of similar social status, they or their kin would usually agree to a marriage if the woman became pregnant. Mobile women by contrast were more likely to become illegitimately pregnant because they usually had affairs with equally mobile and hence untraceable men. And if a woman did not work for a relative, there would be no kin to mediate a marriage. Worst of all, there would be no money to set up a household and feed a child. Communities had no wish to bear the cost of such problems by giving alms to women with bastards. There was widespread agreement that such women had brought these problems upon themselves by lust and lechery; they deserved to be sent begging. At the same time it was obvious that the poverty and shame such a life entailed made it more likely that women would try to terminate an unwanted pregnancy, abandon or even kill bastard children.

So people knew whom to mistrust if bellies swelled and there was news of growths and clogging blood: that is, mobile maidservants, especially if they were from a poor family and aged over 20, the age when most women engaged in serious sexual activity. Swiss maidservants in particular were thought of as disreputable in southwest Germany, since these were the daughters of poor *Häusler*-families in mountainous regions. In 1664, the Leonberg midwife told a Swiss maidservant whose diminished belly caused suspicion, that she deserved "the same reputation Swiss maids are generally said to have".[61] Equally suspect were independently working women, spinners, seamstresses or laundresses, as well as the agricultural day-labourers who were increasingly defamed as "masterless" women, rejecting the household order in pursuit of liberty and lewdness. The language of insult reflects the bitterness and envy that could develop between those within and those outside the household order. In 1648, a Memmingen artisan wife accused her lodger, an independent seamstress, of having "lain with the carpenter's apprentice more often than she herself had lain with her own husband, from whom she had had six children". The seamstress asked whether this was meant to imply that she had aborted that many children. The woman asserted: "it was obvious that she knew well how to do it".[62] Wives therefore invested independent women with their own desires and fantasies; abortion was imagined to be their tactic to avoid marriage and the burdens of childbearing and raising.

Mistrust became a political virtue as authorities put mounting pressure on masters and mistresses to survey and report not only the sexual activities but also the suspected pregnancies of their servants. The fact that suspects would then be examined by midwives returns us to the question of midwives' role in fertility control. Since the late fourteenth century, midwifery had been a public office, supervised by civic and territorial authorities. Like licensed female healers, midwives were therefore vulnerable to exposure and harsh punishment if they administered any form of birth control. Moreover, by the sixteenth century their office was deemed "respectable", so that they belonged to the middling sort and were mostly artisans' wives or widows of good reputation. Groups of four women, called the "sworn" or "honourable women" (*ehrbare* or *geschworene Weiber*), would voluntarily supervise and assist them.[63] Sworn women also enjoyed high status. In cities they were usually patricians', merchants' or richer artisans' wives; in small towns commonly mayors' and pastors' wives. The increasing respectability of midwifery, however, was not wholly dependent on social status (in rural areas the office continued to be fulfilled by poorer women). Rather, it depended on the fact that midwives were increasingly the supervisors of deviant women and mothers.[64] Midwives and sworn women had to exhort women who might otherwise induce miscarriages to carry through their labour properly.[65] They examined and had to report those suspected of hiding pregnancy or attempting abortion. They interrogated single women about the identity of their children's fathers before offering any physical or moral help during birth.[66]

All these measures expressed not only deepening concern about alms wasted on single women and about declining birth rates; they also testify to an intensified religious view of motherhood. A pregnant woman was commonly described as being of blessed body (*gesegneten Leibes*), since those who conceived within marriage were blessed by God. It was a woman's *Beruf* and *Amt*, her profession and office, to bear children given to her by God. Work metaphors (labour pains as *weibliche Arbeit* or the *zum Kind schaffen*) turned the process of giving birth into a kind of special female mission she was expected to fulfil. Sentimental notions of motherliness were built into the supposition, likewise, that motherly love was a natural, inborn and unambiguous sentiment to be found universally in a divinely created world. Those who did not want to carry through a pregnancy were unnatural. In an age that saw the wild and threatening aspects of human nature (such as unbound desire) embodied in femininity, it was the bearing of children – rather than women's contributions to economic reproduction or devotional life – that gained women protection and rights. In order to gain complete respect in society, women needed to dissociate themselves from any who embodied the depraved aspects of female nature: those who led men into temptation, pursued their desires, lived outside the household order or tried to avert the divine punishment of bearing bastard children. The issue of fertility control therefore carried larger social and emotional meanings that shaped people's responses to it.

An unnatural pregnancy

Communal concern about attacks on unborn life affected married as well as single women, however. To establish this, we turn finally to the story of Christina Schauth, who in 1715 claimed to have given birth to eight frogs. The notion that a woman could be pregnant with frogs rather than with a child was not in itself beyond credit in the early modern period, even if it did disturbingly blur the barrier between animals and humans. More important for our purposes is the way the interrogations about the case reveal the public concern about right order in pregnancies. The help that was offered could easily shift into control, and the communal valuation of love and peace coexisted with suspicion and watchfulness.

In July 1715, Christina, wife of the wheelwright Balthasar Schauth in the Württemberg village of Onstmettingen, claimed she had been pregnant for 14 months.[67] On 8 July her crisis at last arrived. She summoned her sister, the parson and his wife, and, from the fields, the midwife. She showed her sister a bucket of bloody matter that had come from her, she said, and as the sister stirred it, she discovered eight frogs in the mess. The midwife cleaned them, as she would have done with a baby, and the parson urged Christina to thank God for helping to end her curious and burdensome pregnancy. None disbelieved the evidence of his or her eyes. That afternoon, Balthasar Schauth took the frogs to the Balingen physician in a small linen bag. "Look, this is the child my wife has had", he said. Rauchendorff was "very surprised" but again not disbelieving. He only wondered whether in springtime Christina had bathed in or swallowed water with frogspawn in it. Balthasar remembered no such thing. When Balthasar was on his way home, Doctor Rauchendorff called on the Balingen pharmacist. He carefully inspected the two large and six little frogs and put them in spirit to preserve them.

Meanwhile the news of the birth spread quickly in Onstmettingen. Not surprisingly, Christina's everlasting pregnancy had been gossiped about for the past two months; it had gone on so long that many suspected that Christina might have given birth secretly, been "unfaithful" to the child (*ihm ein untrew erwiesen*) or even killed it. Instead of dropping these grave suspicions after the birth, the parson reported, there was now great "uproar" among the people. The birth, it quickly turned out, was fraudulent. Someone had seen Christina's half-sister catching the frogs. This was decisive. Christina was arrested and taken to Balingen.

In the course of several interrogations, the story turned out to be this: Christina had been living with her husband for nine years. Before their marriage (the church consistory judges related in their report on the couple's reputation), Balthasar had led a "fine and quiet" life, and everyone had "loved him". By contrast, Christina was the local miller's stepdaughter and had been a rather "cheeky" (*frech*) girl. In 1704 she had come before the church consistory court because she kept meeting a soldier. The soldier owned the key to her bed-chamber and had (nevertheless) been seen climbing in and out of her window. When Christina became pregnant during these episodes, she rather surprisingly named Balthasar as her child's father. He had not wanted to marry her, and was imprisoned for pre-marital sex. His parents, the parson and the church consistory judges persuaded him to marry. After this Christina changed for the better. Although she was still described as audacious, the marriage was peaceful; she often went to church and worked busily. Balthasar was the one who began to slip somewhat. He started to gamble and was sometimes drunk, then swearing and turning violent. But normally he, too, was hard-work-ing, went to church often, took Communion and lived in peace with everyone. They were, in other words, a perfectly normal couple.

Except that for the last eight years she had not conceived. Her peri-ods had been regular, except once, five years ago, when they stopped for eight weeks. The previous Easter, she missed her period for a second time, but felt no pain. She had developed a good appetite and become fatter. Sleeping had become uncomfortable because a lump (*Knüpfel*) developed in the left side of her belly. On St. Gallus Day in September, she felt movement (*herumfahren*) in her belly. Now she believed she was pregnant and that the baby would be born in Feb-ruary. Since St Gallus Day, however, she had gained no further weight (which could be explained by her hard work). In winter she first told other women about her pregnancy at a spinning-bee, and said the child was due soon. The women laughed at her, saying, "Christina, but where is your child", because she was not growing fatter.

Soon after Christmas everyone noticed that she prepared every-thing for the baby, got nappies and other "child things" (*Kindsgeräth*). Then she and her sister-in-law had a washing day, and Christina lifted something very heavy. She felt pain in her back and womb and returned home quickly. Through her window, her neighbour could see that she had labour pains. When Christina's sister Anna Maria was on her way to spin at Christina's that afternoon, she met her brother-in-law, who said that Christina's labour had started. To her surprise, however, Anna Maria found her sister at the spinning-wheel; she did not know whether or not she had labour pains. Anna Maria cooked her a soup, and when she left told Christina to get the midwife. The next morning, a Sunday, Anna Maria anxiously waited to hear whether Christina had given birth; but there was no such news. Christina had been out in the street, and although she did not go to the spinning-bee that night, everything seemed to continue as usual.

In this curious aftermath, Christina and Balthasar continued to feel something alive in her belly and insisted that a birth was imminent, even though by Easter the pregnancy seemed more than a little protracted. One day Christina said to her aunt, the cowherd's wife, "Come with me; I want to talk to you." She hesitated, and then revealed her hopelessness: "Oh aunt, if I were standing on top of the highest mountain in the whole world, I could not see all of my unhappiness. I only wish I could get a child." Then her voice lowered: "There has been this beggar woman here. Two children were running after her, and she carried the smallest in her arms. It is four weeks and a couple of days old. I would like to raise it as if it was mine, if only she would give it to me." "You old fool!" her aunt rebuked her, "Do you think a mother could do that (*es über das Herz bringen*), give you her child; just tell me, where have you put your big belly; has nothing come from you?" "No", Christina answered. She admitted that she did not know what to make of her condition: sometimes she had a big belly and sometimes not, and all she felt was this big *Knüpfel* on her left side.

Between that time and Whitsun, rumours spread that Christina might have given birth in secret or murdered the child. Eleven male witnesses later emphasized not only that the women had been wondering about the whole affair, but that the men also had "quite a few thoughts and opinions" about Christina. What puzzled them was that she and her husband were evidently looking forward to having the child; there was no motive for murder.

When at last Balthasar complained to the parson about all the gossip, some people were called before the church consistory. At first all denied having heard the rumours, then admitted that "every now and then people talked a lot about it"; but they did not know who had started the stories. The judges decided that the midwife should inspect Christina. She too felt something "alive" in Christina's body. She and the councillors advised the couple to go to the civic doctor in Balingen, so that Christina might be helped if her belly contained something "unusual".

She saw Rauchendorff on 26 June. He noted the following symptoms: Christina had not menstruated for more than a year and a small movement could be felt in her belly; but she had neither vomited nor been sick from eating, and she lacked any of the other symptoms pregnant women usually had. He guessed that either something was wrong with her uterus, or it was a "growth of blood", or a mole, which, he later reported, occurred every now and then but was strange for ordinary people. He first prescribed Christina a brown powder with some herbs. But when her body still failed to open, the parson advised her husband to seek Rauchendorff's advice again. This time he prescribed several *Mutterkräuter* or "mother-herbs", and told Christina to be bled at her foot. No pregnant woman ought to be bled, but this was necessary in order to see how "nature" was going to respond. He also warned her that she was probably going to discharge mucus and blood. By now it seemed unlikely that she carried a child. It was after these lengthy and emotionally draining negotiations, at last, that Christina must have decided to give birth to her frogs in order to "quieten the people". She got cows' milk ready, to pretend she had breast milk.[68] After she had taken the prescribed potion (*Mutterwasser*) three times, a strong flow of blood ensued, the *Hertzfluß*: it consisted of *Möckhle*, black blood with little clots. It was now that her sister, the neighbour, the parson, his wife and the midwife stirred up the frogs, which then stirred up the whole story.

There was an epilogue that somewhat rehabilitated Christina by shifting the blame for the conception of the fraud. It was discovered that a week before the birth, a 60-year-old villager, Maria Sautter, had urgently tried to speak to Christina. Christina said that Sautter advised her to put frogs into the bucket once her flow started in order to "shut people up". At first she had not wanted to do so and trusted in God's help. Then the woman had brought her some soup, and as soon as she had eaten it Christina had been convinced that the frogs were a good idea; she told her little half-sister to go and catch some. Sautter denied the charge, but it was well known that she never told the truth.

The fact that Christina had conceived within marriage had never been doubted. Unlike a single woman in this position, she was "honourably pregnant" (*in Ehren schwanger*). This explains the support from the parson, his wife and the midwife. Also, they and the doctor believed in the unpredictable manifestations of "nature" in the female body. Local doctors like Rauchendorff or his Eisenach colleague Storch held that "nature" should be followed, helped and directed – for example by opening the body at a vein to redirect blood flow. It was impossible fully to comprehend nature, however.[69] By the early eighteenth century, medical practice was largely a matter of probing, testing and observing within the limits of this paradigm.

For us, likewise, there is no way of reconstructing Christina's true condition. Perhaps she had not been pregnant at all, or she had lost the child after the exertions of the washing day. It is striking that she did not think she might regain trust by simply telling people either that she had miscarried or that Rauchendorff believed that she suffered from a growth. Since everyone might well have believed that Christina was barren,[70] her sudden pregnancy seemed strange anyway; hence the laughter of the women in the spinning-bee. When it did not result in a birth she became vulnerable to accusations that she had harmed the child. Thus the frogs were more than a means of "shutting people up". The fraud was also a cry for compassion. Women who gave birth to animals were sure to be pitied; some exhibited the animals and received gifts.[71] But in Christina's case the strategy failed. Her disappointment that she was unable to deliver a child went unrecognized. Instead of compassion people had only insisted on knowing what had happened to her body. One can hardly imagine what it must have been like for her to leave the prison and return to Onstmettingen.

Conclusions

In early modern Germany, women's control of reproduction was limited far more by legal and communal regulation than ever it was by medical developments. While many women doubtless continued to influence diagnoses according to their interests (by presenting an illness narrative, for example, rather than by admitting intercourse), by the seventeenth century the mistrust and surveillance of those suspected of hiding pregnancies seems to have been increasing. The ability of women to conceal what happened in their bodies was not only attacked by the authorities; common people, too, insisted on making women's bodies a matter of public concern. The shapes of bellies and breasts, eating habits, work habits, real or imagined flows of water or blood were all closely observed. The desire to look, as it were, beneath women's skin and to discover the truth about their condition was therefore not necessarily confined to doctors or political authorities. The changing attitudes to motherhood in early modern society seem to be crucial for our understanding of this process.

Notes

My thanks to Vic Gatrell for his help in preparing this chapter.

1. Stadtarchiv Konstanz (StAKN), K 64, 9 July and 18 May 1688, Elsbetha Eggenmännin.
2. Cf. in particular J. M. Riddle, *Contraception and abortion from the ancient world to the Renaissance* (Cambridge, Mass. & London: Harvard University Press, 1992); L. Leibrock-Plehn, *Hexenkräuter oder Arznei: Die Abtreibungsmittel im 16. und 17. Jahrhundert* (Stuttgart: Steiner, 1992); R. Jütte (ed.), *Geschichte der Abtreibung: Von der Antike bis zur Gegenwart* (Munich: C. H. Beck, 1993).
3. Cf. especially J. T. Noonan, jun., *Contraception: a history of its treatment by the Catholic theologians and canonists*, 2nd edn (Cambridge, Mass.: Belknap Press of Harvard University Press, 1986); G. Jerouschek, *Lebensschutz und Lebensbeginn: Kulturgeschichte des Abtreibungsverbots* (Stuttgart: Enke, 1988).
4. Cf. A. McLaren, *Reproductive rituals: the perception of fertility in England from the sixteenth century to the nineteenth century* (London & New York: Methuen, 1984), ch. 5; R. Jütte, "Die Persistenz des Verhütungswissens in der Volkskultur: Sozial- und medizinhistorische Anmerkungen zur These von der 'Vernichtung weiser Frauen'", *Medizinhistorisches Journal* **24**, 1989, pp. 214–31; K. Stukenbrock, "Das Zeitalter der Aufklärung: Kindsmord, Fruchtabtreibung und weltliche Justiz", in *Geschichte der Abtreibung*, Jütte (ed.), pp. 91–120.
5. The "demise" of the midwife, we are recently told, "sounded the death knell" of traditional knowledge of contraception – and, it would follow, of the termination of pregnancies – "knowledge historically belonging to women", see L. Schiebinger, *Nature's body: gender in the making of modern science* (Boston: Beacon Press, 1993), p. 210.
6. McLaren, *Reproductive rituals*, p. 6; P. Crawford, "Sexual knowledge in England, 1500–1750", in *Sexual knowledge, sexual science: the history of attitudes to sexuality*, R. Porter & M. Teich (eds.) (Cambridge: Cambridge University Press, 1994), p. 99; H. Wunder, *"Er ist die Sonn', sie ist der Mond": Frauen in der Frühen Neuzeit* (Munich: C. H. Beck, 1992), p.165. For pathbreaking work on conflicts among women to do with fertility cf. L. Roper, *Oedipus and the devil: witchcraft, sexuality and religion in early modern Europe* (London & New York: Routledge, 1994), esp. ch. 9.
7. Cf. McLaren, *Reproductive rituals*, p. 102; B. Duden, *The woman beneath the skin: a doctor's patients in eighteenth century Germany* (London &

Cambridge, Mass.: Harvard University Press, 1984), ch. 4; M. Lorenz, " '. . . als ob ihr ein Stein aus dem Leibe kollerte . . .': Schwangerschafts-wahrnehmungen und Geburtserfahrungen von Frauen im 18. Jahr-hundert", in *Körper-Geschichten: Studien zur historischen Kulturforschung V*, R. van Dülmen (ed.) (Frankfurt am Main: Fischer, 1996), pp. 99–121.

8. Cf. Stukenbrock, "Das Zeitalter der Aufklärung", p. 118.

9. StAKN, K 64, 9 July 1688.

10. Cf. U. Rublack, "Pregnancy, childbirth and the female body in early modern Germany", *Past and Present* 105, 1996, pp. 84–108.

11. B. Duden, "Die 'Geheimnisse der Schwangeren' und das Öffentlichkeits-interesse der Medizin: Zur sozialen Bedeutung der Kindsregung", in *Frauengeschichte – Geschlechtergeschichte*, K. Hausen & H. Wunder (eds) (Frankfurt am Main & New York: Campus, 1992), pp. 117–30.

12. C. Völter, *Neueröffnete Hebammen = Schuhl/Oder Nützliche Unterweis-ung Christlicher Heb = Ammen vnd Wehe = Mütter*, 2nd edn (Stuttgart, 1687), p. 9.

13. *Ibid.*, p. 14.

14. *Ibid.*, p. 235.

15. *Ibid.*, p. 13.

16. A. L. Reyscher (ed.), *Vollständige, historisch und kritisch bearbeitete Samm-lung der württembergischen Gesetze*, vol. 6 (Tübingen, 1842), p. 320.

17. B. Duden, *Disembodying women: perspectives on pregnancy and the unborn*, trans. L. Hoinacki (Cambridge, Mass.: Harvard University Press, 1993), p. 96. On pregnancy diagnosis in legal medicine, cf. E. Fischer-Homberger, *Medizin vor Gericht: Zur Sozialgeschichte der Gerichtsmedizin* (Darmstadt: Luchterhand, 1983), pp. 218–85.

18. A. Oakley, *The captured womb: a history of medical care of pregnant women* (Oxford: Basil Blackwell, 1984), p. 17.

19. Hauptstaatsarchiv Stuttgart (HStASt), A 209, Bü.1559, Barbara Klein-knecht.

20. HStASt, A 209, Bü.1690, 1673, Möckmühl.

21. HStASt, A 309, Bü.127, 1683.

22. E. Ross, *Love and toil: motherhood in outcast London, 1870–1918* (New York & Oxford: Oxford University Press, 1993), p. 106.

23. HStASt, A 209, Bü.1923, 22 July and 30 Aug. 1667.

24. HStASt, A 209, Bü.1345, 7 Feb. 1666, Anna Maria Vischer.

25. L. Leibrock-Plehn, "Frühe Neuzeit: Hebammen, Kräutermedizin und welt-liche Justiz", in *Geschichte der Abtreibung*, Jütte (ed.), p. 74.

26. *Ibid.*, p. 76.

27. The following substances were mentioned: *Lorbeer* and *Poley*, each nine times; *Haselwurz*, seven times; *Sennes*, five times; *Schwalbenwurz*, three times; *Rosmarin*, *Liebstöckl* and *Melissenwasser*, each twice; *Essig*, *Kerbolderbeere*, *Holderlatweg*, *Kallnuß*, *Mutterkraut*, *St. Johannis Kraut*, *Absein*, *Rabänzlein*, *Safran*, *Benedictwurz*, *Sander*, *Wachholderbeere*, *Salbei*, *Erzäppel* and *Merrehtich*, each mentioned once.

28. In 1515, for example, a single woman who was pregnant by a married man took a herbal mixture and "put a root on her heart for two days". HStASt, A 44, U 3749, 27 Sept. 1515, Ursula Wiest.
29. StAKN, BI 81, 12 Aug. 1600, fol. 167r.
30. HStASt, A 209, Bü.1923, 30 Aug. 1667, Margaretha Schmollinger.
31. Stadtarchiv Hall (StAH), K 11, F.39, 1680, Maria Barbara Vischer.
32. StAKN, RP, BI 80, 23 July 1597.
33. One maidservant who had slept with a soldier took vinegar and hoped for the best. StAKN, K 4, Franziska Schenk, c. 1693.
34. HStASt, A 209, Bü.277, 1677. In 1683, one woman therefore confessed that if she "had done what her lover wanted, she would have had no child", for he had "brought her several things to drive it from her". But she could not face taking them. HStASt, A 309, Bü.128, 1683, Anna Katharina Seyboldt. One widowed woman was pregnant by a married man and drank several strong abortifacients; "blood ran out of her mouth". To avoid local suspicion she left the country until the baby came from her dead. HStASt, A 309, Bü.173, 1627, Elisabeth Maurer.
35. HStASt, A 209, Bü.1785.
36. A total of 22 women were consulted: 9 healers, 7 mothers, 2 unspecified women, 2 widows, 1 mistress and 1 midwife; as against a total of 27 men: 9 doctors, 9 healers of various kinds (namely quacks, shepherds, root-diggers, executioners, cowherds, and a *Feldscherer*), 4 pharmacists, 3 unspecified men and 2 barbers.
37. HStASt, A 210, Abt.I, Bü.444, 28 Dec. 1665; for another example of this kind see HStASt, A 209, Bü.2010, 10 Oct. 1679, Anna Maria Gönninger.
38. Later the midwife's daughter brought Anna a sweet drink in a wooden mug, but it had no effect. StAKN, HIX, F.41, 23 June 1597; RP, BI 80, 1596–8, fols 277v–278v.
39. One Constance pharmacist's apprentice dealt like this with a seamstress who claimed to have lost her period in 1691 and demanded "purgatives". When she returned, the apprentice enquired whether the remedies had taken effect. She replied, "no, she needed something strong, a purgative like a horse". The pharmacist "was suspicious of her" and denied any further medication. StAKN, K 4, 28 July 1691, Elisabeth Löfflerin.
40. She insisted that in this woman's case a doctor had to be consulted, and the midwife agreed. StAKN, K 72, 30 July 1697.
41. StAKN, K 5, 16 July 1669, Catharina Bühlerin.
42. HStASt, A 309, Bü.127, Regina Kapphan.
43. HStASt, A 209, Bü.558, 8 Mar. 1699, Anna Dorothea Sailer.
44. StAH, 4/479, 18 Sept. 1566.
45. StAH, 4/79, Fraisch und Malefizrepertorium, Barbara, widow of Jos Weiss.
46. StAH, RP, 1680, 22 Oct. 1680, fols 521r–522v, Maria Barbara Vischer.
47. Contrary to what Jütte believes: "Persistenz des Verhütungswissens", p. 220.
48. Stadtarchiv Memmingen (StAMM), A 44 d, 17 May 1574, Agatha Menzler.

49. HStASt, A 209, Bü.1926, Anna Kaiser.
50. HStASt, A 209, Bü.1564, 28 Feb. 1690.
51. She was banished from the Hall territory for two years. StAH, 4/484, 8 Apr. 1681, fols 115r–v.
52. StAKN, K 41, 23 July 1633, Ursula Gaisser.
53. StAKN, RP, Bl 80, 1596–8, fols 277v–287v.
54. StAKN, K 56, 6 Mar. 1675, Barbara Jäger, for a woman who had been abused by a cleric who gave her money, two herbs, and the order not to confess the abortion to his dean; StAH, 4/479, 22 Aug. 1576, fol. 305r, for a case of pre-marital sex where Hans Schuhmacher had given Anna Seuter "herbs, bread", and other things for an abortion; HStASt, A 209, Bü.277, 1677, Margaretha Frank, for a case in which the man had married someone else instead and brought her abortifacients.
55. When Anna began to feel the child's movements, he purchased a "grey powder" from a pharmacist's apprentice (though because she disliked remedies from the pharmacy, Schreiber pretended he had bought the powder from a Jew). It would do her no harm at all, he said; it would just drive the child away. If she must miscarry, she objected, she would need help. But next day Schreiber again forced her to take the powder with wine. Noticing that some powder was left in the glass, he insisted that she drink up. This time it proved effective. For some time after the miscarriage, Anna was bereft of "mind and senses". She was forever banished from Constance, he was sent away for five years to the Hungarian war. StAKN, K 29, 16 Oct. 1660, Anna Zecklein.
56. StAH, K 11, F.46, Margaretha Hausler.
57. HStASt, A 209, Bü.558, 3 Feb. 1699.
58. HStASt, A 209, Bü.1690, 1673, Anna Maria Hamberger.
59. A. Weckerin, *Ein köstlich new Kochbuch von allerhand Speisen* ... (Amberg: Michel Forsten, 1598; repr. Munich: Heimeran, 1977), p. 139.
60. HStASt, A 209, Bü.1345, 7 Feb. 1666, Anna Maria Vischer.
61. HStASt, A 209, Bü.1471, 12 Mar. 1664, Barbara Sticker.
62. StAMM, A 145/5, 9 June 1648, Maria Meyer.
63. M. E. Wiesner, "The midwives of south Germany and the public/private dichotomy", in *The art of midwifery: early modern midwives in Europe*, H. Marland (ed.) (London: Routledge, 1993), pp. 77–94.
64. Cf. U. Gleixner, "Die 'Gute' und die 'Böse': Hebammen als Amtsfrauen auf dem Land. (Altmark/Brandenburg, 18 Jahrhundert)", in *"Weiber", "Menscher", "Frauenzimmer": Frauen in der ländlichen Gesellschaft 1500–1800*, H. Wunder & C. Vanja (eds) (forthcoming).
65. Cf. Rublack, "Pregnancy, childbirth and the female body".
66. In some places, midwives were even required to examine whether a couple's first child was born nine months after the marriage so as to see whether its parents were punishable for pre-marital fornication: see Wiesner, "The midwives of south Germany", p. 87.

67. The following description of the case is based on several reports in HStASt, A 209, Bü.191.
68. The midwife or her aunt asked her concerned what she was going to do with the milk if she had no child. She was told to stand next to the oven and count the tiles up to nine, and then the midwife or aunt moved her hands across her left, larger breast mumbling something.
69. Duden, *Woman beneath the skin*, ch. 4.
70. Sterility affected about 7 per cent of all couples in similar Württemberg villages at this time and was nothing unusual: A. Maisch, *Notdürftiger Unterhalt und gehörige Schranken: Lebensbedingungen und Lebensstile in württembergischen Dörfern der frühen Neuzeit* (Stuttgart: Gustav Fischer Verlag, 1992), p. 272.
71. In 1509, for example, a vagrant woman was pitied and given alms in Pforzheim when she pretended to have given birth to a toad: see R. Jütte, "Dutzbetterinnen und Sündfegerinnen: Kriminelle Bettelpraktiken von Frauen in der Frühen Neuzeit", in *Von Huren und Rabenmüttern: Weibliche Kriminalität in der Frühen Neuzeit*, O. Ulbricht (ed.) (Cologne: Böhlau, 1995), p. 127.

Chapter Four

ᴥᶊ

Religious dissent and the roots of German feminism

Dagmar Herzog

In the last few years it has become an established consensus among German women's history scholars that the first organized German women's movement had its origins in the religious dissenting movement of the 1840s.[1] Calling themselves *Deutschkatholiken* (German-Catholics, as opposed to Roman Catholics), individuals who opposed the exclusivism and authoritarianism gaining ground within the Roman Catholic Church in Germany established one major strand of the dissenting movement in 1845. They were joined by Protestants disaffected by the conservatism and beholdenness to monarchical authority evidenced by their own church hierarchy – many of whom were organized into a protest movement called "Free Protestants". Inspiring each other, the dissenters stepped out of their respective mainstream churches and founded new, democratically run congregations dedicated to individual freedom of belief, cross-confessional co-operation, and the separation of church and state. Whether themselves initially Catholic or Protestant, the dissenters were united in their alarm at the resurgence of neo-orthodox Catholicism in particular.

Despite both extensive harassment by local police and religious leaders, and legal and political disenfranchisement by most state governments, the dissenting movement gained somewhere between 100,000 and 150,000 official members by 1848, and it had many more sympathizers. It was the largest German protest movement of any sort before the revolutions of 1848 (and indeed, many dissenters subsequently became revolutionaries).

Depending on which German state one looks at, women constituted between 30 and 40 per cent of the membership, and this high level of female participation was undoubtedly a response to dissenting leaders' active concern to address and include women.[2] The movement's male leaders routinely called for greater equality for women; many dissenting congregations granted their female members voting rights, and there was a dramatic proliferation of activist and charitable women's clubs formed within and alongside the dissenting congregations. Women's organization of fund-raising and charitable activities proved essential both to the survival of the movement, and to its practical people-serving vision, and these activities, in turn, gave women's rights activists an institutional base and a great deal of leadership experience. As one contemporary noted, among the important achievements for which the dissenters could take credit was also the *"lifting-up of the female sex*, through expanded participation of the same in childraising and service to the poor, through women's clubs, [and] through the ... free speech they have been granted".[3] Similarly, the most famous women's rights activist in nineteenth-century Germany, Louise Otto, remarked in 1847 that "it is above all the religious movement [of the dissenting congregations] to which we are indebted for the rapid advance of female participation in the issues of the times".[4] In short, contemporaries and scholars alike have agreed: the roots of German feminism were to be found in religious dissent.

But in my own research on the dissenters, I found a much more confusing phenomenon. What I found is that the dissenting movement undermined its own feminist demands in subtle, but unmistakable, ways. Dissenters were indeed intensely preoccupied with gender relations; many of their sermons, tracts and newspaper essays are devoted solely to this topic; scores more touch on it in part; and yet others rely heavily on gendered imagery. A close examination of this plethora of writings by men (for, as so often, it was the male members of the movement who left the paper trail) reveals the ways dissent mobilized various, indeed conflicting, conceptions of womanhood.[5]

Male dissenters did routinely call for greater equality for women within marriage, and for a broadening of women's spheres of activity. But their calls for women's emancipation were always coupled with a celebration of marital companionship and with a reaffirmation of women's difference from men. Furthermore, while dissenters generally rhapsodized about women's unique capacities and characteristics, with striking frequency there was another undercurrent as well. For in dissenting texts, women appear as both a source of salvation and a source of danger, as both loyal and seducible, vulnerable and unreliable. These contradictory valences can, I believe, be best understood when the religious dissenting movement is situated in the context that produced it: a two-decade-long history of fierce controversy between political liberals and a resurgent conservative Catholicism over the politics of the private sphere, and above all over male sexual rights.

The complex ways gender figured in dissenting rhetoric make most sense when this context is kept in mind. The point here is not to make a hindsight-inspired fuss about mid-nineteenth-century dissenters' misogyny. Rather, the goal is to show, by reconstructing the imaginative world dissenters inhabited, how religious conflicts around sexual matters could both produce a feminist vision, and complicate that vision. Male dissenters' battle against the authoritarian forces ascendant within the Roman Catholic Church in Germany – specifically as those were expressed in conservative Catholics' views on sex and marriage – both spurred dissenters to seek to emancipate women and, however paradoxically, to be exceedingly anxious about whether women were worthy of that effort.

Dissenters' views on women could seem so novel and appealing particularly in light of the anti-feminist consensus shared by most mainstream liberals and conservatives in the 1840s. Conservatives, predictably, were unabashed in their portrayal of women as weaker and more susceptible to sin than men, and therefore more in need of control. They openly defended husbands' dominance over wives and denounced any efforts to allow women to step out of the private sphere of the home; this position fitted comfortably with their more general demands for a corporatist, hierarchically ordered society.[6] Liberals had to do more fancy theorizing in order to reconcile their own demands for greater political freedoms for men with their insistence on the exclusion of women from public life. In order to resolve this philosophical dilemma, they, like many of their Enlightenment predecessors, invoked the laws of nature. Nature decreed that all men were born equal; nature also determined that women were different. The health of the state, they insisted, required the maintenance of sexual difference and inequality, for – as the leading liberal encyclopaedia characteristically announced – "those who by unilaterally following an abstract rule of equality ignore the laws and barriers of Nature and demand more rights for women than women, according to those laws and barriers, can possibly want, destroy [that Christian and German family life that is] the holiest and most solid foundation of human and civic virtue and happiness".[7] In sum, for many mainstream liberals, difference and equality were conceived of as irreconcilable.

It is in this situation that the religious dissenters of the 1840s would seem like a marvellous alternative, for they proposed that difference and equality between the sexes were absolutely reconcilable, and their writings were saturated with calls for women's emancipation.[8] Thus, for example, one of the main founders of dissent, Johannes Ronge, while on his first missionary travels, proclaimed that his movement would "loosen the seal for the free participation of the female sex in public life . . . and the effects which this free participation will call forth – buttressed by the sanctifying and overpowering might of the female spirit in world history – will be unimaginable and immeasurable".[9] This sort of rhetoric about the redemptive power of womanhood recurred frequently in other dissenters' statements as well. And, interestingly, it was almost always coupled with calls for equality within marriage. As Ronge put it, a marriage based on love required "equal rights for both spouses". Why? Because "a woman held in tutelage cannot satisfy the free man, cannot complete his being".[10]

While at first this may indeed appear as a great contrast to standard liberal views, on second glance it quickly becomes evident that the dissenters' vision of gender equality was inextricable from their dream of a romantic partnership – and for this vision the maintenance of gender difference was just as essential as it had been for mainstream liberals and their vision of a more patriarchal family.[11] Another dissenting preacher, for instance, declared that "for the concept of marriage as an intimate togetherness . . . only One foundation is decisive and sufficient – . . . it is the equal human dignity and the equal human right that the woman deserves just like the man". Yet the same preacher also assured his listeners that "the whole emotional world of the woman . . . the whole breadth of her duties is utterly divergent from the nature and calling of the man". Thus he intoned: "Blessed is the woman, whose husband is a man, courageous, generous, a man who protects her, a man with whose strength her mildness unites into beautiful harmony."[12] These examples could be multiplied; they are quite characteristic.[13] Over and over again, dissenters presented the mutual complementarity of men's and women's different qualities as the basis for a sound marriage.[14] Equality was possible precisely when difference was maintained.

There were multiple reasons for dissenters' interest in greater equality between the sexes. One important cause was the feminization of religion already being remarked upon in the first half of the nineteenth century.[15] Women were understood to be the backbone of the traditional Christian churches, and no upstart religious movement could afford to ignore this constituency. Another significant reason lay in the dissenters' democratic and anti-authoritarian tendencies, and their rejection of distinctions between clergy and laity. As the interest in advancing women's equality shown by the contemporaneous movement of Reform Judaism reveals as well, there seemed to be an almost necessary relationship between calls for women's emancipation and challenges to traditional religions.[16] This was both because of the perceived links between women and religiosity, and because the questioning of traditional authority arrangements implicit in a critique of traditional religions invariably called all forms of authority and inequality into question. This phenomenon took on even greater significance because of the dissenters' belief (widely held at the time, also by those elsewhere on the ideological spectrum) that the family was a microcosm of society and that social transformation could only be grounded in self-transformation. Democracy had to be practised in the private realm if it was to have any hope of conquering the public realm.

But in order to understand why the dissenters' calls for women's emancipation were also consistently embedded in glorifications of marital partnership and of women's special difference from men, and why that delight in women's difference at times slid over into more negative representations of female nature, it is necessary to place their efforts in the context of religious conflicts of the pre-revolutionary period, especially the increasingly exacerbated polarization between political liberals and religious conservatives that had been evolving since the 1820s. At its centre was an intense contest over male sexual rights in particular.

The polarization first took shape around a conflict over priestly celibacy. Although there were notable initiatives in Württemberg, Hessen and Silesia (as well as Switzerland), the conflict was particularly acute in the Grand Duchy of Baden, not coincidentally the home of many of Germany's most illustrious and influential liberals.

There, leading Catholic professors at the University of Freiburg had launched petition campaigns to encourage the archbishop and the grand duke to abolish priestly celibacy within Baden's borders. (They quite seriously believed this could be achieved.) Calling celibacy "immoral, unlawful and unnatural", an "unnecessary coercion" that robbed the individual of his "personal freedom" and of the "enjoyment" of "one of the most essential natural rights", these reformers managed mainly to bring Rome's wrath down on their own heads, to catalyse the politicization of religious conservatives, and ultimately to lose their jobs.[17] But, along the way, the reformers did gain the fervent support of the liberal luminaries in the famous Lower Chamber of the Badenese diet. Thereafter, throughout the 1830s and 1840s, as the increasingly conservative Catholic hierarchy in Baden and elsewhere worked successfully to crack down on all movements for church liberalization – ascribing any and all efforts at church democratization (even if they had nothing to do with sex) to reformers' apparent "fleshly lust" and "propensity to licentiousness" – the parliamentarians vied with each other to denounce celibacy's "unnaturalness", and to declare how "inhumane it is, to exclude a whole class from the greatest of life's pleasures".[18] That the liberal commitment to combating compulsory celibacy was by no means limited to Baden became quite apparent at the Frankfurt parliament in 1848, when liberals from diverse states recommended that notions such as "the vow of chastity is null and void from the civic point of view" or "religious vows which permanently limit personal freedom are invalid" be written into the Basic Rights.[19]

Although political liberals' efforts to assist Catholic reformers in achieving an abolition of the requirement of celibacy had been in vain, the battle over celibacy caused the notion of men's right to sexual expression to become a major plank in the liberal platform, for the Catholic Church's insistence on priestly celibacy symbolized for liberals its more general denigration of human sexuality. Indeed, conservatives had not only dismissed anti-celibacy activists as "softies" and "woman-craving whimperers" and accused them of displaying "the most vulgar Jewish and pagan . . . weakness" – while sarcastically noting surprise at the notion that "in order to revive the frozen members of the body of Christ . . . one must above all provide for women".[20] They also increasingly warned that, even "within marriage, a brutal, powerful sensuality must be combated".[21] Couples were urged to model themselves on the sexual restraint shown in the marriage of Mary and Joseph, and were told from the pulpit that "matrimony is no place to be beasts".[22] Put on the defensive, liberals became even more effusive about the benefits of sexuality and marriage, arguing that "marital and familial relations belong to the most supreme and noblest life joys. Exclusion from these relations as a rule causes onesidedness, immorality, mental and physical agonies."[23]

Just how much the hostility between liberals and conservative Catholics was growing across the German lands also became apparent at various points in the 1830s and 1840s when Rome initiated a series of conflicts with German state governments over the practice of mixed marriages between Catholics and Protestants – a practice that also came to be interpreted in sexualized terms. From the pulpit, in the daily press, in polemical tracts and even in scholarly reference works, mixed marriages became the subject of the most heated outpourings. The church told priests to pressure particularly Catholic brides about the dangers mixed marriages posed to the salvation of their and their children's souls. Liberals were understandably enraged: free choice in love was a matter of fundamental principle for them, and liberals continually exalted the power of love – marital love – to overcome differences of faith.[24] For liberals, the controversy over mixed marriages was another incarnation of the controversy over celibacy. In both, their preoccupation with individual freedom of choice was conjoined with a programmatic insistence on the joys of married life, in which they continually conflated insistence on every man's right to sexual expression with paeans to domestic bliss.

But the increasingly self-confident conservatives responded to liberal protestations by mounting a major campaign to portray mixed marriages as motivated only by "love of the flesh", and arguing that only a shared Catholic Christianity saved sexual relations within marriage from being purely "animalistic".[25] Although according to conservative Catholics, the purpose of marriage was most definitely procreation and child-raising, sexuality – even within marriage – was nonetheless presented as a problem, a potential evil, which could only be justified through the religious unity of the two partners.

It was right in the midst of this battle, in late 1844 and the first half of 1845, that the dissenting movement arose. The most immediate catalyst for dissent's emergence was a rationalist outrage at the revival of pilgrimages and relic-worship in the supposedly so "enlightened" nineteenth century. And probably the largest reason lay in a widely felt need to create an organized humanist form of Christianity – to provide individuals with a tolerant, supportive community in which they could combine reason and spirituality, and express a faith that was no less fervent despite its disgust at hierarchical control and rigidly exclusivist doctrines. Widespread discontent with both the political authoritarianism of Restoration Germany and the generally growing intervention of Rome in Germany's religious affairs were important factors as well.

But in their numerous tracts and proclamations, the dissenters also made clear that their profound disgust at enforced priestly celibacy, and their alarm at Rome's increasing resistance to mixed marriages in particular, lay at the centre of their concerns. The dissenters particularly welcomed as spiritual leaders priests who wanted to marry, and especially encouraged mixed Protestant–Catholic couples to join their fold, thus directly, and concretely, snubbing the Catholic hierarchy in its stances on sex and marriage – and concomitantly garnering the utter adoration of political liberals across the German lands.

The overheated rhetoric used by religious reformers and political liberals in the earlier battles with religious conservatives were taken up again – and indeed developed further – by the liberals' dissenting heirs. Calling God the "Father of Love", the dissenters self-consciously developed a "religion of love".[26] They criticized celibacy as a "sin against Nature" and referred to sexual love as a "sacred yearning", a "so mighty drive, permeating living organisms by the laws of Nature's Founder".[27] They described marriage as *heaven on earth*", and rhapsodized about "sexual love, that divine and deifying love between man and woman".[28] They ridiculed "the poor pious idiots who think an unmarried life is more sacred than marriage!", and contended that "precisely the combination of man and woman produces the perfect human being".[29] Most importantly, as one dissenting preacher put it: The very notion "that I live, that you live, is proof of the sin of our parents. Against no other church doctrine has my heart so revolted as against this one."[30] With inimitable circumlocutory awkwardness (and circular logic) he concluded: "if love blesses the bond, . . . then this love will . . . ennoble all those pleasures, through which pure lust unfortunately lets so many people sink into animalistic rawness, into the sweet revelations of *a love made holy*".[31]

It was thus also no coincidence that conservatives used sexual rhetoric to denigrate dissent the moment it emerged, calling dissent a "religion of the flesh" and dissenters' notions of marriage "exceedingly vulgar", and claiming that dissenters "know no other God than the God of passion and sin".[32] Thus, for instance, one especially influential ultramontanist put down dissenting congregations by suggesting they had been "germinated in the lasciviousness of radical rabble-rousing". "It is not rationalism which confronts us here", he argued, "it is a disgraceful sensualism, whose wretchedness is glued together with a few rags of humanitarianism of the sort which all lewd people appeal to".[33]

Because conservatives were vociferously denigrating human sexual relations, because conservatives were using sexual rhetoric to denigrate dissent and deny its spiritual validity, dissenters appropriated religious language to defend sexual relations. Their very legitimacy as a spiritual movement turned on their ability to present sexuality in spiritual terms. They worked, in short, to spiritualize sex.

It was in this spirit that dissenters also rushed to congratulate those priests who joined the movement so as to get married. They exulted in the courage these men displayed in making such a "manly, truly Christian decision", in putting their bodies on the line so as to "reject celibacy *also through the deed*", and in transcending that hesitation "that usually keeps weak-minded people stuck at the halfway point".[34] Enforced celibacy, dissenters thought, emasculated men in two ways: it was a sign of their lack of independence, their pathetic subservience to other men within a hierarchical system. (Priests were taunted as "humiliated", "supine", "passive", "Romish choirboys".)[35] And, quite concretely, it meant that they were deprived of any (legitimate) sexual expression. For – as dissenters raged – "through the *commandment of priestly celibacy, marriage in and of itself* is, strictly speaking, branded as an *immoral* relationship".[36]

Whatever advocacy of women dissenters displayed, then, was inextricably bound up with this passionate defence of (hetero)sexuality and marriage, and their glorification of women's special qualities is best understood as part of this larger project. Indeed, dissenters made this connection explicit.[37] For example, one argued that the commandment to be celibate

degrades the entire female sex . . . because in the final analysis it rests on the conviction that *any* association *at all* with a woman in marriage is, seen strictly, a degradation of the man . . . But this then means nothing other than that through the woman the man is defiled. The woman herself is therefore something unclean, the woman is ungodly . . . Is not through this church law the whole female sex declared to be a herd of lepers?[38]

While this again appears to be quite an insightful point, and it has been praised as such by other feminist scholars of the movement, it too must be placed in context, particularly in the context of dissenters' endless rhetorical assaults on the priesthood. Dissenters recurrently inveighed against celibacy as a "school of lechery", and invoked the image of the lascivious priest, contending that "those parents to whom the purity of their daughters is dear, are forced to *forbid* them to go to confession".[39] Above all, dissenters threatened their male listeners with the image of the priest invading the heterosexual dyad – his disruption of matrimonial twosomeness.

Johannes Czerski, one of the ex-priests who founded the movement, expressed particular outrage over the way "the young hot-blooded doubter, worrying about his capacity for self-denial, is told when he enters the priestly life: 'You will not have one wife, but you will have one thousand!' "[40] Anxieties centred on the confessional box – perceived of as the vulnerable valve, the permeable point of entry, into the private sphere – for there, it was said, priests interrogated women about "the secrets of the marriage bed".[41] Or, as another prominent dissenter reminded his listeners, there "the wife is often handled by the priest as though her body and soul belonged to him!"[42]

And it was in this context that the image of the woman as seducible and unreliable appeared. For as one dissenting newspaper intoned, "if the woman is not so honourable and chaste, then obviously confessions about sexual sins must from the depths of the heart call forth stimulations and consequences on both sides, where youth and warm blood assert their power".[43] Ronge himself was most bothered by the way "the priesthood allows the woman to sin and then makes her into its slave through absolution".[44] And yet another contributor to the debates put it this way: "To marry a woman whose soul belongs to another – young man, consider this carefully – that means to marry adultery along with her." For "privy to the innermost secrets of the woman, [the priest] is the master of her soul. Now there is complete sharing between the husbands, for she has two: to one belongs the soul, to the other the body, but whoever owns the soul also in truth owns the body, for thought has the body in its power."[45]

Dissenters' descriptions of the confessional did manage to convey concern for women's vulnerability and that was no doubt the level at which some people interpreted them. But the dissenters' imagery was also indisputably meant to evoke a sense of threat for their male listeners and readers, and to encourage a sense of competition between husband and priest. (Indeed, what dissenters were not naming explicitly was the very real emotional support and often quite beneficial counterbalance to their husbands that priests could offer women.)[46]

Priests were (contradictorily) portrayed by dissenters – depending on whatever larger point they were trying to elaborate – as both undersexed *and* oversexed, as both emasculated *and* predatory (a phenomenon that bore an uncanny resemblance to the contradictory ways homosexual men would be represented just two or three decades later).[47] Criticizing priests was a way for dissenters themselves to assert their own proper – virile but controlled – masculinity; their male listeners and readers were enjoined to define their masculinity in opposition to the symbol of the priest as well. The clearest implication of dissenting rhetoric was that if men wanted happiness in marriage and fidelity from their wives, they would have to break from Catholicism and join the dissenting movement. As the rhetoric also indicated, however, dissenters were a bit worried about whether women would co-operate with this agenda.

Dissenters' recurrent apprehension about women's unreliability was, crucially, inextricably intertwined with misgivings about precisely that purported special difference of women's nature that the dissenters elsewhere celebrated. Dissenters constantly elaborated on the differences between "man's predominating intellect, and the woman's feeling, fervour and capacity to give of herself".[48] But it was precisely women's emotionality that also worried them. One dissenting newspaper, for example, clearly speaking of its old enemy Catholicism, argued that: "the priests of this faith have recognized well that they have little support any more from the enlightened men of the new age ... That is why they have focused particularly on women; for in them emotion predominates, an emotion ... that is easily aroused by images of heaven and hell and ... that can be led along the path of religious rapture."[49]

Similarly, a leading dissenting preacher complained of "the peculiar *affinity* between the character of the old *religion* and the character – that is, the peculiar nature – of the *female being*, the female mind. The old religion was based primarily on ominous dark *emotion*, its wishes and desires, and on the *fantasy* that made itself available to those wishes."

These reflections could not fail to evoke – and this was clearly his intent – a sense of competition between husband and priest for a woman's loyalty, when he further remarked that "the whole external appearance of the [Catholic] religion, the *rituals*, the *architecture* of the churches, and – not to be forgotten – the exceptional position of the *priesthood*, are all designed to captivate and capture the soul of the woman from this [emotional] side".[50] In the same text, then, this dissenter could both hail – as he had done a few moments earlier – women's distinct nature, the warm enthusiasm and fervent engagement of women that had been so indispensable to the growth and survival power of dissent, and decry the dangers brought to dissent by those very same distinctive qualities. As all these remarks suggest, the real life-or-death battle dissenters felt they were engaged in was one between dissenters and priests, and it was precisely women's difference, in particular their emotionality, that was causing dissenters to fear they might lose that battle.

The dissenters, in short, were most definitely directing themselves to their female listeners and readers, but they were as much, if not more so, concerned to address and engage men. A major reason for the dissenters' interest in gender issues lay in the legacy of hostility to conservative Catholicism they inherited – and elaborated. The dissenters' defence of women's equality, and their insistence on women's difference from men, were both deeply embedded in their effort to justify women as worthy love objects, just as their vaunting of the power of love itself was an impassioned response to conservatives' privileging of celibacy and pronounced distrust of sexual attraction and love as the bases for a marriage.

The less appealing images of women that dissenters also mobilized revealed deeper anxieties. On the one hand, the writings on women provided male dissenters with an important venue for articulating their own anguish at institutional religion's power to shape individuals' understanding of themselves and their most intimate choices.[51] On the other hand, and conversely, for both formerly Protestant and formerly Catholic dissenters, attacking institutional Catholicism was also a time-honoured way to process generalized male insecurities about one's own sexuality and masculinity.[52] Criticizing Catholicism was the most culturally acceptable mode for naming their own distress.

I want to propose, then, that the religious dissenting movement of the 1840s, this largest of all pre-revolutionary protest movements, was most seriously and profoundly concerned with questions of sexuality and masculinity. And so, while other recent scholars have praised the male dissenters for their decisive pro-woman stance and for creating the context in which organized feminism was first produced in Germany, I believe a more complex and nuanced picture is needed. Placing the dissenting movement in its proper context – the religious conflicts over sex that spawned it, and that caused sexual matters to become some of its central preoccupations – and taking seriously the ambiguous rhetoric about women other scholars of the movement have ignored, forces us to rethink the roots of German feminism. The point is certainly not to deny the vital relationship between feminism and dissent, but rather to suggest a more equivocal story of the emergence of feminism: by raising questions about the extent to which the dissenting movement's literature on the emancipation of women was in fact more centrally concerned with the rights, hopes and fears of men.

Notes

I would particularly like to thank Ellen Furlough, Isabel Hull, Doris Kaufmann and Kathy Peiss for their perceptive commentary on earlier versions of this chapter. A longer version of the chapter appeared in Dagmar Herzog, *Intimacy and exclusion: religious politics in pre-revolutionary Baden* (Princeton, NJ: Princeton University Press, 1996). Reprinted by permission of Princeton University Press.

1. See esp. S. Paletschek, *Frauen und Dissens* (Göttingen: Vandenhoeck & Ruprecht, 1990); C. M. Prelinger, *Charity, challenge and change: religious dimensions of the mid-nineteenth-century women's movement in Germany* (New York: Greenwood, 1987); and A. Lotz, " 'Die Erlösung des weiblichen Geschlechts': Frauen in Deutschkatholischen Gemeinden", in *Schimpfende Weiber und patriotische Jungfrauen: Frauen im Vormärz und in*

der Revolution 1848/49, C. Lipp (ed.) (Moos & Baden-Baden: Elster Verlag, 1986).

2. For example, for the Grand Duchy of Baden see the Mannheim and Heidelberg *Deutschkatholiken* membership lists of May 1846, in Generallandesarchiv Karlsruhe 362/1342 and 356/566; for other German lands see Paletschek, *Frauen*, p. 244.

3. K. Kleinpaul, in *Kirchliche Reform* (Halle) (Feb. 1847), p. 14. Emphasis here, as elsewhere in this chapter, was in the original.

4. L. Otto, "Die Teilnahme der weiblichen Welt am Staatsleben", in *Vorwärts! Volkstaschenbuch für das Jahr 1847*, repr. in *Die deutsche Frauenbewegung: Ihre Anfänge und erste Entwicklung: Quellen 1843–1889*, M. Twellmann (ed.) (Meisenheim am Glan: Anton Hain, 1972), p. 5.

5. With the exception of one anonymous woman, whose views did not particularly distinguish her from her male contemporaries (indeed she was more conservative in both her theology and her ideas about gender than most of the men), all the published contributors to the debates about women's rights among dissenters in the 1840s were male. In 1850, a few more women's voices joined the fray. See the texts reprinted in the "Anhang" to S. Paletschek, *Die Stellung der Frau im Deutschkatholizismus und in den freien Gemeinden im ausgehenden Vormärz und zu Beginn der Reaktionszeit* (MA thesis, University of Hamburg, 1983).

6. For a sampling of contemporaries' arguments, see J. B. v. Hirscher, *Die christliche Moral als Lehre von der Verwirklichung des göttlichen Reiches in der Menschheit*, 5th edn, vol. 2 (Tübingen: H. Laupp, 1851), pp. 418–20; W. H. Riehl, "Die Frauen: Eine social-politische Studie", in *Deutsche Vierteljahresschrift*, 1852 (3), p. 238; *Süddeutsche Zeitung für Kirche und Staat* (Freiburg), 30 Sept. 1847, p. 1069; Isaak Jolly and Karl Friedrich von Stockhorn's remarks in *Verhandlungen der Stände-Versammlung des Grossherzogthums Baden* (II. Kammer), 30 Apr. 1844, 4. Protokollheft, pp. 241, 249. Also see G. Denzler, *Die verbotene Lust: 2000 Jahre christliche Sexualmoral* (Munich: Piper, 1988), pp. 267–330.

7. C. T. Welcker, "Geschlechtsverhältnisse", in *Das Staats-Lexikon*, K. v. Rotteck & C. T. Welcker (eds), 1st edn, vol. 6 (Altona: J. F. Hammerich, 1838), p. 645. For a related assertion of contemporaries' fears that "women's emancipation" would necessarily involve both a blurring of gender identities and women's abandonment of familial roles, see *Evangelisches Kirchenblatt* (Freiburg), 15 June 1845, pp. 97–8.

8. The only other group of men attempting to implement greater equality for women were left-liberal democrats, but they advanced many of the same ambiguous notions that dissenters did, and indeed, there was tremendous overlap in membership between dissenting circles and democratic ones. On the democrats' gender views, compare C. Lipp, "Frauen und Öffentlichkeit: Möglichkeiten und Grenzen politischer Partizipation im Vormärz und in der Revolution 1848", and C. Lipp, "Liebe, Krieg und Revolution: Geschlechterbeziehungen und Nationalismus", both in Lipp

(ed.), *Schimpfende Weiber*, esp. pp. 295, 364. On the overlap in membership, see Paletschek, *Frauen*, esp. pp. 11, 13, 52–5, 144.

9. J. Ronge, *Rede, gehalten am 23. Sept. 1845 in der Münsterkirche zu Ulm* (Ulm: E. Rübling, 1845), p. 12.

10. J. Ronge, *Maria, oder: Die Stellung der Frauen der alten und neuen Zeit* (Hamburg: G. W. Niemeyer, 1849), p. 12.

11. Ronge, indeed, made his distaste for any blurring of gender differences explicit when he contrasted "that beautiful sanctifying femininity" with (what he called) "emancipation mania"– displayed by those women who thought it was "necessary to take over completely male spheres of activity and imitate . . . male manners". *Ibid.*, p. 10.

12. See F. Albrecht, "Mann und Weib", in F. Albrecht, *Religion: Eine Sammlung von Predigt-Vorträgen im Geiste des neunzehnten Jahrhunderts*, vol. 2 (Ulm: Gebr. Rübling, 1866), p. 470; F. Albrecht, "Ave Maria", *Religion*, vol. 1 (Ulm: Gebr. Rübling, 1857), p. 181; and F. Albrecht, "Das rechte Band der Ehe", *Religion*, vol. 2, p. 479.

13. Another preacher, for example, exclaimed: "How divinely beautiful is a marital life, in which the *man* exists for his calling and for his family, while in the house the woman is *everything* . . . She . . . vitalizes and beautifies the homey hearth, the sanctuary for which the man invests his energies in acting and fighting for the fatherland." H. Rau, "Die Stellung der Frauen in der Christenheit", in H. Rau, *Worte zum Herzen des deutschen Volkes: Vorträge und Gebete* (Stuttgart: Franckh, 1848), p. 149.

14. Dissenters also went to extraordinary rhetorical lengths to present their particular model of marriage as the highest and most desirable goal a woman could attain. (As one dissenting newspaper urged its female readers: "Hang on with gratitude to the reform of our century [i.e. the dissenting movement], it is that which will ransom you." "Die Frau des Christenthums", in *Der fränkische Morgenbote* (Nuremberg), 24 July 1851, p. 66.) In addition, the dissenters continually deployed contrasts between "Oriental" (or "Mosaic") polygamy and "enslavement" of women and Greco-Roman (or Christian, or "Occidental", or "Germanic") "veneration" of women in order to underscore their points about the glories of marriage – thereby both completely ignoring the significant number of single women in their movement, and unreflectingly casting aspersions on their Jewish contemporaries. For the fuller argument, see D. Herzog, *Intimacy and exclusion: religious politics in pre-revolutionary Baden* (Princeton, NJ: Princeton University Press, 1996).

15. For background on the feminization of religion, see H. McLeod, "Weibliche Frömmigkeit – männlicher Unglaube? Religion und Kirchen im bürgerlichen 19. Jahrhundert", in *Bürgerinnen und Bürger: Geschlechterverhältnisse im 19. Jahrhundert*, U. Frevert (ed.) (Göttingen: Vandenhoeck & Ruprecht, 1988); and E. Saurer, " 'Bewahrerinnen der Zucht und der Sittlichkeit': Gebetbücher für Frauen – Frauen in Gebetbüchern", *L'Homme: Zeitschrift für Feministische Geschichtswissenschaft* 1(1), 1990,

pp. 37–58. Cf. also the remarks of a conservative and a radical contemporary: L. Castorph, *Sendschreiben als unterthänigste Petition an die Allerhöchste Badische Staatsregierung und Hohe Badische Stände-Kammer hervorgerufen durch die Motion des Herrn Abgeordneten Zittel* (Baden-Baden: Scotzniovsky, 1846), p. 45; and L. Dittmar, *Der Mensch und sein Gott in und ausser dem Christenthum* (Offenbach a. M.: G. André, 1846), p. 67.

16. Reform Jews, for example, not unlike Christian dissenters, argued for greater equality for women within Jewish religious life and within Jewish marriages, and criticized those elements of Talmudic law that were "an insult to the free personality of women, an insult against religion" (so much so that more orthodox Jews ridiculed the reformers' "chivalrous" efforts to "break a Talmudic lance in honour of the Jewess"). See *Die Reform des Judenthums* (Mannheim), 2 Dec. 1846, p. 285; and *Der Orient: Literatur-Blatt* (Leipzig), 20 Aug. 1846, pp. 538–42. See also W. G. Plaut (ed.), *The rise of reform Judaism: a sourcebook of its European origins* (New York: World Union for Progressive Judaism, 1963), pp. 252–5.

17. See the oft-repeated slogan of Prof. Heinrich Schreiber, cited in H. Maas, *Geschichte der katholischen Kirche im Grossherzogthum Baden* (Freiburg i. B.: Herder, 1891), p. 52; and the petition by Profs Heinrich Amann and Karl Zell, signed by 23 Catholic laypeople, reprinted in *Verhandlungen* (II. Kammer), 9 May 1828, 4. Protokollheft, pp. 59–73. Cf. also A. Franzen, "Die Zölibatsfrage im 19. Jahrhundert", *Historisches Jahrbuch* 91, 1971, which documents the conflicts over celibacy in the other German states.

18. Letter from Archbishop Bernhard Boll to Pope Gregory XVI, 26 Oct. 1832, quoted in Maas, *Geschichte*, pp. 52–3; Philipp Ludwig Seltzam and Johann Baptist Bader's remarks in *Verhandlungen* (II. Kammer), 16 Dec. 1831, 35. Protokollheft, pp. 20, 22.

19. Remarks by Heinrich Friedrich Wedekind (from Hanover) and Karl Alexander Spatz (from Bavaria) in F. Wigard (ed.), *Stenographischer Bericht über die Verhandlungen der deutschen constituirenden Nationalversammlung zu Frankfurt am Main*, vol. 3 (Frankfurt am Main: J. D. Sauerländer, 1848), pp. 2015, 1750.

20. M. Häusler, *Noch ein nachdrückliches Wort über das ernstliche letzte Wort eines Cölibat-Feindes und eines würdigen Consortens, der um die hohe Erlaubniss des Rücktrittes in den Laienstand wehmüthig flehet* (no place, no publisher, 1815), pp. 48, 64–5; J. A. Möhler, "Beleuchtung der Denkschrift für die Aufhebung des den katholischen Geistlichen vorgeschriebenen Cölibates: Mit drei Aktenstücken" (1828), in *Dr. J. A. Möhler's gesammelte Schriften und Aufsätze*, Johann Josef Ignaz Döllinger (ed.), vol. 1 (Regensburg: G. J. Manz, 1839), pp. 190–91, 180.

21. *Süddeutsche Zeitung für Kirche und Staat*, 29 Nov. 1846, p. 1077.

22. On the Mary and Joseph ideal, see anon., *Die Musterehe und die Nothwendigkeit einer Wiederherstellung der Ehe nach der Musterehe* (Freiburg i. B.: Herder, 1850); and "Familie", in *Real-Encyclopädie des Erziehungs-*

und Unterrichtswesens nach katholischen Prinzipien, H. Rolfus & A. Pfister (eds), vol. 1 (Mainz: Florian Kupferberg, 1863), pp. 562–3. On "beasts", see J. Dürr, *Predigten auf alle Sonn- und Festtage des katholischen Kirchenjahrs und bei besonderen Anlässen*, vol. 2 (Villingen: F. Förderer, 1843), pp. 246–7; and cf. A. Stolz, "April", in *Mixtur gegen Todesangst: Kalender für Zeit und Ewigkeit Erster Jahrgang 1843: Für das gemeine Volk und nebenher für geistliche und weltliche Herrenleute*, 16th edn (Freiburg i. B.: Herder, 1868), pp. 36–7.

23. C. T. Welcker, "Verbotene Ehen, insbesondere Priester-Cölibat", in *Das Staats-Lexikon*, Rotteck & Welcker (eds), 1st edn., vol. 15 (Altona: J. F. Hammerich, 1843), p. 665. For an explicit example of liberals' disgust at neo-orthodox restrictions on sex within marriage, see *Seeblätter* (Constance), 29 Apr. 1845, p. 210.

24. In other words, love between individuals was seen as socially transformative. A classic example was provided by one liberal government minister who earnestly discoursed on "the reconciling power of marriage" and elaborated that mixed marriages had helped to

   overcome the damaging mutual prejudices, antipathies and hesitations, interwoven the physical and spiritual interests of families of different confessions in the most intimate way, and therefore in all these ways like almost no other thing worked towards the inner unity and strengthening of the life of the state and the life of the *Volk*.

   [K. F. Nebenius], *Der Streit über gemischte Ehen und das Kirchenhoheitsrecht im Grossherzogthum Baden* (Karlsruhe: G. Braun, 1847), p. xvii. Again, debates at the Frankfurt Parliament in 1848 would reveal in how very many different German states liberals had become obsessed with defending mixed marriages. See Wigard (ed.), *Stenographischer Bericht*.

25. Anon., *Die Musterehe*, p. 17; Hirscher, *Die christliche Moral*, vol. 3, pp. 513, 516.

26. Handwritten "Trauungsrede" of 14 May 1846, from a dissenting marriage ceremony, in the Heinrich Schreiber papers, Stadtarchiv Freiburg K1/27 2/9; and H. Jellinek, *Die religiösen, socialen und literarischen Zustände der Gegenwart: In ihren praktischen Folgen untersucht. Erster Theil: Die religiösen Zustände der Gegenwart, oder: Kritik der Religion der Liebe* (Zerbst: Kummer, 1847).

27. "Die Ehe, vom bürgerlichen und kirchlichen Standpunkte aus betrachtet", *Katholische Kirchenreform* (Berlin) (June 1845), p. 164.

28. L. Uhlich, *Die Ehe: Eine Erörterung* (Magdeburg: Selbstverlag, 1857), p. 16; J. Kinorhc, "Ueber die Ehe zwischen Juden und Christen", *Kirchliche Reform* (Oct. 1846), p. 1.

29. Uhlich, *Die Ehe*, p. 6.

30. Albrecht, "Erbsünde", *Religion*, vol. 1, p. 290.

31. F. Albrecht, "Ueber die Ehe", in F. Albrecht, *Predigten, Aufsätze und Mittheilungen*, vol. 5 (Ulm: G. P. Geuss, 1846), p. 8.

32. A. Stolz, "Der neue Kometstern mit seinem Schweif oder Johannes Ronge

und seine Briefträger" (1846), in A. Stolz, *Gesammelte Werke*, vol. 8 (Freiburg i. B.: Herder, 1913/14), p. 60; F. A. Staudenmaier, *Das Wesen der katholischen Kirche: Mit Rücksicht auf ihre Gegner dargestellt* (Freiburg i. B.: Herder, 1845), p. 184; J. H. Mehlmann, "Einige Worte über deutschkatholische Praxis", *Mannheimer Morgenblatt*, 20 July 1847, p. 964.

33. F. J. Buss, *Das Rongethum in der badischen Abgeordnetenkammer* (Freiburg i. B.: Herder, 1846), pp. 72, 21.

34. See *Trau-Rede, am 21. Februar 1845 bei der kirchlichen Trauung des katholischen Predigers Czerski in Schneidemühl gehalten von dem evangelischen Ortspfarrer Grützmacher* (Berlin: W. Hermes, 1845), p. 6; *Oberrheinische Zeitung* (Freiburg), 5 July 1846; *Seeblätter*, 21 May 1846, p. 257.

35. J. Ronge, *Zuruf* (Dessau: H. Neuburger, 1845), p. 12; J. Ronge, "Letter to the inferior clergy", in anon., *John Ronge, the Holy Coat of Treves and the new German-Catholic Church* (New York: Harper, 1845), pp. 129–30.

36. *Unsre Antwort: Abgedrungene Erklärung der Mannheimer Deutsch-Katholiken auf das Manifest des erzbischöflichen Ordinariats in Freiburg* (Belle-Vue: Verlags-Buchhandlung, 1846), p. 16.

37. For example, cf. Ronge's remarks in *Maria*, p. 8.

38. C. Scholl, "Unsere Reform und die Frauen" (12 Nov. 1848), in *Aus hohen Tagen: Das Erwachen der Geister in Oesterreich* (Berlin: H. Lüstenöder, 1891), p. 93.

39. G. v. Struve, *Briefe über Kirche und Staat* (Mannheim: J. Bensheimer, 1846), p. 53; *Unsre Antwort*, p. 16.

40. J. Czerski, *Rechtfertigung meines Abfalles von der römischen Hofkirche* (Bromberg: L. Levit, 1845), p. 14.

41. "Die Ehe", *Katholische Kirchenreform* (Apr. 1845), p. 87.

42. Scholl, "Unsere Reform", pp. 94–5.

43. "Die Ehe", *Katholische Kirchenreform* (June 1845), p. 167.

44. Ronge, *Maria*, p. 7.

45. "Der katholische Priester in seiner Stellung zum Weibe und zur Familie von J. Michelet: Aus dem französischen", *Katholische Kirchenreform* (May 1845), pp. 140 and 142. Cf. the quite similar remarks in F. Albrecht, "Die Trauung", in *Religion*, vol. 2, p. 498; and *Keine Ohrenbeichte mehr! Zeitgemässes Wort eines Rhein-Hessischen Katholiken an seine Glaubensgenossen* (Frankfurt am Main: C. Körner, 1845), p. 7.

46. Cf. on this point J. R. Watt, *The making of modern marriage: matrimonial control and the rise of sentiment in Neuchâtel, 1550–1800* (Ithaca, New York: Cornell University Press, 1992), p. 11.

47. See J. C. Fout, "Sexual politics in Wilhelmine Germany: the male gender crisis, moral purity, and homophobia", *Journal of the History of Sexuality* 2, 1992, pp. 388–421, here pp. 404, 413, 416. Cf. J. D'Emilio, "The homosexual menace: the politics of sexuality in cold war America", in *Passion and power: sexuality in history*, K. Peiss & C. Simmons (eds) (Philadelphia: Temple University Press, 1989), p. 232.

48. Scholl, "Unsere Reform", p. 98.

49. *Deutschkatholisches Sonntags-Blatt* (Wiesbaden), 5 Mar. 1854, p. 39.

50. C. Scholl, "Die Frauen in der Religion", *Es werde Licht!* (Nuremberg & Leipzig) (Oct. 1875), pp. 5–6.

51. It is possible, for instance, that in elaborating on the vulnerabilities of women in the confessional box, the dissenters were actually thematizing their own sense of vulnerability. Thus, for example, dissenters indignantly labelled the confessional "that torture-chamber of the conscience" and argued that the obligation to confess was "a Roman presumption and tyranny" that "made a farce out of the autonomy of thinking people, [and produced] a loss of self, debilitation and desacralizing of the innermost human being, a repression, enslavement and smothering of the free spirit". Struve, *Briefe über Kirche*, p. 53; *Unsre Antwort*, p. 23.

52. For example, a good deal of the dissenters' rhetoric harked back to Reformation times. What was new, however, was the imprint these views were leaving on such specifically modern, nineteenth-century political formations as liberalism and feminism.

Chapter Five

જ

Companionship and conflict: the negotiation of marriage relations in the nineteenth century

Lynn Abrams

On 6 May 1842 Theodore Janssen was granted a divorce from her husband Gerhard by the Cleve regional court under Article 231 of the *Code civil* that permitted a dissolution of marriage on the grounds of "cruelty, ill-treatment or serious insult".[1] The couple had married eight years previously but within a few months Gerhard, who was a cabinet-maker by trade, developed a serious drink problem. Thereafter, Theodore testified, she was subjected to almost daily verbal and physical abuse until April 1838 when Gerhard, having lost all his customers on account of his drinking and therefore being unable to provide for his wife and children, deserted his family for his home town of Xanten and then proceeded across the border to Belgium. Theodore left to stay with her parents. Gerhard's return to the area some four years later and his resumption of a regime of torment towards his wife prompted Theodore to take her marriage to the divorce court.[2]

The substance of Theodore Janssen's case consisted of eight detailed instances of cruelty and abuse that had allegedly occurred between the summer of 1835 and December 1841. She described how, in the late summer of 1835, Gerhard had returned home drunk at around 11 pm, and exclaiming that she and her parents should be hanged, hurled several chairs around the room and threw Theodore to the ground with the words, "yes you hussy [*Luder*] I'll murder you". Fortunately, she was rescued by Janssen's apprentice and their domestic servant. Gerhard, who had moved to the bedroom, proceeded to throw everything out of the bed with the exception of the straw mattress upon which he lay, ordering his wife to do the same. But as he cursed her with the words "whore and slut" she fled the room, narrowly avoiding injury from a knife that Gerhard threw after her.

Furthermore, Theodore testified that for many months during 1837 Gerhard had taken a knife to bed every night, threatening to cut his wife's throat while she was sleeping. On another occasion, dated precisely as Ash Wednesday 1838, Gerhard again rebuked his wife for being a slut and a whore, threatened to kill her by placing a knife in front of her face and forced her wedding ring from her finger. Theodore was able to count on no fewer than 26 witnesses to her husband's brutal and threatening behaviour, ranging from her mother and the local pastor to various maidservants, apprentices, neighbours and acquaintances.[3] There was no doubt that Theodore's life was in danger, that the ill-treatment had been persistent, that cohabitation was no longer possible and that Gerhard had attempted to defame the honour and good name of his wife. Thus, Theodore Janssen received her divorce.

Theodore Janssen was typical of women living in areas of Germany under the *Code civil* who used the divorce court, not only to escape violent and abusive marriages that clearly did not conform to their expectations but to articulate publicly their beliefs about the nature of the marriage relationship. Such women held a marriage ideal that bore some resemblance to the notion of companionate marriage, and they consistently rejected husbands' use of physical violence to reinforce their dominance within marriage.

In recent years the so-called companionate or affectionate marriage has become one of the great movable feasts and arguably one of the most imprecise concepts of Western historical scholarship on marriage and the family.[4] This model of a marital relationship which incorporates attributes such as companionship, mutual affection and respect, and equality is frequently identified as an indicator of significant social and economic change, and of an improvement in the position of married women. However, although Lawrence Stone spoke of the companionate marriage not appearing until the eighteenth century (in England) amongst the upper classes, it would appear that in Reformation Europe the idea that a marriage should be based at least partially upon affection and companionship was not uncommon.[5] Certainly in Germany, as Lyndal Roper has shown, the Augsburg Council regarded marriage as a "natural, complementary hierarchy of masculinity and femininity" that incorporated harmonious productive and emotional relationships within the artisanal household.[6] Of course, the Reformation conception of companionate marriage was still predicated upon a gender hierarchy, despite the fact that, as Roper argues, patriarchal marriage appeared to be constantly challenged or undermined.[7] In the eighteenth and early nineteenth centuries, David Sabean shows how marriages in rural Neckarhausen were conceived as a contract within a network of reciprocal relationships. In Sabean's words, "a simple patriarchal solution to running a household was not enforceable".[8] Marital companionship was an issue for debate once more in the early nineteenth century, as Dagmar Herzog's contribution to this collection shows. Although male Protestant and Catholic dissenters advocated greater equality within marriage and spoke of marriage based on love or affection as opposed to the property considerations of arranged marriages, they continued to affirm natural difference between the sexes. Indeed, sexual difference was the basis for complementarity within the marriage relationship.[9] Some prominent female dissenters, however, held a more radical view of the companionate marriage. For the liberal Protestant dissenter Louise Dittmar, for instance, the economic and political dependence of the wife upon her husband was the main cause of unhappy marriages.[10] It followed from this that "Marriage, as a free community of individuals, can only function when the right to individuality and freedom without the hierarchical gradation of the gender of both partners is defended in the political arena."[11] According to Dittmar the law was the very foundation of women's subordination within marriage. She demanded a revised Civil Code to replace what she called "this two, three or even five-headed monster" (referring to the patchwork of law codes extant in the separate German states) which in fact reduced women to slaves.[12]

> He [the husband] is the political, moral and economic representative of her political, moral and economic position. She is nothing, he is everything. He is the custodian of her property and at the same time, her guardian . . . Legal protection of the female is a constitutional saying . . . the man in fact holds all the power, he is the representative of political sovereignty, of absolute monarchy, of autocratic government.[13]

So, in Dittmar's view, legal protection of the female by her husband was a pretence if there were no safeguards against the abuse of power by him.[14] Dittmar's analysis was based on the notion of fundamental human rights and a rejection of the traditional liberal position that qualified the demand for equality for all individuals by an insistence on natural gender difference.[15]

After the turn of the century and after the introduction of the new Civil Code (*Bürgerliches Gesetzbuch* or BGB) in 1900 that had much to say on marriage and divorce, the "problem of marriage" was addressed by a number of prominent feminists who had been prompted into a serious consideration of the marriage institution and women's position within it by the BGB's reinforcement of patriarchal relations and its incorporation of the notion of the passive and obedient wife. Writers like Marianne Weber – who could be described as a moderate feminist – and the socialist feminist Lily Braun, began to talk explicitly about the notion of companionate marriage: a model that they predicated upon an improvement in the legal status of the wife. "Once the female has turned into a human being, that is, an individual personality, with views, judgements and life-goals of her own, then she has been spoiled for the average marriage", wrote Lily Braun in 1905.[16] Two years later Weber noted that women were striving for greater independence and many were "standing on their own two feet" and in these circumstances the patriarchal model of marriage was no longer tenable.[17] By 1914 she was arguing that "companionship . . . is a child of our time", characterized by "the foundation of the relations between husband and wife not only on their sexual differences but on the things they have in common. Companionship can naturally only exist when husband and wife relate to each other not just as sexual beings but as human beings."[18] Clearly then, Weber and Braun, although in political terms on opposite sides of the fence, were in agreement on one thing: they rejected difference as the basis for companionship.

There are clearly a number of quite different notions of what constituted a companionate marriage being used here. However, a cursory look at the evidence from the early modern period through to at least the nineteenth century suggests some continuity of common expectations on the part of both spouses of mutual affection, harmony and respect that might loosely constitute a companionate model of marriage but that did not exclude (and often assumed) a hierarchy of the sexes. That is, a harmonious and respectful marriage still required the wife successfully to fulfil her allotted role and still permitted the husband to punish transgressions with a "modicum" of physical abuse. The following analysis of severe marital disharmony in the early to mid-nineteenth century, therefore, does not attempt to locate the definitive emergence of the companionate marriage in this period but rather confirms the observation of James Hammerton that "patriarchal and companionate marriage were never stark opposites".[19] The tensions experienced by the couples described below were partly a consequence of the existence of a rather slippery concept of marriage within which the balance between patriarchy and companionship was continually being negotiated. Moreover, to take the continuity theme one step further we might note that although the precise causes of domestic conflicts can generally be found in historically and regionally specific social, economic and political conditions, the manifestations of conflict are remarkably consistent over time. Lyndal Roper for the sixteenth century and David Sabean for the eighteenth, to take just two examples, describe instances of marital misconduct concerning sexual behaviour, the control of money and the household, and violence, that will be repeated in the nineteenth century.[20]

I want to suggest that spouses, and especially women (and not just the educated middle classes and feminist activists), held notions of marriage as a harmonious partnership long before the end of the nineteenth century. Drawing upon the statements of those whose marriages had broken down and who had sought a formal separation or divorce through the courts it is clear that husbands *and* wives held expectations of marriage characterized by companionship, affection and mutual respect (albeit within the boundaries of separate gender roles) and that women, aided by a relatively liberal divorce law, continued a long tradition of challenging their husbands' authority at a time when men were trying to maintain a patriarchal notion of marriage to bolster their declining power in the economic sphere.[21] Women who petitioned the courts for a divorce on the grounds of cruelty in particular – and women were in a massive majority here – were saying they were not prepared to tolerate their husbands' violent assertion of patriarchal power.[22] By taking their marriages to the divorce court women were not only escaping marriages that did not live up to their expectations but, in speaking about their severely troubled and dysfunctional marriages, they were often implicitly publicly articulating their beliefs about the nature of the marriage relationship. This is not to say that the patriarchal marriage gave way to a companionate model, but women's public resistance signalled to men, the community and the legal system, that excessive violence within marriage was intolerable while, at the same time, they affirmed their opposition to husbands' violation of a more incontestable (at least in court) set of expectations: autonomy over housewifely functions, access to the house and particular spaces and functions within it, and recognition of their chastity.

The evidence presented below does not suggest that women's resistance to male exploitation of the power that was invested within them in the marriage institution was new in the nineteenth century, although the arena – the secular divorce court – was. Indeed, the resistance documented below belongs to a long tradition of similar action taken by wives albeit manifested in different ways. During the Reformation, the Reformation Councils were responsible for adjudicating marital disputes which, although not explicitly permitting beaten women a voice and in spite of condoning the right of a husband to chastise his wife, did acknowledge that some marital violence reached an intolerable level.[23] Joy Wiltenburg shows how early modern street literature, ballads and the like, permitted women a degree of power in the household and acknowledged women's legitimate call on community support in the case of severe cruelty.[24] In the eighteenth century, church (*Kirchenkonvent*) and secular courts (*Schultheissamt)* that heard cases of marital conflict allowed battered women to speak out against their husbands.[25] Thus, well before the introduction of secular separation and divorce, women have had some access to arenas in which they could articulate their expectations of marital behaviour. In nineteenth-century Germany, however, relatively liberal divorce laws – at least in comparison with much of the rest of Europe – provided women (and indeed men) with a public platform for the articulation of marital grievances and ideals.

Why focus on probably the most disturbing indicator of marital breakdown, domestic violence? It might be objected that the moment of physical abuse is an unreliable indicator of spouses' expectations of what constituted "normal" relations. For some time now, historians of the family and of women have used domestic violence cases as indicators of the shifting nature of gender relations in the past. There now exists a substantial canon of such work that, for the most part, seeks to counter the contemporary belief that wife-beating was caused by pathologically violent men or the "rough" working class in conditions of poverty and squalor.[26] Following Linda Gordon who, in her examination of domestic violence in nineteenth-century America, argued that violence was "not the total, undifferentiated and predictable tyranny of men and helplessness of women",[27] but a product of complex struggles and negotiations that are historically specific, historians of Britain, Europe and North America have constructed a scenario that relates domestic violence to changing socio-economic conditions and discourses upon marriage and the ways in which these impacted upon relations between the sexes. Thus, violence between the sexes in the nineteenth century is often explained as a manifestation of the breakdown of the old certainties of pre-industrial society. In the words of Robert Griswold speaking about nineteenth-century America, "Where women had once been respected they were now dominated by men who, caught in social and economic changes they could scarcely fathom let alone control, channelled their impotency and frustration into a new control over their wives."[28] Physical abuse, then, is an index of external factors impacting upon personal relations and here I aim to use cases of abuse against wives as an indicator of profound economic and social change that in turn acted to alter the basis of the marriage contract.

Historians have also tried to chart the position of women through the discourse and reality of domestic violence. Far from demonstrating the decline of women's power within the family, some have suggested that cases of wife-beating, particularly in the mid- to late nineteenth century, illustrate women's agency – women did not passively submit to husbands' domination, rather they asserted their power within the household, helping to fuel domestic spats and occasionally more serious violent incidents that the women then used to prosecute or divorce their husbands.[29] However, with the rise of the notion of companionate marriage and the ideology of domesticity in the late nineteenth century, it has been asserted that women were less likely to experience physical violence at the hands of their husbands but the cost was their acceptance of female passivity.[30]

More recently, A. James Hammerton in an analysis of marital conflict and attitudes towards marriage in nineteenth-century Britain maintains that such patterns and explanatory frameworks are misleading and that the level of conflict and violence within marriage was probably fairly consistent throughout the century. However, Hammerton is not setting out to dehistoricize domestic violence, to argue that spousal cruelty exists in all societies and that therefore historical explanation is unnecessary. What changes, he argues, is the public discourse on domestic violence. In the mid- to late nineteenth century the husband who used violence to assert his authority was publicly criticized as a relic of an outmoded culture of aggressive masculinity.[31] David Sabean has suggested that a similar process was underway in Germany as wife-beating as a legitimate means of enforcing male authority within marriage was rejected and men who beat their wives were now regarded as exceptional characters whose behaviour was uncontrolled and thus had to be controlled by the state.[32] It is the purpose of this chapter to examine some of the dynamics of gender relations within marriage during the nineteenth century through the prism of cases of domestic violence and spousal cruelty presented before the Cleve *Landgericht*. In particular it analyzes the consequences of a contradiction between a legal conception of marriage, enshrined in the Civil Code, which upheld a patriarchal model of marriage and thus provided men with some justification for their use of physical violence against wives, and an alternative model of marriage that envisaged a softening of the hierarchy, greater emphasis on respect, harmony and reciprocity, and that allowed women to reject a marriage governed by authoritarian relations. A close reading of these divorce depositions does provide a more nuanced insight into the nature of marital relations and shifting expectations in the predominantly rural Cleve county in the Düsseldorf district during a period in which economic and social change was seriously impacting upon gender roles, while the marriage law remained patriarchal and married women's legal status was, to quote a commentator on the French *Code civil*, "lamentable"[33]. By the mid-nineteenth century, then, what was at stake were power relations within marriage: who exerted power and who obeyed. And it was predominantly women who placed this on the public agenda expressed in terms of expectations of a form of marriage that would entail a more equal distribution of power and authority.[34]

It should be noted that poverty, or at least economic instability was an experience common to many of the couples cited here. Cleve was a predominantly rural area located in the Düsseldorf administrative district of the Prussian *Rheinprovinz*. Its economy was based on agriculture and the artisanal trades. Under the *Code civil* peasants had been emancipated and the guild system abolished, which gave the economy of the *Rheinprovinz* an initial stimulus. However, the area suffered from an inegalitarian social structure with day labourers outnumbering agricultural proprietors and tenant farmers and an overcrowded artisan sector. The decades preceding the harvest failure of 1845–6 and the revolution of 1848 were characterized by falling real wages, intense competition and mass impoverishment.[35] By the 1840s it was said that the impoverished and those living on the edge of poverty formed the majority of the *Rheinprovinz*'s population.[36] Poverty and insecurity must have had a corrosive effect on marital relations – certainly the scarcity of work and the fragile nature of the household economy featured in many divorce cases – but the explanation of domestic violence is not to be found in these conditions alone. Rather, two themes occur frequently in the context of marital conflict and wife-beating in Cleve county: female independence and sexuality, and authority in the household. It was in these spheres that men were acutely aware of the shift of gender roles and in which they attempted to reassert their control.

Although spouses did not necessarily anticipate their marriages to be a bed of roses, they did expect to be treated with respect and to enjoy a reasonably harmonious and possibly affectionate partnership. The marriage between Wolff Simons and his wife Elise was described as "tolerable, if not especially happy", but the relationship had become intolerable for Elise owing to "the vehemence and brutality of her husband".[37] Elisabeth Heiming formally separated from her husband Rüttgerus on the grounds of cruelty and failure to provide. Rüttgerus was described in court as "unkind to his wife, argued with her at every opportunity, and spoke to her harshly."[38] The power of words to harm or ruin a reputation appears still to have been taken seriously here, with women especially complaining that their husbands called them whore (*Hure*), bitch (*Biest*) and slut (*Luder*), although men too expected their wives to speak to them respectfully.[39] The shopkeeper Franz Hellen succeeded in gaining a separation from his wife Dorothea on the grounds of her unseemly behaviour and foul language. "The marriage contract had hardly been signed when [her] malevolent disposition, quarrelsomeness, common, vulgar behaviour became so obviously apparent ... that superhuman self-denial was required by the plaintiff, to maintain quiet, moderate behaviour in order to escape the most vulgar emotions of his wife."[40] But actions spoke louder than words, and although women may have expressed dismay at their husbands' coarse language, only amongst the upper classes would this have sufficed for a divorce. Lower- and middle-class women, however, articulated their conception of the marriage contract by signalling their unwillingness to endure physical cruelty.

The women in Cleve who used the divorce law to challenge the dominance of their husbands often took this step from sheer desperation. For women of all social classes, the wives of farm labourers to the aristocracy, a legal dissolution was the only means by which they could permanently escape a violent and abusive marriage, as a decision in their favour might also make provision for maintenance payments and permit them to remarry.[41] But as we examine these women's depositions it becomes clear that women were attempting to renegotiate marriage relations, or at the very least hold on to a marriage model that permitted them some autonomy, while men were trying to maintain or re-establish their dominance in the face of economic and social problems that threatened to undermine their position. This process is clearly outlined in David Sabean's study of the Württemberg village of Neckarhausen between 1700 and 1870. It is around 1800 that Sabean suggests a shift in the nature of domestic violence, from what he terms "systematic chastisement" to "reactive striking out".[42] "Rather than using a rod to enforce compliance or staging a carefully prepared beating", writes Sabean, "husbands boiled over in anger and wreaked immediate vengeance."[43] The reason for this change, suggests Sabean, was a shift from a patriarchal, economy-based marriage to a marital relationship based more on companionship. As husbands began to lose the economic and political right to their *Herrschaft*, they translated their impotence and frustration into assertion of power in other ways. Thus we witness men turning to what was termed *liederlich* lifestyles, drinking, attempting to assert their position in the household by questioning the wife's control of this sphere and resorting to violence and abuse to re-establish their *Herrschaft*. The relative paucity of research into the relationship between marital relations and local socio-economic conditions in Germany means we should take care in drawing too many parallels between Sabean's Württemberg community and this one in the *Rheinprovinz*. Yet the comparability in terms of economic change manifested in alterations in the sexual division of labour predicated upon the emergence of what is termed a "makeshift economy", particularly during the first four decades of the nineteenth century, suggests the forms of marital conflict observed in Cleve might bear many similarities to those occurring in Neckarhausen and elsewhere.[44]

What we are seeing in Cleve is a process of renegotiation of reciprocities in which women were more skilled in the negotiation process, or more adaptable, than the men. In other words, wife-beating and a divorce case signal the end-point of a process of struggle that has often lasted for a number of years. As Linda Gordon states: "Had women consistently accepted their subordinate status, and had men never felt their superior status challenged, there might have been less marital violence."[45]

At first sight the evidence presented by women in their divorce depositions seems merely to describe a common litany of domestic violence that appears to change little over time. Women were slapped, punched and kicked, thrown against walls and furniture, down staircases and to the floor, and beaten with household implements; pots and pans, cutlery, plates of food, shoes, stones and items of furniture were hurled across rooms, while scissors and razor-blades as well as knives were used to threaten and sometimes to injure women. Women had the clothes they were wearing torn from their bodies, they were pulled by the hair, thrown out of bed and locked out of the bedroom or the house. All of this was frequently accompanied by a torrent of verbal abuse. If they did not manage to flee the house or alert the neighbours with their cries for help, women were knocked unconscious, received black eyes, bruises, cuts and diverse injuries at the hands of their husbands. But these women's depositions suggest a pattern of marital conflict and violence that was firmly rooted in the political economy of a nineteenth-century rural society experiencing structural change. Few men seem to have struck their wives in a systematic and predetermined way; rather, husbands' actions were informed by specific circumstances and events that encouraged them to demonstrate their *Herrschaft* symbolically and physically.

One indication that women had expectations of greater reciprocity within the marriage relationship was their resistance to being treated like servants by their husbands. It has been plausibly argued that the early to mid-nineteenth century saw the emergence of a new ideology of *Häuslichkeit* that placed emphasis on orderliness, cleanliness and diligence within the home.[46] A wife was increasingly judged according to her ability to adhere to the new standards of domesticity and this became a node of conflict within marriages. The majority of violent incidents occurred within the home and we frequently find women's household management being scrutinized, criticized and challenged by husbands as a prelude to an outburst of abuse. The wife of Wilhelm Spiegelhoff described in 1851 how her husband had "withdrawn from all domestic life, inhabited his particular room, spoke at the most a couple of words with his wife about food and drink [and] treated her like a servant".[47] Similarly, the Heimings' household economy was at the centre of their domestic disputes. Rüttgerus Heiming had physically and verbally abused his wife throughout their two-year-old marriage, but for Elizabeth the marriage became intolerable when Rüttgerus "took away the running of the household from his wife and transferred it to the daughter of his first marriage since when he has ceased to say a friendly word to his wife . . . banished her from his table and forced her to eat alone in her room".[48] The final indignity for Elizabeth was being forced to beg for food and drink from neighbours when Rüttgerus deprived her of even these basic necessities. Behind these disputes around *Häuslichkeit* lie more far-reaching changes in the division of labour, at least amongst the artisanal and labouring classes. With many men unable to secure stable employment, wives were forced to play a larger role in providing for the family by taking in lodgers or caring for apprentices without the additional help of a housemaid, or by working in the family business in addition to undertaking household responsibilities. When women's labour became crucial to the survival of the household they threatened the husband's position and thus contributed towards an imbalance within the marriage relationship.[49]

The control of space within the household also seems to have become an issue for marital strife. The interior of the home was regarded as the woman's domain, thus male incursion into this space and exclusion of women from it was one way in which husbands sought to reassert their power. Anna and Johann Maassen fell out over her allegation that he had dissipated her property, in particular by spending more than a thousand thalers on his own needs. One June day in 1832 Johann proceeded to lock up the house, making sure he had possession of all the keys. He eventually changed the locks so Anna Maassen could no longer gain access.[50] Maria Tollschneider suffered the ultimate indignity when her husband Wilhelm not only conducted an affair in the conjugal home, and beat his wife forcing her to flee, but she admitted she was forced to slip into the house at night while her husband was in bed with his concubine in order to obtain food to take back to her lodging.[51]

Mealtimes were economically exposing occasions. The meal-table was a focus for the reciprocal duties of husband and wife and while husbands complained about the preparation of meals, wives vented their anger at husbands who arrived home drunk at mealtimes or who failed to acknowledge the work that had produced the meal. Bernhard Riehs returned home drunk at midday, looked into the pot and was apparently dissatisfied with what his wife had prepared for the meal. "In a thrice, as she lifted the pan from the fire, Riehs took hold of a chair and hit her with it over the head . . . the chair flew into pieces from the blow."[52] Theodore Janssen described to the court an incident in which her husband came home at midday, lay down on the bed and told her to bring his meal to him there. "After she had carried out his wishes, he ordered her to eat but when she did this he threw a plate of meat and vegetables towards her, saying that he should be given raw steak."[53] Apparently Gerhard Janssen was in the habit of eating raw meat as a hangover cure. Catharina Hülsken was preparing food in advance for the arrival of guests the next day when her husband Engelbert began to rain insults upon her in his rage, grasped a stick of sausages that was hanging over the oven and threw them to the floor at Catharina's feet, causing the sausages to fly all over the kitchen.[54]

Household finances were unmistakably at the root of many domestic disputes. A successful marriage depended on mutual management of resources and the husband often attacked the woman's ability to manage resources wisely or else he denied them altogether, either by drinking to excess or leading a dissolute lifestyle or both as in the case of Dominicus Mottmann. Dominicus was a master cabinetmaker and small businessman in Cleve. He married Agnes in 1847 and shortly after he began to drink and undermine the marriage on account of his "idleness and wastefulness" according to Agnes's deposition. He also began to beat his wife as well as venting his aggression on the contents of the household: various household items including the porcelain were destroyed by a drunken Dominicus. Around Christmas 1853 "Mottmann hit the plaintiff in the face and over the head . . . with a pair of overshoes because his wife had remarked she had not needed the shoes which Mottmann had bought without her knowledge."[55]

Drink was often at the heart of financial disputes and violent conflicts, but drink in itself is not a sufficient explanation for men's violent behaviour towards their wives. As Linda Gordon argues, there is little evidence to support the view that alcohol in itself causes violent and aggressive behaviour.[56] Rather we should focus on the cultural role of drinking and the social relations it fostered and destroyed. While women did drink, they were more likely to do it at home and in smaller quantities than their husbands. Taverns were a male preserve and in any case women were less likely to have the time or the money to drink for pleasure. In Cleve only one woman challenged this trend and she did not become violent. She was merely considered a public nuisance and a bad mother.[57] While not all male drinkers beat their wives, however, the association between alcohol consumption and violence is close enough to warrant closer examination. Men drank in public and often in company. All of the towns and villages in the Cleve district had their taverns, offering men like Johann Dohmen the opportunity to drink much of the day. Johann neglected his business, spent the whole day going from one tavern to the next, and would return home to his wife in the evening to hurl insults and to beat her.[58] Gerhard Janssen habitually visited several taverns in the area around Xanten in one day, so that the innkeepers were well acquainted with his violent disposition. On one occasion while in one of these taverns Gerhard reportedly exclaimed that he was going to stab his wife and "because I know that I will then have to die, I shall kill myself at the same time". He did not carry out his threat but regularly beat his wife while under the influence of drink.[59]

While there is no indication that the all-male company these men undoubtedly enjoyed in the taverns encouraged domestic violence, tavern culture probably helped to reinforce a sense of male dominance or an atmosphere of patriarchy under siege. In the tavern men were out of reach of women, they were spending their money as they wished and reinforcing a patriarchal system that they felt was being challenged by economic pressures and a new model of contractual obligations. Women, on the other hand, were resentful of the time and money spent by their husbands in taverns and probably played some part in escalating marital conflicts.[60] The stereotypical image of the wife as an innocent victim of her husband's drinking and brutality – an image frequently conjured up by lawyers in divorce depositions – was simplistic and misleading, as it did not take account of women's assertiveness in domestic power struggles.

In their vivid descriptions of the physical cruelty they endured, Cleve women also added that they were verbally insulted by their husbands. Along with words of abuse such as dog, bitch, pig and slut, whore (*Hure*) was the most frequently cited term of abuse. This insult implies an undercurrent of sexual antagonism within these marriages and in particular suggests husbands' resentment of women's relative autonomy.[61] Thus, whore as a term of abuse need not imply a wife's sexual infidelity but could be a reference to women's increasing sphere of influence and autonomy in this period just as the men were experiencing a relative decline in economic and therefore political power. Yet, in Cleve, use of the term "whore" was often accompanied by physical cruelty and allegations of infidelity. Matthias Bletschen was alleged to have "mistreated his wife in a drunken condition, reproached her most unjustly, [said] that she was a whore, had given herself in a bad way to all the men where she lives and in that way earned money [to buy] her clothes".[62] Similarly Johann Langen accused his wife of having had intercourse with other men before their marriage, "he insulted her, whore, slut, bitch, etc, hit and punched her with his fists . . . and ripped her clothes from her body". On another occasion he tore her clothing, threw her out of bed and threw the bedding into the hall and threatened to throw her out of the house.[63]

Sexual relations were also a focus of the element of exchange implicit in the marriage contract and thus this arena was likely to feature as another node of conflict. Women were often attacked, beaten and insulted in the bedroom, accused of adultery and threatened with violence while they lay in bed. Men used the accusation of adultery to assert their dominance. Margaretha Boll described how her second husband, Johann, regularly beat her and threw her out of the house on account of his almost daily assertion that she was adulterous.[64] Wilhelm Bego, who was an itinerant tailor, beat his wife on his infrequent visits home, accused her of adultery while he was away and explicitly called her a "*Bürgermeister*'s whore".[65] And suspicion fuelled by acquaintances who testified to having seen men enter the house while he was away led the shopkeeper Wolff Simons to accuse his wife of entertaining another man. Elisa Simons's story was somewhat different. She claimed that the marriage had become intolerable owing to the "vehemence and brutality" of her husband and furthermore he had insulted and abused her on account of his "unfounded suspicion of his wife's infidelity".[66]

Some husbands took their wives' pregnancy to be an indication of sexual infidelity and/or female autonomy. Childbirth was still very much the woman's sphere and men seemingly resented the solidarity that developed between women and children in the community.[67] It was not uncommon for women to be beaten when pregnant; Theresa Eirman was beaten by her husband while pregnant and while she was breast-feeding her child,[68] and Elisabeth Schreiber's husband, who was described as an "uncouth and violent man", had thrown his wife down the stairs when she was heavily pregnant.[69]

In nineteenth-century Cleve, and other similar rural communities, it would appear that in response to husbands' attempts to shore up their dominance within the family and the community that was being undermined by economic crisis and changes in the relations of production, women were using their rights under the *Code civil* to demand respect and greater equality in marriage, even asserting a more egalitarian model of companionate marriage, and were challenging their husbands' "right" to beat them. These women's complaints, although articulated within a distinct socio-economic environment, cannot be entirely disengaged from more general discussions and criticisms of marriage that became louder and more widely disseminated as the century progressed. Yet, the new German Civil Code of 1900 reasserted the central importance of marital stability by restricting the grounds for divorce. At the same time this Code privileged the marital crime of adultery over that of cruelty by subjecting cruelty claims to the interpretation of the courts. Thus, almost a century of evidence from women who had used the separation and divorce courts in the Rhineland and Prussia to state indirectly their preference for a different kind of marital relationship based on mutual respect and reciprocity rather than patriarchal dominance, was ignored. The state implicitly condoned husbands' use of physical violence against their wives and thereby upheld a patriarchal model of marriage that conflicted with the realities of married life. Wives were reshaping their expectations of marriage along semi-companionate lines. When they encountered serious and in particular, violent resistance from husbands, they used the divorce court to nullify the contract. But when the opportunity arose for the legal system to reflect decades of change in marriage relations, it failed to do so and instead the individual needs of women were relegated beneath the bourgeois ideal of marital stability.

Notes

I would like to thank Elizabeth Harvey and Eve Rosenhaft for their valuable comments on earlier versions of this chapter.

1. The *Code civil*, or Code Napoléon, was in force in the Prussian *Rheinprovinz* from 1814 until 1900. It permitted divorce on four grounds: adultery, mistreatment, imprisonment of a spouse, or by mutual agreement. One French commentator on the Code Napoléon noted that "cruelty" referred to "acts of violence which endanger life or injure the health of the person". Ill-treatment furthermore was interpreted as "being of a duration, the treatment being of such a kind to expose to physical danger, rendering conjugal life impossible". Insult, on the other hand, was a vaguer term incorporating diverse forms of abuse including defamation of character and "any words, writings or acts by which one of the parties reflects on the honour and good name of the other". V. Marcade, *Explication du Code Napoléon* (Paris, 1868), p. 577.
2. Hauptstaatsarchiv Düsseldorf (HStAD), Zweigarchiv Kalkum, Cleve Landgericht, Rep 7/254: 6 May 1842.
3. HStAD, Rep 7/254: 6 May 1842.
4. See L. Stone, *The family, sex and marriage in England, 1500–1800* (London: Weidenfeld & Nicolson, 1977); J. Finch & A. P. Summerfield, "Social reconstruction and the emergence of companionate marriage, 1945–59", in *Marriage, domestic life and social change*, D. Clark (ed.) (London: Routledge, 1991), pp. 7–32; E. Roberts, *Women and families: an oral history, 1940–1970* (Oxford: Basil Blackwell, 1995).
5. See M. E. Wiesner, *Women and gender in early modern Europe* (Cambridge: Cambridge University Press, 1993), p. 60.
6. L. Roper, *The holy household: women and morals in Reformation Augsburg* (Oxford: Clarendon Press, 1989), p. 165. Cf. S. D. Amussen, who uses the concept of "benevolent patriarchy" in *An ordered society: gender and class in early modern England* (Oxford: Basil Blackwell, 1988).
7. Roper, *Holy household*, p. 205.
8. D. W. Sabean, *Property, production, and family in Neckarhausen, 1700–1870* (Cambridge: Cambridge University Press, 1990), pp. 171 ff.
9. See D. Herzog, "Religious dissent and the roots of German feminism", Chapter 4 in this volume.
10. L. Dittmar, *Das Wesen der Ehe nebst einigen Aufsätzen über die soziale Reform der Frauen* (Leipzig, 1849).
11. Dittmar, *Das Wesen der Ehe*, repr. in R. Möhrmann (ed.), *Frauenemanzipation im deutschen Vormärz* (Stuttgart: Reclam, 1978).
12. Dittmar, *Das Wesen der Ehe*, p. 94.
13. *Ibid.*, p. 132.
14. Indeed, it has been acknowledged that the duty of a husband to protect his

117

wife was largely symbolic whereas his right to obedience had great practical significance in everyday life. H. Dörner, *Industrialisierung und Familienrecht: Die Auswirkungen des sozialen Wandels dargestellt an den Familienmodellen des ALR, BGB und des französischen Code civil* (Berlin: Duncker & Humblot, 1974), p. 143.

15. On male liberal writings on sexual difference see K. Hausen, "Family and role-division: the polarisation of sexual stereotypes in the nineteenth century – an aspect of the dissociation of work and family life", in *The German family*, R. J. Evans & W. R. Lee (eds) (London: Croom Helm, 1981), pp. 51–83.

16. L. Braun, *Selected writings on feminism and socialism* (Bloomington, Indiana & Indianapolis.: Indiana University Press, 1987), p. 125.

17. M. Weber, *Ehefrau und Mutter in der Rechtsentwicklung* (Tübingen: J. C. B. Mohr, 1907), p. 413.

18. M. Weber, "Eheideal und Eherecht", in M. Weber, *Frauenfragen und Frauengedanken* (Tübingen: J. C. B. Mohr, 1919), p. 146.

19. A. J. Hammerton, *Cruelty and companionship: conflict in nineteenth-century married life* (London: Routledge, 1992), p. 2.

20. Roper, *Holy household*, pp. 165–205; Sabean, *Property, production, and family*, pp. 124–62.

21. A very similar situation is described by Sylvia Möhle for Göttingen during a period of economic crisis: "Ehen in der Krise: zur Bedeutung der Eigentumsrechte und der Arbeit von Frauen in Ehekonflikten (Göttingen 1740–1840)", in *Familie und Familienlosigkeit: Fallstudien aus Niedersachsen und Bremen vom 15. bis 20. Jahrhundert*, J. Schlumbohm (ed.) (Hanover: Hahnsche Buchhandlung, 1993), pp. 39–50.

22. Of 60 cases heard in Cleve between 1818 and 1870, 31 plaintiffs cited Article 231 of the *Code civil* as grounds for a total dissolution (30 of whom were female), and another 7 cited mistreatment as grounds for a legal separation.

23. Roper, *Holy household*, pp. 185–94.

24. J. Wiltenburg, *Disorderly women and female power in the street literature of early modern England and Germany* (Charlottesville, Va. & London: University Press of Virginia, 1992), pp. 97–103.

25. Sabean, *Property, production, and family*, pp. 124 ff.

26. See, for example, S. D. Amussen, " 'Being stirred to much unquietness': violence and domestic violence in early modern England", *Journal of Women's History* 6 (2), 1994, pp. 70–89; L. Gordon, *Heroes of their own lives: the politics and history of family violence* (London: Virago, 1989); Hammerton, *Cruelty and companionship*; M. Hunt, "Wife-beating, domesticity, and women's independence in eighteenth-century London", *Gender and History* 4, 1992, pp. 10–33; N. Tomes, "A 'torrent of abuse': crimes of violence between working-class men and women in London, 1840–1875", *Journal of Social History* 11, 1978, pp. 328–43.

27. Gordon, *Heroes of their own lives*, p. vi.

28. R. Griswold, *Family and divorce in California, 1850–1900: Victorian illusions and everyday realities* (Albany: State University of New York Press, 1982).

29. See E. Ross, "Fierce questions and taunts: married life in working-class London", *Feminist Studies* 8, 1982, pp. 575–602; Tomes, " 'A torrent of abuse' ".

30. See C. Backhouse, " 'Pure patriarchy': nineteenth-century Canadian marriage", *McGill Law Journal* 31, 1986, p. 303.

31. Hammerton, *Cruelty and companionship*, pp. 2–3.

32. Sabean, *Property, production, and family*, p. 168.

33. E. Blackwood Wright, *French civil code* (London: Stevens, 1908), p. vi.

34. Women formed the majority of plaintiffs in divorce cases in a number of jurisdictions. In Hamburg, for example – where cruelty was not a valid ground for a divorce – between 1816 and 1879 women accounted for 60 per cent of petitioners. Similarly, in Frankfurt/Oder, under the Allgemeines Landrecht, drunkenness and assault were the most common grounds cited by women, prompting Blasius to argue that divorce appeared to have a "safety-valve function" for women. D. Blasius, "Bürgerliche Rechtsgleichheit und die Ungleichheit der Geschlechter", in *Bürgerinnen und Bürger*, U. Frevert (ed.) (Göttingen: Vandenhoeck & Ruprecht, 1988), pp. 77–8.

35. J. Sperber, *Rhineland radicals* (Princeton, NJ: Princeton University Press, 1991), pp. 16 and 28.

36. H. Lademacher, "Die nördlichen Rheinlande von der Rheinprovinz bis zur Bildung des Landschaftsverbandes (1815–1953)", in *Rheinische Geschichte*, F. Petri & G. Droege (eds) (Düsseldorf: Schwann, 1976), p. 487.

37. HStAD, 7/265: 27 July 1848. In a similar case heard in Hamburg, it was said of the divorcing couple: "They lived together, not always very happily, but they got along, so that one could speak of a good marriage." Staatsarchiv Hamburg, Niedergericht 5488: 25 July 1879.

38. HStAD, 7/225: 23 July 1844.

39. On the power of words, see Sabean, *Property, production, and family*, pp. 139–46; L. Roper, "Will and honor: sex, words and power in Augsburg criminal trials", in L. Roper, *Oedipus and the devil* (London: Routledge, 1994), pp. 53–78.

40. HStAD, 7/231: 17 July 1822.

41. The social background of female plaintiffs mirrors that of the area as a whole, the majority being wives of farm labourers, artisans and small shopkeepers. However, in nearby Düsseldorf a famous divorce case involving Sophie von Hatzfeldt and her husband the Graf von Hatzfeldt demonstrated that divorce was an option even the aristocracy made use of. HStAD, Rep 4/260.

42. Sabean, *Property, production, and family*, p. 133.

43. *Ibid.*, p. 134.

44. *Ibid.*, ch. 5 and ch. 6. See also Möhle, "Ehen in der Krise" for a comparable situation in Göttingen.
45. Gordon, *Heroes of their own lives*, p. 286.
46. Sabean, *Property, production, and family*, pp. 179–80.
47. HStAD, 7/270: 21 Feb. 1851.
48. HStAD, 7/255: 23 July 1844.
49. This is clearly demonstrated by Sylvia Möhle for Göttingen for the end of the eighteenth and beginning of the nineteenth century: "Ehen in der Krise", pp. 44–6.
50. HStAD, 7/237: 25 July 1832.
51. HStAD, 7/234: 30 June 1824.
52. HStAD, 7/249: 1839.
53. HStAD, 7/254: 6 May 1842.
54. HStAD, 7/255: 8 Feb. 1844.
55. HStAD, 7/225: 7 May 1853.
56. Gordon, *Heroes of their own lives*, p. 264.
57. HStAD, 7/282: 20 May 1858.
58. HStAD, 7/225: 25 Mar. 1850.
59. HStAD, 7/254: 6 May 1842.
60. Sabean shows that the number of marital cases in which the husband's drinking was mentioned increased dramatically in the nineteenth century. This increase does not necessarily indicate greater alcohol consumption on the part of men but rather lower tolerance by wives that was partly due to women's greater role in the labour market. *Property, production, and family*, pp. 174–9.
61. Sabean writes, "*Hur* is . . . individualising and stresses her own power and character." *Property, production, and family*, p. 144.
62. HStAD, 7/240: 20 Nov. 1833.
63. HStAD, 7/268: 16 May 1850.
64. HStAD, 7/247: 27 Sept. 1838.
65. HStAD, 7/266: 2 Nov. 1848.
66. HStAD, 7/265: 27 July 1848.
67. See E. Ross, *Love and toil: motherhood in outcast London, 1870–1918* (New York & Oxford: Oxford University Press, 1993); contrast with the situation described by U. Rublack for early modern Germany, "Pregnancy, childbirth and the female body in early modern Germany", *Past and Present* 105, 1996, pp. 84–108.
68. HStAD, 7/267: 11 Dec. 1848.
69. HStAD, 7/278: 7 Feb. 1856.

Chapter Six

The sick warrior's sister: nursing during the First World War

Regina Schulte
Translated by Pamela Selwyn

Problems of approach

Since the 1970s, women's history has sought to discover women's place in history, to give women a voice, and to make them visible. It has sought to examine history as a site of female, specifically "other" experiences and thus not simply to add women to historiography as it had been conceived up until then, but also to confront and challenge the historical record with the specific difference of female experiences and perceptions. This "other" historical discourse was intended not only to bring forth new questions, approaches and methodologies along with new fields of research, but also to read traditional historical fields against the grain of an inherently masculine viewpoint. Finally, with "gender history", women's historians left the separate "room of one's own"[1] that had been important for consolidating their research and feminist interests, in search of a more general discourse aimed at undermining the apparently natural polarity of the sexes in history, by historicizing it.

This historicizing process implies two additional steps: studying the commonalities and complementarities in gender relations as well as differences at any given period, and their dependence upon cultural and social factors. Thus the place of gender relations in so-called general history may be established, thereby underlining the specific role of gender relations in history and enriching our understanding with new and critical elements. The wars of the modern period are, in the emphatic sense of the word, thresholds of this general history. For that reason I have spent the past few years engaged in individual studies on the historical anthropology of war experiences from the seventeenth to the twentieth century. The First World War marks a deep break in continuity in modern German history. For that reason I have chosen an absence in the literature on the First World War as the subject for this chapter, while trying to suggest how this gap might be filled using the tools of gender history.

Strangely enough, an old polarity of early women's studies has continued to guide the women's and gender history on the First World War that has appeared up until now. Woman's role in the family, household and workplace is contrasted to that of the soldier at the front line. Home front and front line thus appear as two blocks, identifiable as feminine and masculine, facing each other and yet growing ever further apart. This research – by Ute Daniel on working-class women, by Susanne Rouette on demobilization, by Karin Hausen on war widows – has been solid and impressive.[2] But where are the women who shared the soldiers' experiences, participating in their life at the front and demonstrating their own strength when the soldiers were stricken – the nurses?

Recent literature on the organization of total war only mentions the nurses in passing, and even in analyses of war experiences they remain objects of masculine attribution. Even Robert Whalen's *Bitter wounds* portrays front-line nursing staff only in the form of male orderlies and otherwise in gender-neutral terms.[3] Belonging neither to the heroic brotherhood of the trenches nor to the female community of household and work back home, they appear to exist in a no-man's-land. What remains is an almost salacious but apparently dominant image of front-line nurses as the "angels in white" or the angels of death of the male imagination.[4] This allegorical complement to the soldier has apparently stymied women's historians as well, who have tended to look for the emancipatory content of war experiences, or to assume that approving of the war or serving voluntarily at the front were things foreign to female nature. Thus front nurses could be identified neither as victims of male war nor as heroines whose war experiences brought out "women's innate pacifism".[5] To that extent they also mark an embarrassing point in the history of the bourgeois women's movement, whose leaders formulated ideals in 1914 that seemed to be virtually personified in the figure of the front nurse.

Why is it that British gender history avoids treating its "heroines" so shamefacedly? How is it that Anne Summers, Sandra M. Gilbert and others manage to explore this topic, with all its ambivalences of class and gender, in all its complexity, using it to evoke an image of society at war?[6] The explanation may lie in the greater self-confidence born of a less broken feminist and left-wing tradition, as well as the national context of a victor state. The work of these historians exists in the context of the English cult of Florence Nightingale as "the lady with the lamp", and serves to demythologize the "lady-nurses".

Is the contrast connected to a specifically German experience? At first glance this very experience seemed to invalidate the most readily available sources, or to make it easier to ignore them. The diaries published by the Red Cross in 1916 and 1917[7] and the autobiographical documents by front nurses published in 1934 and 1936[8] were stamped from the outset as unauthentic, since their publication was clearly intended to serve the propagandistic ends of, respectively, supporting one war and preparing for the next. On closer inspection, though, they represent a multi-layered and rich body of texts, ripe for critical deciphering rather than dismissal.[9] Comparison with research in Britain can help us develop an approach to the sources and offer background for conceptualizing further research. German research, in contrast, has so far yielded only a few works along these lines: above all, an article by Herbert Grundhever from the field of critical medical history, and as background the history of the nursing profession by Claudia Bischoff: the latter, however, does not examine the specific role of nurses in war.[10] We do not even possess anything approaching precise basic social historical data, such as the number and social origins of the nurses, or the location and duration of their duty, let alone studies of biographical cohorts, analyses of the different types of nurses or microanalyses of individual military hospitals or sectors.

The mother houses and the supply of nurses

The nurses and assistant nurses (some 92,000 in all) employed during the course of the war by the "Imperial Commissar and Military Inspector for Voluntary Nursing" represented about two-fifths of medical personnel, most of whom were male stretcher-bearers, orderlies and physicians.[11] They came from or through various organizations. The most important were the Red Cross nurses' associations and the mother houses of the Lutheran deaconesses (*Diakonissen*) in the Kaiserswerth nurses' association, in which even before the war

25,000 and 11,000 nurses, respectively, worked. The Lutheran nurses – whose history records an inspiring visit to Kaiserswerth by Florence Nightingale – also went to war under the flag of the Red Cross. In smaller numbers, but from similar structures came the sisters of the Orders of St John, the Silesian and Rhenish-Westphalian Knights of Malta, the Royal Bavarian Knights of Saint George, and the mother houses of the Sisters of Mary and the Grey Sisters of St Elizabeth in Breslau. These were actual or quasi-conventual orders devoted chiefly to nursing. The Red Cross associations had also adopted this traditional structure and discipline. They worked, however, on an interdenominational basis and focused more on preparedness for war work. The only other interdenominational nurses' organization was the Professional Organization of Nurses in Germany that had only been founded in 1903 and worked together with the Federation of German Women's Associations (*Bund Deutscher Frauenvereine*) and the National Women's Service (*Nationaler Frauendienst*). Organized rather like a trade union, it only achieved a membership of some 2,500. Although prepared for service, it was not admitted to wartime medical service in 1914 because this lay in the hands of the Red Cross, which at the beginning of the war could fall back both on an enormous supply of quickly trained unpaid volunteers and on co-operation with the religious nursing orders. The professional association thus turned at first to Austria, but with growing need during the course of the war it was also used on all fronts in the Reich as well.

The organization dominating wartime medical care was the Red Cross, under whose banner the medical service stood. Its pillars were the nursing sisterhoods that since the founding of the Patriotic Women's Associations (*Vaterländische Frauenvereine*) by Queen Augusta in 1866 after the Austro-Prussian War had been pledged to war work and known thereafter as the "Empress's Army".[12] They viewed their duty, alongside social and disaster relief work, as training women for war work in particular.[13]

Although we do not yet have the empirical studies to prove it, we may assume that the orders and sisterhoods provided a classic field of activity for unmarried daughters of the upper and middle classes. To this extent the sisterhoods may be regarded as a nationalized substitute for convent traditions, including their discipline and the sense of purpose gained through a quasi-familial activity in a broader social field. The Mother Superiors were almost all of the aristocracy or the educated middle classes. The Red Cross and the Lutheran nurses' orders were regarded as institutions for young ladies of good family (*höhere Töchter*). Even in the trade-union-like Professional Organization of Nurses more than half of the 2,650 members reportedly came from the upper classes. "Their fathers were higher civil servants, military officers, professors, lawyers, physicians, apothecaries, manufacturers and large landowners."[14] The rest came from the middle classes and the rural population.

Nurses' training was in the hands of the orders and associations or hospitals and private nursing schools. The length of training varied, but after 1906 in Prussia and most other states there was an examination after a one-year training. Studies have shown that this training consisted mainly of 10–12 hours of heavy and dirty housework a day for room and board and 10–20 marks pocket money per week. Even after completing training, most nurses' wages were on a par with those of domestic servants. Nurses were expected to display an endless willingness to work, including night duty, frequently every night. Nursing personnel were expressly required to perform "all work", particularly cleaning and other housework. Because they had to be ready to work at all times, nurses had scarcely any leisure or holiday time. Tied to the mother house by the obligation to accept room and board, they lived in almost complete dependence. Bound to absolute obedience to matrons and doctors, there was little scope for them to assert their own interests. Claudia Bischoff has rightly pointed out the similarities in the situation of nurses and domestic servants in the Kaiserreich, except that the former tended to come from more genteel backgrounds and were confined to their nurses' quarters.[15]

Thus it is not improbable that the female volunteers of 1914 were hoping that war work would provide an escape from pent-up frustrations and thwarted expectations. The hard reality of nursing in the pre-war period contrasted sharply with a widespread idealization, beginning with children's books, which had made many aristocratic and middle-class girls dream of nursing as a fulfilling social use of their femininity, and not simply a respectable alternative for those without a husband or profession.

In any case, what the propagated role model of the nurse came down to – in Britain, incidentally, as in Germany – was that women could develop their "true, natural" femininity particularly well in this field. Serving, caring and selfless, the nurse – at once mother and sister

– could use her capacity for love, chastity and self-sacrifice. Her work was "voluntary", which meant that it was unsullied by shabby materialism or professional ambition. Nurses were not there to compete with doctors on the plane of scientific knowledge and rationality, but rather to serve obediently and supplement their work as care-givers, and to fuse with the desires and needs of patients. Humility and a good upbringing would allow them to perform any task with dignity. "The principle that a nurse, even one from the highest aristocracy, must not fail to perform, automatically, any task, however arduous or repellent, for the well-being of the patient represents . . . the most essential foundation for the training of good nurses." [16]

The Patriotic Women's Associations considered that the Red Cross nurses were particularly qualified for military service because of their strict socialization in the hierarchical conditions of the mother houses with their ethos of asceticism, obedience, renunciation and sacrifice. These values were exaggerated in an image of ideal femininity and motherliness, which helped to conceal the exploitative nature of nursing and deny the common assumption that it was a substitute for marriage and motherhood. Only more precise information about the lives of unmarried women in the Wilhelmine middle and upper classes could give us a deeper understanding of the extent and the subjective significance of women's willingness to volunteer for medical service in the First World War.

Setting out, or the "other" volunteers

On 2 August 1914 the Red Cross, which during the following four years was to send 19,073 voluntary female auxiliary personnel to the area behind the lines, and whose wartime publications remained consistently pro-war and pro-nationalist, printed the appeal of the Patriotic Women's Associations:

> War has been forced upon us. Germany's army is drawing its sword for Kaiser and Reich, to defend our dear Fatherland. Our husbands, sons and brothers hasten to the standard, joyfully prepared, with God's blessing, to risk their blood and their lives for King and Fatherland. The Fatherland expects of Germany's girls and women the same devotion, the same readiness to sacrifice as of its sons. [17]

They were expected to perform labours of love, fulfilling a mighty duty for the nation by tending the wounded and raising the fighting morale of the troops.

This pathos, every bit as inflated as the outpourings of military volunteers and of those who called them up, was by no means unique among organized women in 1914. It is far more likely that the associations and sisterhoods volunteering as military nurses shared the standpoint of the Red Cross Patriotic Women's Associations. Even the Professional Organization of Nurses, rejected as a quasi-union, struck the same note in its publication *Unterm Lazaruskreuz* on 8 August 1914: "Let 'I serve' be our battle cry!"[18] It was not only functionaries who adopted this tone. If we look at the autobiographical accounts and diaries of those who volunteered as war nurses we find, in less stereotypical language, even greater impatience and desire to work near the front lines. "The impatience with which we [members of the Baden Red Cross nurses] await that great moment when we are called to the area behind the lines, is indescribable", wrote Emmy von Rüdgisch in her war diary.[19] The same fear is echoed in other accounts: "If only I didn't fear getting there too late",[20] or "I shall never forget the day. The long wait was finally over – we were off to the field."[21] Bertha von der Schulenburg noted, when the big moment finally came: "We were so impatient that the railway journey seemed quite endless."[22] And another nurse recalled: "My heart was thumping . . . it was a day of honour for us all: the F2 was the first hospital train off to the front, from behind the lines to the theatre of operations, into the line of fire . . . Our faces were positively transfigured, all petty concerns forgotten."[23]

It is clear that there was a female counterpart to the Langemarck generation,[24] not only in the polarity between front and home front, but in the same impulse to break out and away from the obstacles and disappointments of everyday life into something that seemed more real, to be consumed by fire, to live close to danger and significance. What moved young women of the bourgeoisie and aristocracy to volunteer in droves as military nurses at the beginning of the First World War, and why did so many nurses from the mother houses press as close as possible to the front lines? The phrase they repeat again and again, in common with male volunteers, was the urge to be "off to the field". This implies a desire to leave behind urban civilization and their routine subjection to the obstructive discipline of the mother houses, and to participate in the soldiers' escape into a world in which reality and significance coincided, blood was spilt and sacrificed for a higher purpose, and where they could assuage and comfort. Their task suddenly takes on an archaic and fantastic quality. They had not yet encountered the reality of war.

I would like to indicate with two quotations the two paths along which we must search for an understanding of nurses' projections and fantasies as they set off on what they saw as a great adventure. In them, nationalist stereotypes and professional perspectives are intertwined in a manner that is simultaneously parallel and in contrast to the utterances of comparable men. The first is by Gertrud Bäumer, a champion of the bourgeois women's movement, who in the face of war put aside her long-time work on behalf of women's rights and later recalled

> the unprecedented sense of liberation once we felt that we were living under an order different from the materialistic–technological one of the nineteenth century. An order not of work and payment, risk and profit, investment and advantage, but of life and death, blood and strength, of commitment itself, absolutely, no matter what . . . The feelings of the entire people were torn from the moorings of calculation and raised up to the world of values: home, soil, . . . [25]

The other quotation comes from the organ of the comparatively dispassionate Professional Organization of Nurses, *Unterm Lazaruskreuz*, and is dated 1 December 1914:

> . . . one is free of the narrowness of home, can try one's hand at a great task, one can turn a situation that is often worse than nothing into a large hospital ward . . . And one can stand by the poor men in their suffering, who with their bodies have been protecting our German homeland! . . . Each of us must ask herself . . . whether she has developed her character sufficiently to become what the slaughter of nations is destined to make of her: a person worthy of the great times in which she is privileged to live, and in which we nurses, together with the army and the doctors, are most directly involved.[26]

Cinderella in the engine of war

The place where female nursing staff were supposed to be employed was behind the lines: in military hospitals. The military medical service was organized to move casualties from the front lines to the military hospital – and, statistically, each German soldier went there at least twice – via several intermediate stops: from the field dressing station to the ambulance-corps' main dressing station, from the field hospital to the military hospital and, where necessary, by hospital train back home. Military hospitals were set up in schools, churches, convents and castles. During the course of the war, though, this scheme broke down and after 1915 nurses also worked in hospitals at the front where, as some reported with something like pride, they endured their trial by fire.[27]

Those nurses who were not qualified surgical nurses were mainly employed tending the wounded or in the contagious diseases hospitals or psychiatric wards. It was these places that shaped the nurses' experiences. While surgical units under the direction of doctors often resembled assembly-line operations, it was the nurses who, with their constant presence in the wards, were closest to the wounded soldiers. Their work consisted of easing pain and dressing disgusting stinking wounds (a subject mentioned by many women), and of remaining calm when the hospital came under fire and panic spread among the wounded men, even when an entire sick ward or a church could not be evacuated at short notice. "I refused to abandon our wounded", one sister emphasized, speaking for many, and another added, "It was a good thing that I was with my soldiers in the church."[28]

The sick wards were also places of death. "The wounded they bring us are almost all dying. All of them very young men. I am seeing mass death for the first time. Horrifying!"[29]

> Seeing the suffering and the dying is hard. At home one never thought it would be so difficult. Our hospital is overcrowded. The casualties are four deep now, over 400 hundred of them, some on sacks, some just on straw. Most are head injuries who roll back and forth on the floor, unconscious. Many are bleeding to death . . . Although our limbs are stiff we are all working ceaselessly until, at one in the morning, we collapse dead tired on to our dormitory beds.[30]

The following passage from a war diary provides a report that seems at once very condensed and typical in its portrayal of the radical gap between the nurses' expectations and their concrete experiences "in the field":

> We must contend with terrible conditions. We are supposed to care for up to 300 wounded here, but there are absolutely no supplies! In the morning helpful soldiers found us some mattress ticking. We began by tearing it up for bandages, since there was no material for dressings. Later we took down the curtains and made bandages of them. Our charges are starving, and all we can give them is dry army bread. We have only a few buckets of water to slake their thirst, from which the wounded always suffer the most. They must only drink it boiled for, it is said, everything is poisoned.
>
> The wounded men, with their bodies shot to pieces, would like to lie on something soft, but we do not have enough straw. They are sticky with blood and dirt; they have been unable to wash for six weeks. We have no water, no basins, no soap or towels – nothing! Many die without our being able to do anything to ease their pain . . . Instead we get fresh casualties, most of them terribly maimed. Four tables have been set up at the entrance. There, wounds are dressed day and night, without interruption. We do not know the doctors. They come from the front lines and work in silence. We must be very close to the front lines, for the wounded come direct from the battlefield. . . . I was on night watch today . . . So many died in the night. It is so terribly cold and frightful here.[31]

Nurses rarely remained in the same sector throughout the war. In many war diaries, in which travel accounts represent important passages, the transfer from the western to the eastern front symbolizes a radical change of war experience. If the journey to the western front, with its euphoric ignorance, was illuminated by the glow of late summer, the journey to the eastern front was an experience of icy cold, halting trains, hunger and the desolation of abandoned railway stations. Here, cold and darkness hung over bullet-riddled quarters overflowing with half-starved, neglected soldiers infested with mosquitoes and lice. Above all, the eastern front meant working in the contagious diseases hospitals with soldiers suffering from malaria and typhus. Overworked and exhausted, many sisters also fell ill and died.

Under the extreme conditions of the front (particularly during the second half of the war), where increasing misery and intense pressures on the medical services required solidarity, and knowledgeable and effective co-operation, experienced and increasingly self-confident nurses began to criticize loudly, and even to boycott, incompetent or arrogant doctors who did not respect their own experience and achievements, until "even the surgeon had to capitulate before the nurses' caps".[32] A close reading of the nurses' publications suggests that there may have been many more conflicts between doctors and nurses. Intensive research on individual hospitals, sectors and time periods would be useful here. Until now such references have been few and far between, since it was not in the interests of the associations to allow rebellious nurses or the open airing of conflicts to call into question the idealized image of the Red Cross.

Reconstituting the fantasy of the family at the front

Another level of experience runs through the accounts of front-line nurses, though, one that counteracted perceptions of the anonymity and mass character of pain and death. The engine of war and the encounters at the front were translated onto the plane of archaic family relations. In the case of nurses, the familial structure provided a framework for making sense of their experience and as such was a crucial source of strength. This strength should not be underestimated: anyone studying the front-line nurses must recognize their extraordinary efforts and their capacity to keep working and caring even in the face of continual extreme situations.

The nurses wanted to be "sisters", and not only in the sense of the community of the mother houses, sisters among sisters. They also wanted to be the sisters of brothers, of soldiers. One of them sings a soldier to sleep, just as she used to do for her own little brother. "The finest reward for my work was the name 'our sister', given to me at the time by the men and officers."[33] They wanted not only to be the big sisters of brothers grown small and weak; they also wanted to be part of the brotherhood of warriors, accepted as a comrade, "comrade sister". The community of the front seemed to offer them as unmarried women what the childhood world of play had denied them – the status of an equal among equals. To march arm in arm, and to be photographed with doctors and officers, in particular, but also with orderlies and common soldiers, was proof for them of their recognition and importance as part of the great events of war. "There is a fine, comradely spirit in our hospital. Doctors, nurses, soldiers and ambulance men all stand shoulder to shoulder to get the job done."[34] And they were so proud when one of their number was awarded the Iron Cross, or was buried, as a warrior among warriors, in a military cemetery.[35]

On the other hand, nurses were also mothers and regarded the young soldiers, in particular, as their children:

> A large hall is the "infants' ward", so called because it is populated solely by eighteen-year-olds . . . I must comfort my children well. When they are better and have recovered from the shock they will make just as good soldiers as anybody else. In the evenings . . . I sing to them "Sleep, my little prince, sleep."[36]

The sister-mother comforts and sings her child-heroes to sleep and recovery. It is her tender caressing hands that relieve their shock. The wounded man "instinctively feels the woman's hand which tames the madness and rage within him".[37] She gives him food and drink: "it keeps body and soul together, and our lads need mending in both to defend our fatherland".[38] Finally, it is the sister-mother who watches by the dying child's bedside. "Our young volunteers were our particular problem-children . . . Many a one went to sleep in my care, with the word 'Mother' the last upon his lips . . . Once one of these lads asked me: 'Please, Sister, sing me a song, so I can sleep.' I sang softly . . . 'Guten Abend, gute Nacht'. As I finished the last verse, a smile crept over the boy's features which had been contorted in pain, and he fell asleep, forever."[39]

In some memoirs it seems as if the mothers at the front were competing with the mothers at home. The nurses staged family festivities at Christmas and the Kaiser's birthday "just like at home with mother", they said. "We nurses were happy . . . and these big lads are so very grateful for any little thing."[40]

The hospitals behind the front seem to have revived the intimate space of the bourgeois family centred on mothers and sons. In this fantasy the nurses were the mothers of infants whom they rock, caress, feed and even sing lullabies to. They nourish them so that their "sons" may become heroes when they return to the front. The interior world of the family staged at the front restores the battered warriors

Figure 6.1   "The greatest mother in the world" (Imperial War Museum, London).

for the battle in and against the outside world, a battle portrayed as a defence of the actual interior world of the family. Thus the nurse participates in the glory and greatness of the soldiers – and here

133

usually they mean the volunteers – by becoming the mother who keeps them alive, reproducing sons for the front. With her the heroes can regress for a little while, becoming small and helpless. At Christmas time this family of little sons is enacted, and the magical power of "German Christmas" invoked. Helene Mierisch, for example, organized an appearance of Saint Nicholas, meting out punishment and praise. "Can one bring a familiar childhood figure into places of horror?" she asks. "Yes indeed, life must triumph!" And then "soon everything is just as it is at home".[41] But the sister-mother is also the mother of the dead warrior. A reflected light from her smile remains on his face, his peaceful death another fulfilment of her duty. And in this attitude his heroism immortalizes her as well.

Avoiding insight

Those nurses who wrote about their return from the front after the defeat experienced it as humiliating and disappointing. "The Moor has done his duty, the Moor may go", wrote Helene Mierisch[42] and for many the question of demobilization, of where they were going to go, must also have been a frightening one. Not all had come from mother houses; many had left behind a frustrating family situation where they felt superfluous. Was their future the past? The research on English nurses points to this conclusion, but we do not yet know what the future of most war nurses in inter-war Germany looked like. Much social historical and biographical work remains to be done here.

The surviving autobiographical documents point to another, political dimension of homecoming, for instead of being welcomed, as they had expected, they were scorned. Contemptuous eyes met the nurses who returned from the eastern front "because we looked like dirty soldiers".[43] "How differently we had imagined our homecoming and reception!"[44] Once home they found themselves amidst the turmoil of revolution, but – still living in the fantasy of the soldier's mother and officer's sister – they felt nothing in common with the mutinous sailors and demonstrating workers of the home front. One nurse who had tried under the soldiers' councils to continue working in military hospitals that were being dismantled, wrote: "This cannot possibly be the end of such a heroic struggle. Where are the leaders? . . . Proud

Germany, which stood up to a world of enemies for four and a half years, destroyed?"[45] Another felt deeply humiliated when she returned by train from Antwerp in the company of soldiers' council members she referred to as "drunken sailors" and "deserters".

> Oh, one would rather see nothing more – just to get home, to hide away for shame and shattered idealism ... We did not return as victors, we had lost not only the war, but our honour ... I thought back on my war years in Russia, how often we had imagined peace and our entry into Germany. "When peace comes", the General always told me, "Sister Elfriede will ride beside me through the Brandenburg Gate!" And now? I clenched my teeth.[46]

What effect did the war have on the nurses? Those who were able to return to their mother houses would go back to their old work. But they had lost their great undertaking, and felt betrayed. Their accounts are marked not by mourning for the masses of dead or hopes for the radical changes of revolution (which had brought women the vote, of which 90 per cent of women took advantage), but rather by shame and disappointment. Had they learned nothing that might have caused them to question the war? Their war experiences had apparently taken place exclusively in a space that excluded or suppressed the political, that is in the private sphere of familial structures transferred to the front. And yet it was precisely there, where the private was put to public use, that they had discovered their own importance. But their version of "emancipation", freeing them for comradeship and national significance, had taken place within the old structures, those very structures that now relegated them to subordinate status within the mother house or on the margins of the family. The fact that many of them offered their diaries, field-post letters, loose notes and memories for publication in 1936 in a German book honouring the war nurses – a book of commemoration "for a great era"[47] – shows that they remained tied to war, for they were involved in preparing for the next one. Helene Mierisch, who published her war diary on the occasion of a Red Cross nursing veterans' meeting in 1934, wrote in the Afterword:

> Thus did our comradeship survive the revolution and the post-war period.
> Let us remain in future what our comrade, Sister Elisabeth, admonishes us to be in the song:

"And if a leader's word should call us,
Man or woman, we know but one honour –
To be a comrade, a comrade."[48]

In conclusion, I would like to return to a question posed at the beginning that refers to the seemingly polarized structure of wartime society as it has been portrayed by some women's historians. Did life at the front perpetuate or eliminate this structure? Did the private sphere of the family pack up and move to the front, and do we encounter there a structure inherent to war, at once imperial and populist, which was specific to bourgeois society at the beginning of this century? It is only since the middle of the nineteenth century that women have worked as nurses at the front. It might appear that female war nursing, with all it implies, also represents a counterpart to the specific figure of the modern soldier, particularly the volunteer of 1914. In contrast to earlier mercenaries, they committed their entire person, their strength and emotions, engaging and identifying completely with the national cause, and often went to the front as mere boys. If they took the familial part of their bourgeois ego, with its dependence upon the emotional space of women and mothers, to the front with them, did they need it when they were injured, and is this interior space then a precondition for the reproduction of the bourgeois man as warrior?

Theweleit's *Male fantasies* has provided us with a reflection of this perception on the part of officers who could not get enough of war.[49] In the self-perceptions and experience of nurses this desire also seemed to be commonplace. In 1937, the International Red Cross adorned a certificate of honour for a German war nurse with an impressive figure, similar to one used in 1916 as "the greatest mother in the world" on Allied posters to recruit nurses: the nurse with a soldier on her lap – whether dead or severely wounded is unclear – unmistakably based on a pietà, under a crown of thorns on a devastated battle field. In her tender concern for the soldier's pain and death, she appears as a universalized and exalted fusion of the private and the public, the religious and the national, embodying in a nun's habit the duty of the war nurse. The certificate was issued in 1937 in Geneva, but it refers back to the continuity of the allegory, for the "Diplôme Florence Nightingale" had already been established and awarded in all countries in 1912.

Figure 6.2 Diplôme de la médaille Florence Nightingale (Archiv des deutschen Roten Kreuzes, Bonn).

Notes

A German version of this chapter appeared under the title "Die Schwester des kranken Kriegers: Krankenpflege im Ersten Weltkrieg als Forschungsproblem", in *BIOS: Zeitschrift für Biographieforschung und Oral History* 7(1), 1994, pp. 83–100.

1. V. Woolf, *A room of one's own* (London: Hogarth Press, 1929).
2. U. Daniel, *Arbeiterfrauen in der Kriegsgesellschaft: Beruf, Familie und Politik im Ersten Weltkrieg* (Göttingen: Vandenhoeck & Ruprecht, 1989); S. Rouette, *Sozialpolitik als Geschlechterpolitik: Die Regulierung der Frauenarbeit nach dem Ersten Weltkrieg* (Frankfurt am Main & New York: Campus, 1993); K. Hausen, "The German nation's obligations to the heroes' widows of World War I", in *Behind the lines: gender and the two world wars*, M. R. Higonnet et al. (eds) (New Haven, Connecticut & London: Yale University Press, 1987), pp. 126–40.
3. R. W. Whalen, *Bitter wounds: German victims of the Great War 1914–1939* (Ithaca, New York & London: Cornell University Press, 1984).
4. K. Theweleit, *Männerphantasien*, [2 vols] (Frankfurt am Main: Rowohlt, 1978) trans., *Male fantasies*, vol. 1, *Women, floods, bodies, history*; vol. 2, *Male bodies: psychoanalysing the white terror* (Cambridge: Polity, 1987 (vol. 1); 1989 (vol. 2)); M. Hirschfeld & A. Gaspar, *Sittengeschichte des Ersten Weltkrieges* (Hanau, 1929); E. Domansky, "Der erste Weltkrieg", in *Bürgerliche Gesellschaft in Deutschland: Historische Einblicke, Fragen, Perspektiven*, L. Niethammer et al. (eds) (Frankfurt am Main: Fischer, 1990), pp. 285–319, here p. 317; S. von Hoerner-Heintze, *Mädels im Kriegsdienst: Ein Stück Leben* (Leipzig: F. V. Hase, 1934).
5. See, for example, L. Heymann & A. Augspurg, *Erlebtes – Erschautes: Deutsche Frauen kämpfen für Freiheit, Recht und Frieden 1850–1940* (Meisenheim am Glan: Anton Hain, 1977); on the "mythology of war's gender", see the introduction to Higonnet et al. (eds), *Behind the lines*, pp. 1–17.
6. A. Summers, *Angels and citizens: British women as military nurses' 1854–1914* (London: Routledge & Kegan Paul, 1988); S. M. Gilbert, "Soldier's heart: literary men, literary women, and the Great War", in *Behind the lines*, Higonnet et al. (eds), pp. 197–226; J. Gould, "Women's military services in First World War Britain", in *Behind the lines*, Higonnet et al. (eds), pp. 114–25; G. Thomas, *Life on all fronts: women in the First World War* (Cambridge: Cambridge University Press, 1989), pp. 30 ff. A crucial source on British women's front-line experiences in the First World War is Vera Brittain, *Testament of youth: an autobiographical study of the years 1900–1925* (London: Victor Gollancz, 1933); see also her *Chronicle of youth: the war diary 1913–1917*, A. Bishop with T. Smart (eds) (London: Victor Gollancz, 1981).

7. E. von Rüdgisch, *Unterm Roten Kreuz. Erlebnisse und Schilderungen*, in *Aus dem Völkerkrieg 1914–1916: IV* (Lahr in Baden: Schauenburg, 1916); E. Albrecht, *Aus meinem Kriegstagebuch* (Heidelberg: Wolff, 1917).

8. H. Mierisch, *Kamerad Schwester 1914–1919* (Leipzig: Köhler & Amelang, 1934); E. von Pflugk-Harttung (ed.), *Frontschwestern: Ein deutsches Ehrenbuch 1936*, 2nd edn (Berlin: Bernard & Graefe, 1936). The latter collection contains diary and memoir fragments by 51 women, of whom 16 came from aristocratic backgrounds.

9. On the critical use of autobiographical writings and memoirs on the First World War and the experience of war, see P. Fussell, *The Great War and modern memory* (New York & Oxford: Oxford University Press, 1975), and M. Hettling & M. Jeismann, "Der Weltkrieg als Epos. Philipp Witkops Kriegsbriefe gefallener Studenten", in *Keiner fühlt sich hier mehr als Mensch . . . : Erlebnis und Wirkung des Ersten Weltkriegs*, G. Hirschfeld, G. Krumeich, I. Renz (eds) (Essen: Klartext, 1993), pp. 175–98.

10. H. Grundhever, "Die Kriegskrankenpflege und das Bild der Krankenschwester im 19. und frühen 20. Jahrhundert", in *Medizin und Krieg: Vom Dilemma der Heilberufe 1865–1985*, J. Bleker & H.-P. Schmiedebach (eds) (Frankfurt am Main: Fischer, 1987), pp. 135–52; C. Bischoff, *Frauen in der Krankenpflege: Zur Entwicklung von Frauenrolle und Frauenberufstätigkeit im 19. und 20. Jahrhundert*, rev. edn (Frankfurt am Main & New York: Campus, 1992); see also her "Krankenpflege als Frauenberuf", *Jahrbuch für Kritische Medizin* 8, Argument Sonderband 86, 1982.

11. D. Riesenberger, *Das Internationale Rote Kreuz 1863–1977: Für Humanität in Krieg und Frieden* (Göttingen: Vandenhoeck & Ruprecht, 1992), pp. 80 ff.; H. Grundhever, "Von der freiwilligen Kriegskrankenpflege bis zur Einbindung des Roten Kreuzes in das Heeressanitätswesen", in *Medizin und Krieg*, Bleker & Schmiedebach (eds), pp. 29–44; see also C. Misch (ed.), *Geschichte des Vaterländischen Frauen-Vereins* (Berlin: Heymann, 1917); L. Kimmle (ed.), *Das Deutsche Rote Kreuz: Entstehung und Leistungen der Vereinsorganisation seit Abschluß der Genfer Konvention im Jahre 1864*, vol. 3 (Berlin: Boll & Pickarott, 1910); *Bilder und Beiträge aus der Geschichte der Deutschen Mutterhäuser vom Roten Kreuz* (Düsseldorf: Rhenania, 1929).

12. H. Stahr, "Liebesgaben für den Ernstfall: Das Rote Kreuz in Deutschland zu Beginn des Ersten Weltkrieges", in *August 1914: Ein Volk zieht in den Krieg*, Berliner Geschichtswerkstatt (ed.) (Berlin: Nishen, 1989), pp. 87 ff.; Herbert Grundhever, "Von der freiwilligen Kriegskrankenpflege", in *Medizin und Krieg*, Bleker & Schmiedebach (eds), pp. 37 ff.

13. *Ibid.*, pp. 37 ff. The national Red Cross organizations proved not only in Germany but also in other European states to be indispensable to the waging of modern industrial war. Red Cross personnel were seen as "soldiers without weapons". Riesenberger, *Das Internationale Rote Kreuz*, p. 80.

14. Bischoff, *Frauen in der Krankenpflege*, pp. 108 ff.

15. *Ibid.*, pp. 124 ff.; R. Schulte, "Dienstmädchen im herrschaftlichen Haushalt: Zur Genese ihrer Sozialpsychologie", *Zeitschrift für bayerische Landesgeschichte* 41, 1978, pp. 879 ff.

16. Mendelsohn, cited in Bischoff, *Frauen in der Krankenpflege*, p. 89.

17. Cited in Stahr, "Liebesgaben für den Ernstfall", p. 83.

18. *Unterm Lazaruskreuz: Mitteilungen der Berufsorganisation der Krankenpflegerinnen Deutschlands* 9(16), 8 Aug. 1914, p. 191.

19. von Rüdgisch, *Unterm Roten Kreuz*, p. 42.

20. Mierisch, *Kamerad Schwester*, p. 12.

21. Minna Stöckert, in *Frontschwestern*, von Pflugk-Harttung (ed.), p. 47.

22. Gräfin Bertha von der Schulenburg, in *ibid.*, p. 39.

23. Margarete Schmidt, in *ibid.*, p. 227.

24. On the Langemarck generation and the Langemarck myth, see B. Hüppauf, "Schlachtenmythen und die Konstruktion des 'Neuen Menschen'", in *Keiner fühlt sich hier mehr als Mensch*, Hirschfeld, Krumeich, Renz (eds), pp. 43–84, here pp. 54 ff.

25. G. Bäumer, *Lebensweg durch eine Zeitenwende*, 2nd edn (Tübingen: Wunderlich, 1933). On the "insatiable desire for authenticity", see E. Leed, *No man's land: combat and identity in World War I* (Cambridge: Cambridge University Press, 1979), pp. 62 ff.

26. *Unterm Lazaruskreuz: Mitteilungen der Berufsorganisation der Krankenpflegerinnen Deutschlands* 9(23) 1 Dec. 1914, pp. 243 ff.

27. Elfriede Schulz, in *Frontschwestern*, von Pflugk-Harttung (ed.), p. 182; C. Altgelt, "Feldsanitätswesen", in *Die Organisationen der Kriegführung, Zweiter Teil (Der große Krieg 1914–1918 in zehn Bänden*, vol. 9), M. Schwarte (ed.) (Leipzig: Barth et al., 1921), pp. 401–539; H. Braun, "Organisation, Ziele, Zweck und Arbeitsweise des Roten Kreuzes", in von Rüdgisch, *Unterm Roten Kreuz*, pp. 9–33.

28. Bertha von der Schulenburg, in *Frontschwestern*, von Pflugk-Harttung (ed.) p. 40; Lonny Hertha von Versen, in *ibid.*, p. 45.

29. Minna Stöckert, in *ibid.*, p. 50.

30. *Ibid.*, pp. 48 ff.

31. *Ibid.*, pp. 47 ff.

32. Mierisch, *Kamerad Schwester*, p. 258, also pp. 44 ff.

33. Elfriede Scherhans, in *Frontschwestern*, von Pflugk-Harttung (ed.), p. 157.

34. Anna Groth, in *ibid.*, p. 90.

35. For example, "Im Überfall von Löwen: Ein Bericht mehrerer Johanniterschwestern", *ibid.*, p. 28; Elfriede Scherhans, "Bei der fechtenden Truppe als Regimentsschwester", in *ibid.*, pp. 155 ff.

36. Mierisch, *Kamerad Schwester*, p. 295.

37. Elfriede von Pflugk-Harttung, in *Frontschwestern*, von Pflugk-Harttung (ed.), p. 102.

38. von Rüdgisch, *Unterm Roten Kreuz*, p. 96, see also p. 79.

39. Elfriede von Pflugk-Harttung, in *Frontschwestern*, von Pflugk-Harttung (ed.), p. 99.

40. Anna Groth, in *ibid.*, p. 89. See also, on the Kaiser's birthday, von Rüdgisch, *Unterm Roten Kreuz*, pp. 95 ff.; on Christmas celebrations, *ibid.*, pp. 86 ff., and Mierisch, *Kamerad Schwester*, pp. 48, 92; for a photograph of Christmas celebrations, see Albrecht, *Aus meinem Kriegstagebuch*, p. 28.

41. Mierisch, *Kamerad Schwester*, pp. 41 ff.

42. *Ibid.*, p. 295. This famous quotation is from Schiller, *Die Verschwörung des Fiesko zu Genua* (1783).

43. Mierisch, *Kamerad Schwester*, p. 297.

44. *Ibid.*

45. *Ibid.*, p. 274. The soldiers' councils were set up as organs of revolutionary government in November 1918.

46. Elfriede Schulz, in *Frontschwestern*, von Pflugk-Harttung (ed.), pp. 142 ff.

47. "Vorwort", in *ibid.*, p. 6.

48. Mierisch, *Kamerad Schwester*, p. 300.

49. Theweleit, *Male fantasies* (cf. Note 4).

Chapter Seven

Wise women, wise men and abortion in the Weimar Republic: gender, class and medicine

Cornelie Usborne

> Frau R.
> gives advice on all intimate matters
> and guarantees absolute discretion
> menstrual blockage, discharge, etc.
> treated by unique method
> safe results guaranteed.
> Practice hours daily 12–3 and 4–7 pm.[1]

This was typical of the way *weise Frauen* (wise women) or *Engel-macherinnen* (angel makers), as the public or the authorities called them, advertised their abortion services in Weimar Germany. Advertisements were usually carefully worded. First, they had to steer clear of formulations that could lead to prosecution under Paragraph 219 of the German penal code;[2] secondly, they had to be explicit enough to attract potential customers. Although "menstrual blockage", "delayed period", "menstrual irregularities" were euphemisms for a suspected pregnancy, in the 1920s – before reliable pregnancy tests were available – these usefully ambiguous terms could equally apply to nothing more than a late period. Midwives featured frequently in such advertisements. For example, during the 1920s a certain Frau K. appeared almost daily in the small-ad section of all four local newspapers in her home town in the Ruhr, calling herself a "retired midwife" and promising "a kind welcome, advice and help for all single women and girls" and recommending "treatment of women's complaints of all kinds".[3] Although apparently typical, the advertisement at the top of this chapter is nevertheless of special interest to the historian of gender because Frau R. was in fact a man. It raises the question why he felt it paid to advertise as a wise woman rather than a wise man, as contemporaries often called male lay abortionists,[4] as well as why it paid to advertise as a lay practitioner at a time when German society seemed to have been thoroughly medicalized.[5] This in turn opens up two issues: the role of gender in situations when an abortion was desired and the relationship between lay practitioners and the medical profession. Both these issues address the question of power and the following discussion will attempt to disentangle this complex web of power relations.

The history of abortion has succeeded in addressing questions of gender and in bringing to light the inequality inherent in the relationship between women and the medical profession. However, it has nevertheless been a history written from above that focuses on the politics of reproduction control and elite discourse and marginalizes or ignores grassroots attitudes altogether. Indeed my own research has contributed to this historiography.[6] During the 1920s and early 1930s the dominant discourse about abortion law reform divided into two camps: on the one hand those, usually on the Left, who wanted the law liberalized or even abolished and on the other hand those, usually on the Right or moral Right, who wanted the existing law upheld but better policed.[7] Yet this division into reformers and their opponents obscures a different division of equal significance, that between official disdain for abortion *per se* and popular acceptance of it as a necessary method to end an unwanted pregnancy. In this new constellation of official versus popular views we find the old adversaries united against common foes, the "deviant woman" neglecting her duty to procreate and the "quack abortionist" leading her astray and ruining her health because of greed.[8] But unlike the drama between abortion reformers and their opponents, which was played out before the public in parliament, street demonstrations, party political rallies, newspapers, on stage and film, the second drama was never enacted in the open. Instead, it appeared in the public discourse only obliquely because the main protagonists were in agreement: the medical profession, politicians, churchmen and -women, even sex reformers and feminist leaders all regarded the voluntary termination of a pregnancy as problematic. Even for those who sought to legalize it, abortion remained a necessary evil needing the strictest regulation and medical control. But the assumptions behind this judgement were rarely questioned.

Historians, even feminist historians who might be expected to interpret the body politic from the standpoint of the individual woman, have often adopted uncritically the view – largely shaped by the medical profession – that all so-called quack abortions were by implication dangerous and bad. I have pointed out elsewhere that the demonization of the "back-street abortionist" was a useful strategy by doctors in their campaign to medicalize birth control and abortion. In reality the picture was far more complex.[9] If we are to reconstruct it we need to challenge the hegemony of academic medical thinking and the positivist heritage we have internalized for so long. Only if we approach the history of abortion from below and try and discover the voice of individual women and men can we begin to understand how they viewed an event that was part of their daily life because they themselves had terminated a pregnancy or knew this from friends, relatives or neighbours. By looking at abortion through the prism of gender and class, and by applying anthropological concepts such as pollution images and the distinction between nature and culture or between professional and lay medicine, I hope to shed light on a number of puzzling phenomena: why were official views about aborting women always tinged with disapproval even when women terminated their pregnancies on justifiable grounds? Why were doctors' attitudes to abortion so contradictory, on the one hand regarding it with disdain and on the other pressing for the profession's exclusive control of the practice?[10] There was concerted medical opposition to abortion becoming a routine operation: doctors despised the act of abortion even when it was "medicalized".[11] Yet most doctors insisted on their right to terminate a pregnancy on medical grounds long before this was formally legalized in 1927.[12] This was despite the fact that the principle of medical indication entailed a dramatic departure from official Christian dogma by ascribing to the life and health of a woman a greater value than to the foetus.[13]

This chapter is based on the preliminary findings from some 200 criminal abortion cases, some of which are made up of substantial records including police interviews of pre-trial investigations and the interrogations during the main trial. The chapter does not aim to provide a complete account of all aspects of abortion practice and its legal aspects. Instead, it explores some of the changes in the practice of and attitudes to termination of pregnancy after the First World War. In this it is inspired by recent writing on feminist history and social and medical anthropology.[14] In adopting concepts and methods from anthropology, it is an initial exploration, needing further elaboration; meanwhile, it is to be hoped that other social historians of the twentieth century too will continue to follow the lead of historians of earlier periods who have long used such an approach.[15]

Finding an abortionist: a woman's quest

According to a study completed in 1938 of the complete files on criminal abortion cases investigated and tried at the *Landgericht* Duisburg between 1910 and 1935, there was a standard procedure for a lower-class woman to find an abortionist: once she suspected she was pregnant she asked around for suitable names. If she did not hear of an appropriate person immediately, then one of her woman friends undertook to continue the search and very soon she would have come up with the name and address of a "wise woman" or "wise man". The initial search was made easier because commercial operators advertised widely and many women already had an address as a kind of insurance policy long before the need arose. But it was not just a question of an address: for most women of the lower classes it was nearly always a question of money, too. Abortionists charged different amounts and unless women were financially supported they had to find somebody whom they could afford.[16] Even though a minority of the surviving criminal files are explicit about the process of decision-making, those cases that do give such details, and others from which the information can be deduced, confirm this procedure. My research also suggests that women preferred the help of a female operator and only turned to men as second best.[17] If a wise woman had proved satisfactory she would be used repeatedly, if necessary. For example, one former midwife, a well-known wise woman who had had eleven children herself, was said to have calmed down a worried client with the words: "Don't worry. Wherever I go nothing goes wrong. I have been attending Frau G. for the last eight years and get my 20 marks there every time."[18]

The preference for female help is further suggested by the evidence that many women who had ended up with a (male) doctor had in fact originally consulted a midwife but had then been referred for "expert" treatment. Two doctors in Berlin with exceptionally large abortion practices serve as good examples. Both doctors obtained their abortion patients through contracting a number of midwives or masseuses as touts (*Schlepperinnen*). One midwife actually lived in the same house and even shared the telephone number with the doctor she worked with. She advertised as follows: "Confidential examinations. Doctors, private patients, midwife Halder, Berlin–Lichterfelde". Her contractor, Dr Joachim, was a gynaecologist and family doctor who had apparently been driven to specialize in terminating pregnancies when he failed to gain a health insurance practice. At his trial for criminal abortion in 1918 he justified his use of touts by declaring that Berlin's top gynaecologists all did the same in their efforts to gain access to women who had had "miscarriages" or needed terminations of pregnancies. "The path to the gynaecologist", according to Dr Joachim, "does after all lead via the midwife. That is how the female psyche works, women turn to a woman first." Of course, he also acknowledged that economic deliberations played their part because doctors were usually more expensive than non-doctors.[19] When the *Berliner Morgenpost* reported this trial it received a number of readers' letters from women keen to "clear their own conscience" and confessing that they, too, had used a midwife as *Zuführerin* (tout) to obtain a termination of pregnancy. Indeed, in an expert opinion, the Medical Society of the Province of East Prussia stated that women generally sought the help of midwives for abortion services, that they found them through advertisements or gossip in *Kneipen* (pubs) and that midwives would then pass on their clients to a doctor who was known to be lax about the rules governing abortion.[20] Many midwives, however, did considerably more than act as go-betweens. They also examined their clients and carried out pregnancy tests; they would even supply abortifacients or induce a miscarriage themselves before referring the patient to a doctor for dilatation and curettage. The second example from Berlin concerned the 33-year-old Dr Metall who called himself an obstetrician. In reality he worked almost exclusively as an abortionist, attracting his patients also through touts. In his trial no less than 17 midwives and two masseuses were found guilty of aiding in criminal abortions by sending women for terminations. They did this because Dr Metall obviously made it worth their while and despite the fact that he was well known for his "unprofessional" attitude and his practice for being exceptionally "dirty". As one midwife put it, she "never sent the better class of people" to him.[21]

Women found an abortionist usually through an informal female network of information that operated in the countryside and in towns. In the early 1920s in a village in Upper Bavaria, Therese Hauer (not her real name as indeed all names in this chapter are pseudonyms), a farmer's wife in her forties, found herself pregnant by a Russian prisoner of war. In her "shame" she consulted an acquaintance, the seamstress Frau Eger in Endorf, a village nearby, who told her about the midwife Frau Engele in Munich who was known to induce miscarriages reliably. She also heard about this midwife from another source, a neighbour, through whom she met the neighbour's daughter-in-law, Frau Schuster, who was on a visit from Munich. Thus it was arranged that when Frau Schuster returned home to Munich, Therese Hauer would accompany her and stay in her flat to have the pregnancy terminated there. It turned out that the midwife already knew Frau Schuster (also through Frau Schuster's mother-in-law) and had indeed terminated one of her pregnancies in the past. She now came to attend Therese Hauer in Frau Schuster's flat. It was necessary to come two or three times to complete her task. Although Therese Hauer was about four months pregnant she suffered no hardship. That is why she gladly recommended the same midwife to her sister when she had an unwanted pregnancy. Unfortunately, Frau Engele's operation on the sister was not successful and the latter was forced to attempt the operation herself with the help of friends.[22]

In another example from Munich, from the mid-1920s, the address, though not necessarily the name, of the wise woman was carefully passed on from person to person, preferably in the discreet form of one satisfied client accompanying the next potential client to the woman in question. This way there was little danger of incriminating testimony in the form of written notes with names and addresses and there was also a chance to earn pocket money. In most cases the act of leading somebody to an abortionist was remunerated and this seems to have been accepted as a fair exchange. In 1925 the 19-year-old Maria Zentner, waitress in the *Ratskeller*, a pub in central Munich, suspected that she was pregnant. She had missed her period only a month after she had started an affair with the carpenter, Andreas Hinterhofer. Without hesitation she consulted Mathilde Bender, a 35-year-old divorced dressmaker. Maria knew the dressmaker as a potential abortionist ever since she had been a tenant with her sister in Schwabing, an area of Munich close to the university. The dressmaker did not disappoint her and administered a douche on the sofa in her kitchen. She repeated this a few days later but although Maria did not feel any undue pain she was too frightened to come for a third injection. As a result she only miscarried ten weeks later during her fifth month of pregnancy in her parents' flat apparently after her sister had "kicked her in the stomach". The dressmaker who originally came from Vienna had learnt her abortion skills as a nurse during the First World War when she had had the "opportunity to study women's diseases, pregnancies and how to terminate them".[23] A few weeks after Maria's miscarriage her colleague at the *Ratskeller*, Anny Wacker, also found herself pregnant and since she knew of Maria's abortion turned to her for help. Maria took her to the dressmaker, taking the precaution of never revealing the latter's full name. Unlike her colleague, Anny completed her course of treatment and found that soon her period was fully restored. Obviously satisfied with the dressmaker, Anny in turn recommended her as an abortionist in September of the same year to one of her acquaintances, Frau Mathilde Schaber, a married woman of 34. Mathilde already had three children and was keen to avoid another one. Without telling her husband, she followed Anny Wacker to Schwabing and before the dressmaker started to induce the abortion handed over 30–50 raw eggs, lard and butter as remuneration. She returned twice to Schwabing on her own before she had a miscarriage two weeks later. When asked by the police whether she had passed the address of the dressmaker to others she replied that she "could not remember".[24]

Sometimes, however, the passage to the wise woman or man was less smooth. Then the pregnant woman would be sent from one well-meaning relation or acquaintance to another, each attempting in turn to procure an abortion. Only when every attempt failed was a "professional" abortionist called in. This happened to Maria Stuck, a 36-year-old unmarried bookkeeper, employee of the *Vereinsbank* in Munich. In 1920 she suspected herself pregnant by her then boyfriend, the piano teacher Spatz. He turned to his aunt for help who came up with the name of a Dr Mann who was known to comply with abortion requests for money. Dr Mann eventually procured an abortion but not before several neighbours and friends had had a go themselves and failed. They had used Maria's own instruments, a uterine sound (*Mutterspiegel*) and a catheter. Spatz's aunt, the 46-year-old Therese Gleicher was the first to try but gave up because she apparently "could not find the uterus". She then accompanied Maria to a friend, Frau Braun, who was confident she would succeed because she had induced her own miscarriage some time ago. However, she also failed, as did another friend to whom all three women turned for help. Frau Braun then made another two unsuccessful attempts.[25] When Maria became pregnant again in 1922, this time by a cattle merchant, her subsequent lover, a married plumber, arranged and paid for an abortion by a doctor. Pregnant again in 1923, this time by the plumber, Maria finally asked a woman colleague at work who promptly recommended a 57-year-old divorced midwife struck off the register since 1921 because of illegal abortions.[26]

Some women approached fortune-tellers (*Kartenlegerinnen*) to find out whether they were pregnant and if this was the case they were likely to be offered an abortion there and then. Since *Kartenlegerinnen* seemed to have been predominantly women attracting women clients, fortune-telling and procuring miscarriages were often conveniently linked. This is certainly how Frau Spitzer, the wife of a janitor in a working-class area of Berlin, attracted her clients in the 1920s. Frau Schrader, the wife of another janitor, for example, had been introduced to Frau Spitzer five years earlier by a woman friend. When she asked Frau Spitzer to tell her fortune she was in her seventh month of pregnancy. Frau Spitzer said to her, she "was really stupid to carry the child to term" and she should "let her induce an abortion instead". Frau Schrader, however, refused because it was wrong to "do anything like that" and because her husband "would not stand for it". Frau Margarete Schmalzer, on the other hand, and many other women, too, responded to Frau Spitzer's overtures. Margarete Schmalzer had been married only three years with one child aged three. Finding herself pregnant again she decided on a termination on economic grounds. In fact, so determined was she not to have a second child that she had made enquiries about a wise woman long before her second pregnancy. She had heard about Frau Spitzer from a neighbour. As soon as she had missed her period, she paid Frau Spitzer a visit that had the desired effect.[27]

In the Rhineland, fortune-telling and an abortion practice were often run as a family concern. For example, a 63-year-old widow of a railway clerk and her two grown-up daughters operated a thriving business consisting of procuring abortions and fortune-telling, augmented by multiple petty crimes such as theft and fraud. The abortion practice followed a routine pattern. The mother acted as a fortune-teller and once her clients expressed their concern about a possible unwanted pregnancy she dispelled their fears, promising she knew of a woman who could help. "There is advice for everything except death!" Whereupon her daughter Bertha, who lived in the same house, would enter the room and offer her services and if accepted the abortion was performed immediately. Apparently Bertha had learnt her skills from a widow in the neighbourhood. Her sister was also active as an abortionist. She operated similarly to her mother but instead of *Kartenlegen* she used palmistry to attract abortion clients. In another case, a woman abortionist, also in the Rhineland, worked together with her daughter who acted as the *Kartenlegerin* and sent her mother potential clients. Similarly, two middle-aged sisters, both married to manual workers and with grown-up children, built up a flourishing business through mutual co-operation. They would each work as a *Kartenlegerin* and once a pregnancy was revealed the woman would be sent to the other sister for an abortion.[28]

A case from Munich from the early 1920s illustrates the way many women may have had the name of an abortionist at the ready in case this was needed. Here the name at hand happened to be of a male practitioner. When Frau Margarethe Hackerl, the wife of a mechanic, found herself with an unwanted pregnancy she remembered the name of a certain "masseur" Zargel who was known to perform abortions and lived nearby. She had originally come across his name and address by chance and had decided to make a note "just in case". Since he was both cheap and efficient, "restoring the periodic bleeding soon after" the consultation, she also recommended him to a friend Frau Seidl, who also desired an abortion and accompanied her to him. Later on, Frau Seidl in her turn took other women to the same address, most probably in return for a small fee. She admitted to her police interrogator that she "could well have also passed the address on to others". She recounted how she was in the habit of visiting the Theresienwiese (the venue of the *Oktoberfest*) every day in the summer and how she met many women there and that of course they would gossip about "such things, too". Frau Seidl's protestations that her memory failed her and that she could not remember whether she was paid for either the addresses or for accompanying pregnant women to the masseur in itself reveals how customary this habit of paying for such an information service was. The fact that Herr Seidl earned very little indeed and that she had four adult dependent offspring makes this highly probable.[29]

When women consulted male abortionists, this often seems to have been through coincidence rather than choice. For example, two women typists working at the police station in Berlin-Spandau decided quite independently of each other to approach a homeopath, Ferdinand Stroh, when they desired an abortion. When asked how they had heard of him they said "through work", probably because he had a police record for posing as a registered doctor when he had in fact trained as a chemist. Another of the homeopath's clients, a worker in the china factory in Spandau, was told about him by two colleagues at work, and a further client, a salesgirl in a butcher's shop, went to him because "an acquaintance" had recommended him.[30]

Finding an abortionist: the man's choice

When husbands or lovers took the initiative to terminate a pregnancy they usually picked a male abortionist, a lay practitioner or a doctor who was known to co-operate.[31] They usually picked up a lead from a male acquaintance. Indeed, men had their own male networks, too. The trial of the Munich train driver Anton Schnaller, who faced multiple charges of criminal abortions in 1926, reveals just such a male support group. In fact, since Schnaller's first and second wife as well as his mother were also sentenced for having aided and abetted illegal abortions, Schnaller's male network was seen to exist in parallel to a female network. Schnaller operated an abortion practice for his own domestic purposes but later also hired out his skills to other male colleagues and acquaintances. He had learnt the skill in Belgium during the First World War. After demobilization he had practised it mainly on his first wife, Therese. In spite of Therese's opposition, Schnaller subjected her to no less than four abortions in 1919, twice in 1922 and again in the summer of 1923. In 1924 Schnaller divorced her for his future second wife Karolina, who had been his mistress since early 1920. She had also suffered two abortions by his hand, one in 1920 and another in 1921 before she gave birth to a child in 1925, a year before Schnaller married her. Notwithstanding these two juxtaposed relationships, Anton also had affairs with other women, at least one of whom (the servant girl Maria Weber) had also become pregnant by him. Schnaller also attempted to procure her abortion but failed and she bore his illegitimate child.

While Therese, Schnaller's first wife, with the initial help of Schnaller's mother and a midwife, was busy establishing a thriving abortion exchange – in which she encouraged many women to consider abortions and put them in touch with the midwife in question – Schnaller himself exploited his own surgical skills through his own male connections at work. When August Bratzl, a fellow train driver, found that his girlfriend, a kitchen maid in a Munich pub, was expecting a baby he turned for help to Schnaller who had after all boasted many times of his great success in terminating pregnancies. Schnaller agreed to help his mate by hiring out his abortion instruments, a uterine sound and a catheter, for two weeks. Furthermore, Schnaller conducted a kind of remedial lesson for his colleague in what one could describe as "do-it-yourself abortion". Using the engine of the train to prop up his sketch, he drew a diagram of the female abdomen and indicated the necessary gynaecological procedure. The juxtaposition of the engine and the sketch of the female anatomy in the style of a technical drawing evokes neatly the metaphor of the body as machine often characterizing popular attitudes in the 1920s. Schnaller also assisted another colleague, the train driver Vetter, when the latter confessed during a visit to the *Oktoberfest* in 1925 that his girlfriend was pregnant. In the presence of his wife, Schnaller explained there and then exactly how to insert the sound and the catheter. But for the operation to go smoothly, he should "first to try and sweet-talk the woman pretending to be wanting sex and then quickly insert the catheter".[32]

Gender conflict and co-operation

This statement, attributed to Anton Schnaller, would suggest that he practised what he preached, that is an enforced abortion performed by himself on his unsuspecting wife or mistresses. We know that Therese was an unwilling partner to his abortion attempts; the other women might well also have been tricked into an unwanted operation. Of course it is rare to have positive proof of such gross abuse of a spouse's or partner's rights and feelings and this is why even oblique references should be taken seriously. There are a number of examples where men's abuse of a woman's right over her body is less explicit but strongly implied. Take, for example, the case of the 38-year-old Munich photographer August Wucher, tried in 1927 for attempted abortion in at least two cases. With his various mistresses posing as nude models, Wucher produced and traded in pornographic pictures.[33] He was a philanderer who had a number of short-term sex affairs but also maintained several long-term sexual relationships simultaneously, unbeknown to the women in question. For example, the typist Auguste Scherzl was his mistress at the same time as the accountant Karoline Dietel, and the latter affair overlapped with that of the 27-year-old singer Maria Ritter. According to Wucher's neighbour, all three women had become pregnant and in each case Wucher had induced a miscarriage himself in his own flat and with his own instruments. A careful reading of the case records shows that at least two of the abortions performed were contested. In Auguste Scherzl's case it was an extraordinarily rushed job carried out even before the pregnancy was established (she had not even missed her period once!), simply because she had apparently "lost her appetite, suffered from sleeplessness and looked ill". This might well have been a ruthless precautionary measure against an eventuality. According to Auguste herself she had consented to the operation because "they could not marry" and because she was worried about her "parents' reaction". However, no reason was stated why a marriage was not possible. Karoline Dietel stated quite plainly that the abortion was performed against her wish. She had been pleased when she found herself pregnant but August wanted it "stopped" because "he suffered from syphilis which would also affect the child". Karoline seems to have agreed only after considerable pressure by Wucher.[34] Only Maria Ritter, the singer, denied the accusation of abortion and with the help of her mother avoided a charge. But Wucher also used his abortion skills to help his male acquaintances and earn something on the side. His friend Rummel, director of an electrical engineering firm in Nuremberg, had asked for help because "his mistress [later to become his wife] had really landed him in it". Wucher also complied with the request of another acquaintance, Schlegel, who worked in the local industrial inspection board and was accused of seeking an abortion for his wife because she already had four children. Herr and Frau Schlegel, however, denied this allegation.[35]

What are we to make of this case? It seems to me not too far-fetched to suggest that for this photographer the female body was a disposable commodity useful for commercial exploitation and sexual gratification. The machine paradigm of the body had bred the idea that each model needed a back-up (hence the promiscuity) and once a model became inefficient (when pregnant after inadequate contraception) a hurried repair job was undertaken or it was scrapped and replaced with a newer model, as happened when the mistress was dropped shortly after she underwent an abortion. The cash-nexus that ruled the relationships extended to the do-it-yourself abortions: they saved the photographer time and money and minimalized the risk of detection.

Coercive abortion by men on their own mistresses was obviously not uncommon, as is shown by the following case from 1926, also from Munich's world of petty crime. The locksmith Ernst Schacher, who had already served two years' gaol for criminal abortions, had terminated the pregnancy of his fiancée. From the records it is clear that this had occurred without the woman's consent.[36] But assaults by men on women happened not only between lovers. There is indeed evidence of abuse by male abortionists, too. Women were blackmailed into having sex or more shockingly simply raped, as was the case with a printer/abortionist in the Rhineland who forced his patient to have sex because she was "too cold" for the operation.[37]

The cases just cited illustrate the discord that arose when women were forced into having unwanted abortions. There were also probably many instances of discord when the aborting woman decided unilaterally to have her unwanted pregnancy terminated, especially when she was expecting a child after an illicit love affair. Such disagreements might also have arisen over children conceived within stable relationships and marriage, but explicit references to discord are very rare because women normally stated that their partners/husbands did not know of or opposed the abortion, in order to protect them from prosecution as an accomplice. By contrast, they usually admitted that their sisters or mothers knew about their abortions. Indeed, when questioned by police, these female relations knew about the operation in great detail including the instruments used and the price paid.[38] Sometimes they even helped to do away with the foetus.[39] When Magdalene Wimmer, wife of a postal clerk, decided to terminate her eighth pregnancy, she consulted a woman acquaintance,

Frau Schneider. The latter duly took her to a midwife. The statements made to the police were, however, contradictory. Wimmer said she had told her husband about her decision but that he was against it. Her husband, however, denied any knowledge of it. Frau Schneider on the other hand reported that Frau Wimmer had pleaded with her not to tell Herr Wimmer, but Frau Schneider had then found Herr Wimmer waiting for his wife outside her (Frau Schneider's) house anyway.[40] By assessing police or courtroom interrogations carefully for un-witting testimony we do, however, indeed find hints of gender discord about abortion decisions. For example, in 1926, Sophie Pechriedel, a woman in her mid-forties, was accused of having had a criminal abortion shortly after her marriage in 1923. By then she already had two children by other men as well as having had an abortion by a mid-wife. Pechriedel recounted that her husband used to go round and tell everybody, especially Freisinger (the man who had denounced her to the police), that she had been pregnant and had the foetus destroyed, a story corroborated by one of Pechriedel's friends who heard him saying that "he will make sure that his wife ends up where she belongs because she had had an abortion". Herr Pechriedel's revenge was probably caused by his intense jealousy of his wife's previous and possibly continuing affairs, but there is also a sense that he was angry because she had done away with his future child and that this had exacerbated their quarrel.[41]

We have seen that the decision to seek abortions led at times to manifestations of tension and even violent behaviour between men and women, both between husbands/lovers and their wives/mistresses or male abortionists and their women clients. But there were as many, possibly more incidents of co-operation between the sexes. This seems to confirm what many historians believe, namely that repro-ductive control brought couples closer together – through mutual decision-making they could achieve small families.[42] The most suc-cessful co-operation between male and female abortionists was a husband-and-wife team from Hesse.[43] In 1924 at the *Landgericht* Limburg, Hesse, the Nauheim carpenter Ferdinand Adolf Kastner and his wife Hermine, both in their late thirties and with four teenage children, faced trial for having performed in the years 1920–24 alto-gether 71 criminal abortions. With them another 91 other persons stood accused of aiding and abetting in attempted abortion of which 88 persons were finally convicted. Herr and Frau Kastner's activities were remarkable for a number of reasons. To start with there was the sheer number of women they had helped in just four years; then there was the comprehensive service they had offered to a complete cross-section of the population in a wide area covering all the neighbouring villages and small towns of Nauheim, Heringen, Neesbach, Werschau, Dauborn, Kirberg, Beuerbach, Höchst, Hahnstätten and Oberbrechen. They had helped women of any marital status: married women (the majority), single (15 women) and two widows. The occupations of husbands ranged from farming, skilled crafts such as brick-laying and shoemaking to unskilled manual work. Most single women were domestic servants. Then there was the astonishing success of the operations themselves: only two women experienced minor discomforts. All the rest were trouble-free with not a single serious injury and certainly no death,[44] defying the usual allegations by the medical profession that quack abortionists were always dangerous. But lastly, Herr and Frau Kastner were remarkable for having co-operated so closely as a team and involving the close co-operation of women with their husbands or partners. Although the trial revealed Hermine Kastner as the protagonist responsible for the vast majority of abortions, with her husband only having performed two, the trial also showed that her husband usually assisted her and vice versa. In fact they complemented each other well: women obviously trusted her and had originally sought her advice and help. Herr Kastner, however, provided the link with husbands or lovers in cases where they had decided on abortion and had undertaken the responsibility of organizing it.[45] While his wife was at the forefront carrying out the actual operation he was in the background as the assistant, preparing the solution to be inserted into the uterus, passing the instruments and so on. He also organized the financial side, negotiating for payment and, since much of it was in kind during the inflationary years, it fell on him to make sure quantities of wheat, potatoes, etc. were delivered as promised.[46]

But the trial also showed that most women were supported by their husbands or partners from the moment they suspected conception to the actual operation. Many couples seem to have discussed what to do and consulted Frau Kastner together. Most men accompanied women to the operation and at least 18 husbands and 7 lovers were also present during the operation, giving moral support and even practical help like holding the lamp.[47] On several occasions, when

Frau Kastner had declined to induce a miscarriage because a pregnancy was too far advanced, the husband or lover would undertake it himself. For example, Ida Poll's lover performed a "douching" (*Ausspülung*) himself in his father's stable – by all accounts successfully – after Frau Kastner had declined Ida's request for an abortion in her fourth month of pregnancy. Frau Eigel's husband borrowed Frau Kastner's syringe. When she went to see them at lunch-time she found the front door locked – a rarity in the countryside. Herr Eigel greeted her, addressing her with the familiar "Du": "You are just in time!" He had been in the middle of administering a douche on his wife. He asked Frau Kastner to take over, which she did.[48] This shows that the extreme situation of an unwanted pregnancy could induce a genuine sense of mutuality in a sexual relationship without any obvious sign of male reluctance to witness those most intimate female physiological processes that we today expect to inspire extreme discomfort if not disgust in most men in urban communities.

But there was also co-operation by family members. At least six mothers arranged abortions for their daughters and stayed there during the operation, one man made all the arrangements for his sister and sisters supported each other. Members of the community also contributed to solving the problem of unwanted pregnancies. For example, when the 23-year-old domestic servant Philippine Ranniger had become pregnant, her lover, Theodor Bosel, refused to marry her and told her to seek an abortion. In her misery she turned to Frau Held, the wife of a poor bricklayer with seven children. Frau Held told her not to be stupid and expect Bosel to marry her. Instead she advised her to go to Frau Kastner in Nauheim who had already helped many people. Philippine followed this advice and went there, accompanied by her mother.[49]

Gender, knowledge and power: the medical profession

The world of the lay abortionists provides us not only with examples of co-operation between women, and between women and men, to the benefit of the aborting women, but also with many instances of men abusing women patients. However, there is evidence to suggest that doctors were more prone than lay practitioners to abuse their power, since their social position as the professional expert gave them much more opportunity to ignore patients' wishes. Moreover, in the judicial records I have consulted, I have found only very few cases of lay abortionists but quite a number of doctors involved in gross malpractice, even though I suspect that many doctors' misdemeanours were ignored and so never officially recorded. Even when they are, they are often buried amidst other more mundane details of a court case, whereas lay practitioners' wrongdoings seem to have been made explicit. A family practitioner, for example, who practised in a small town in the Rhineland, regularly offered termination of pregnancy in exchange for sex. In most cases the women involved were very young (between 18 and 21), inexperienced and terrified. In each case intercourse took place immediately and without any kind of prophylactic.[50] Some of these cases have come to light but there may have been many more undetected. The majority of doctors who decided to terminate unwanted pregnancies no doubt behaved correctly. Nevertheless, the fact that incidents of assault occurred which were apparently condoned by the courts, since there was no comment about or punishment for them, suggests that such abuse was tacitly permitted and that women might well have been aware of the risks they took when visiting a male practitioner unaccompanied and in an emotionally volatile situation that laid them open to blackmail. Doctors were looked up to as authorities in all physical matters and often in moral decisions as well; but they were also known to act in an authoritarian way. Male gynaecologists were often criticized for "reducing women to mere objects", especially when it came to deciding which woman "deserved" to have her pregnancy terminated. Then these men usually judged their female patients, as one woman doctor put it, simply as medical cases without reference to their psychological state or social milieu.[51] Not only top gynaecologists but general practitioners could treat women without due respect. They condescended particularly to women from the lower classes who were often diffident when faced with a professional expert. If women were too shy to stand up to their doctor, they were also mostly too shy to complain about him officially, an important reason why there are so few records relating to medical malpractice. Sometimes doctors' own diary entries are a surprisingly useful source of incriminating testimony unwittingly supplied. If we know how to read between the lines, this kind of source can give us rare glimpses into the at times autocratic and misogynist world of official medicine. This is the case with a family doctor whose diary was published posthumously and anonymously as a shining example of an idealist and a friend of the poor. The doctor in question had a country practice in a small north German town. He had performed over 400 abortions in a single year and portrayed himself as a humane friend of women in need. However, his own notes suggest otherwise.[52] He tended to make decisions on subjective rather than objective grounds and there was a strong streak of arrogance and sadism. Even when a pregnancy was not certain he would submit a patient to a "precautionary curettage" which on occasion revealed that she had not been pregnant at all. Worse still, at least three women were given a so-called "libido curettage", a painful procedure designed to improve their sexual performance. This doctor's most extraordinary treatment, however, was his sadistic habit of administering a "palliative curettage" in order to teach a woman a lesson "to take more care in the future". In these instances he also seems to have dispensed with an anaesthetic, possibly to heighten the impact. In one case he entered into the medical records the following:

> Salesgirl. Not yet twenty. Had a boyfriend in the army. I was moved. I do not know if this is true. But I feel sorry for the girl. Examination: uncertain. She returned this morning, wants to be sure. Examination: pregnancy uncertain but cannot be excluded. Abrasio. Of course this hurt her very much, but she pulls herself together. I am convinced that she will now take more care. In my experience a palliative curettage has an excellent pedagogical effect with *nulliparas* [women who were never pregnant].[53]

This doctor also provides a good example of the tendency of many members of the medical profession to exploit their power in more subtle ways by adjudicating rather than executing women's requests. This would not necessarily have been apparent since this doctor seemed at first sight to have given abortions on demand. On closer inspection, however, this was not so. Many women were sent away as "undeserving", often because of a doctor's personal whim rather than on the basis of any rational criteria.[54]

Was this abuse of medical power over women a consequence of gender or was it a function of class and the professional/lay divide? It is tempting to conclude that the working-class aborting woman (she seems to have been the prime target of abuse) who had opted for academic medicine was only safe with a female doctor. A survey conducted in the early 1930s suggests indeed that many women preferred female doctors especially when they needed gynaecological advice. This was for a number of reasons; it was obviously less embarrassing, but there was also a sense that women doctors tended to treat the "whole person".[55] However, there is also evidence that women doctors overstepped their remit, too, proving that in cases of medical control and coercion gender was less decisive than professional power. Sometimes women doctors performed operations that had not been requested. Even if this was done "in the best interest of the patient" it constituted a serious breach of trust. The Munich gynaecologist Dr Hope Bridges Adams-Lehmann is a good case in point. A court case just before the First World War revealed that this popular doctor had performed hundreds of terminations of pregnancy, many of them on poor women. But while they were anaesthetized, 19 women were also sterilized, apparently without consent. Dr Adams-Lehmann's aim seemed at first sight plausible and honourable. She believed a permanent form of birth control would improve poor women's health and quality of life particularly if they had already had a large number of children. She was also convinced of the curative value of sterilization itself. From our vantage point today, however, Adams-Lehmann's action is indefensible on two counts: first, she did not opt for the relatively minor method of sterilization such as laparotomy or tubal ligation, which was widely practised at the time, but chose the much more risky and intrusive hysterectomy, that is the removal of the entire upper womb (*Porro* in her records). Secondly, she failed to consult her patients before or inform them after the operation. They only found out by chance when they came back asking for contraception. There is no indication of whether Dr Adams-Lehmann's popularity suffered as a consequence.[56]

This is not an isolated case. There are others where this kind of autocratic behaviour is explicit, but there may have been many more that were never discovered.[57] Similarly, some doctors seemed to have decided on abortion and/or sterilization according to the alleged genetic "value" of potential offspring rather than in compliance with a woman's own wishes. Often it is impossible to determine whether informed consent had been sought beforehand. Take, for example, the practice of two women doctors, Lotte Fink and Hertha Riese, in charge of the Frankfurt sex counselling centre of the radical feminist organization League for the Protection of Motherhood. They arranged a large number of terminations for their women patients at the local university clinic. But at least a third of these were sterilized at the same time. Both the extent of this operation and its justification suggests that the two doctors were as much motivated by eugenics as by feminism. They were responsible for the sterilization of altogether 435 women in just five years. They had recommended this because they believed contraception had failed with the poorest section of the community "partly because of the women's indolence, partly because of the lack of proper facilities at home".[58] Although Fink rejected the idea that their decision was taken on eugenic grounds, the preponderance of sterilized patients belonging to the poorest social strata and the medical assessment would suggest otherwise.[59]

The question of sterilization on eugenic grounds was to exercise the medical and the legal professions and increasingly the informed public in the second half of the 1920s. When the Depression hit Germany the support for legalized eugenic sterilization gained ground and by 1930 questionnaires revealed that a substantial number of clinicians had carried out eugenic sterilizations, some of which were almost certainly without consent.[60] This habit of taking decisions about a woman's fertility with minimal or no attempt to take her views into consideration seems to have been confined to academic medicine and was almost unknown among lay practitioners who would seldom have possessed the medical know-how to perform such a major operation. According to the judicial files consulted, only one "quack" offered a woman abortion *and* sterilization.[61]

Does it follow that aborting women avoided the medical profession? It is striking that doctors on the whole appear with much less frequency in criminal files. This was partly no doubt to do with detection because they found it easier than wise men and women to conceal illegal operations or, once they were suspected, to stop police investigations leading to a prosecution. But I have no doubt that it also revealed the preference of women, particularly of the lower classes, for lay practitioners.[62] Considerations of money, inclination and gender were important and probably decided most women against choosing a doctor. A medical termination was invariably much more expensive, many doctors declined abortion requests because they opposed abortion on principle or feared prosecution, or because they had too little experience; and the vast majority of doctors were still male.[63] Women doctors seem to have been very reluctant to risk their hard-won professional privileges by becoming involved in illegal practices. So far, I have only come across two cases of women doctors indicted for criminal abortions.[64] But women, especially from the lower classes, seem to have preferred to consult wise women rather than women doctors, even if they were able to find any sympathetic to their request. As I have discussed elsewhere, apart from monetary considerations and the fear of being turned away, there was a shared culture between patient and lay practitioner that must also have given women greater confidence that their predicament would not be exploited. This sense of trust is likely to have given wise women an important advantage over academically trained doctors.[65]

Abortion as "pollution"

Consulting a member of the medical profession entailed an unequal power relationship between doctor and patient or the professional male expert and the typical young woman in a vulnerable position. This in itself would explain the strikingly arrogant treatment of aborting women by doctors. However, medical perceptions of abortion are perhaps worth exploring in a little more depth. The profession's attitude to abortion was contradictory. In public it demanded total control of the practice in the interest of population strength, public health and morality. However, privately most doctors seem to have shunned the operation.[66] Colleagues who had succumbed to the lure of easy money were regarded with contempt and denounced as belonging to the "despised guild of scrapers".[67] But doctors often also looked down on the aborting woman and such cases of blatant misogyny and sadism I have described must be seen as attempts, albeit often unconscious ones, to punish her.[68] Especially the political Left usually described women desiring an abortion, particularly if they were poor, as pathetic victims of an unjust society and the many examples of 1920s abortion art and theatre usually adopted this image of innocent suffering.[69] Yet the same women also evoked fear in men. To many in reality they seemed strong-minded and active rather than weak and passive, especially when they demanded an operation knowing the physical and judicial risks involved and often going it alone against the wishes of their partners or family. As Rosalind Pollock Petchesky puts it, they were making a choice and were seen as "active agents of their fertility and not merely victims of their biology or pawns of 'natural forces' like population movement".[70] This impression was strengthened by the assertion of some high-ranking doctors that most abortions were in fact performed by women themselves without any expert help.[71] This kind of determination, if not wilfulness, threatened the traditional power relationship between (mostly male) doctors and female patients but also between men and women in society at large. Not only were women dispensing with professional or personal guidance but the prospect of their controlling their fertility at will had always conjured up visions of sexual anarchy. A healthy woman whose menses were restored could "draw on abilities and capacities that are not related to the values of ovulation and child-bearing but that are instead related to that other side of her nature, of independence of thought and action".[72] But the nineteenth-century medical assumption that women's physical and mental inferiority derived from their reproductive function lived on in the ideology of maternalism that dominated the welfarism of Weimar Germany, an ideology that doctors actively helped construct.[73] The majority of the profession reacted against feminist agitation for reproductive rights and they were not above punishing women for failing to conform to the prescribed feminine role.

Moreover, women were characteristically dichotomized, regarded as both morally superior to men in their maternal nurturing role and morally inferior because they were controlled by a dangerous sexuality needing containment. Abortion revealed women as sexually active and their wish to remove the consequences of intercourse conjured up visions of women's unbridled lust. This is why many nineteenth- and twentieth-century feminists rejected contraception, fearing it would mean a regression into a "base animalism" and reduce women to mere objects of lust.[74] Woman's nature, identified by her biological function and therefore considered volatile and dangerous, needed to be controlled by male culture to become acceptable: doctors liked to see themselves as the upholders of social order by mastering nature in the form of the female body. They often used harsh therapies to control both men's and women's dangerous sexuality. Vasectomy on male sex offenders, developed in the USA long before the First World War,[75] is a good example and I have already quoted examples of how female sexuality was subject to forms of disciplining.

The medical profession's quest for a monopoly of abortion was important to ensure its vision of "order", but it presented difficulties. Abortion shared important characteristics with childbirth in this respect. Childbirth had been an area of medicine avoided by male doctors because it was regarded as "women's business": as Ornella Moscucci puts it, "the perceived messiness and immodesty of child-birth rendered man-midwifery unpalatable to medical men". Male physical contact with female genitals had always been problematic. Such contact was a violation of women's modesty but it was also considered an indiscretion on the part of women who allowed it. The protection of women from such indelicate interference had of course been the main reason why women had campaigned for female doctors.[76] If childbirth was associated in the eyes of male physicians with impropriety, abortion was doubly so: it was still commonly associated with illicit sex and the medical act was unredeemed by the prospect of preserving life.

The dichotomy nature/culture has long provided a framework for explaining attitudes to gender. But it has also shaped ideas about pollution, a metaphor that is extremely gendered. Ever since Mary Douglas first introduced it in the mid-1960s, social and medical anthropologists have invoked pollution beliefs to explain male hostility to women of childbearing age in general and to menstruating women in particular.[77] Anthropological studies of healing rituals, for example, frequently describe cultural views of women's reproductive substances as representing uncontrolled and thus dangerous forces and as embodying the boundary between nature and culture on the one hand and disorder and order on the other.[78] Even today many men and some male doctors believe that menstrual blood is dirty and intercourse during menses should be avoided for aesthetic and medical reasons.[79] Douglas defined dirt, the matter that pollutes, as "a matter out of place", a wider definition than our contemporary understanding of it which is dominated by the knowledge of it as a "pathogenic organism". Douglas implies that dirt is a contravention of order and thus a by-product of a systematic ordering and classification.[80] Polluting women are seen as a threat to social order and need to be civilized or marginalized. The menstruating or pregnant woman is often subjected to careful controls to avoid her contaminating others. Ann Oakley cites as examples the physical segregation of parturient women in southern India, the "churching" of women after childbirth or the Jewish prohibition against the handling of food by menstruating women.[81] We have come to perceive these beliefs as being more typical of Third World countries and as having been dispelled in Europe by scientific research. But as the anthropologist Henrietta Moore puts it, the categories nature and culture and pollution are not value-free and unmediated, but "derive from Western society, and, as such, they are products of a particular intellectual tradition and of a specific historical trajectory".[82] Certainly such notions were expressed explicitly by some doctors in the 1920s and very probably many others held them unconsciously, too. For example, Ludwig Fraenkel, a well known German gynaecologist, wrote in the standard textbook on women's biology and pathology, published in 1924, that he was convinced that the female organism during menstruation had to expel poisonous substances such as sulphur and calcium. He referred to a German scientist, Schick, whose research had shown that newly flowering roses would wilt if held for ten minutes by a menstruating woman.[83]

I would like to suggest that pollution images could also be used to understand hostility to the aborting woman. Just as late-eighteenth-century population policy has been said to have influenced the notion that menstruation was unnatural because it signified the waste of a substance that should have been used for procreation, many doctors may have clung unconsciously to the belief that women's natural role was childbirth and that an artificial miscarriage was a sin against nature. If menstruation was a pathology, then so was abortion as this restored a woman's menses. The aborting woman was deviant and needed disciplining, especially, as we have seen, since she was also associated with dirt and danger.

Since abortion brought to the fore all the unacceptable facets of gynaecology – orifices, blood and body juices – which doctors found so odious, then doctors had to protect themselves from direct contact. This is strongly reminiscent of pollution beliefs which hold that danger is transmitted from the polluting person by touch. By using instruments and administering anaesthetics to ensure total control, most doctors removed themselves as far as possible from the woman's body and the aborted matter. Doctors attached enormous importance to surgical techniques of dilatation and curettage, thanks to the late nineteenth-century inventions of laminaria tents or tools such as the curette that physicians claimed as their prerogative.[84] By dilating the cervix by means of laminaria tents or the later invention

of the Hegar metal clip, and then removing the aborted foetus completely by scraping uterine walls with the curette, they distanced
themselves from the messy substances and the woman's haemor-
rhaging body.

The application of such instruments could also be dangerous: sometimes doctors inserted them carelessly so that wombs were punctured
or lacerated and many women suffered from pelvic infections and
long-term pain. Many also died.[85] Although Georg Winter, the professor of gynaecology from Königsberg and the generally acknowledged
authority on medical termination, made it quite clear that most terminations did not need anaesthetics,[86] it is surprising to find that most
medical practitioners administered them even if they had no expert
help, as if they suspected antagonism from their patients. The lack of
anaesthesia usually had a purpose: to punish or teach the woman a
lesson as we have seen with the country doctor mentioned above. In
this context it is also interesting that it was not a doctor but a chemist
who had made an important discovery in abortion technique that
promised a safe result without the need of instruments. But as a
number of medical authorities with a more open mind on the problems of abortion remarked, the medical profession was on the whole
not interested in doing research in this field.[87]

By the exclusive use of certain instruments and anaesthetics doctors
also hoped to establish clear boundaries between medicine and
quackery and to define their own procedures as superior to the
methods used by midwives or lay practitioners. Lay practitioners had
recourse to few instruments. The most common method was injecting
boiled water or a soap solution by means of a syringe or douche to
which a long thin catheter of either glass or rubber was attached. All
these were easily obtainable by mail order or from chemists, sometimes even hairdressers or door-to-door salesmen.[88] Midwives and
wise women liked to investigate the womb with their hands and often
they would massage the woman's stomach during the operation to
help her relax and to stimulate contractions. They acted empirically
relying on their senses whereas male medicine was anti-empirical and
indirect. Many female abortionists asked their patients to examine
the aborted matter and report what they had seen. At least one
wise woman asked her clients to return with the aborted foetus to
make sure that everything had been expelled. As far as I can see,
women complied.[89] The different treatment of the aborting woman

by doctors and wise women is reminiscent of the differences between female and male midwives in the eighteenth century as described by Barbara Duden.[90] Whereas doctors avoided physical and emotional contact with both the woman and her foetus, wise women were tactile and involved their client through talking to her, massaging her, feeling inside her and finally inspecting the aborted matter. But if doctors avoided contact because they thought abortion a messy business, then by implication wise women and men who did not avoid contact appeared to doctors sullied and inferior. This is exactly what happened. Medical opinion did its best to denounce lay practitioners as dirty backstreet abortionists, and untrained men and women as ignorant and evil.[91]

Conclusion

This chapter has tried to re-examine abortion as an everyday phenomenon for millions of women in the Weimar Republic. It has shown that whereas the official discourse focused on moral questions, professional interests, party politics and population policy, popular opinion was concerned with practical solutions, such as finding an abortionist who was reliable, effective and cheap. Seen from the viewpoint of the aborting woman, the issues of gender and of class were both crucial factors in shaping her options and her experience.

Abortion was shaped in many different ways by gender relations. An unwanted pregnancy constituted a crisis that activated single-sex networks. If women desired an artificial miscarriage they turned to a female network of information and support and they preferred a female to a male abortionist. Men consulted a male network to find help for their wives or mistresses and they clearly preferred male practitioners. At the same time, an unwanted pregnancy also affected heterosexual relationships. It could lead, as we have seen, to women finding strong support from their male partner/husband, often to an extent unimaginable in contemporary urban society. But in other cases the need or desire by either partner for a termination of the woman's pregnancy exacerbated existing tensions between partners. In such cases, the woman was in a weak position and she became particularly vulnerable to sexual abuse, not only by her husband/lover but also by the male abortionist.

In the relationship between the aborting woman and the abortion-ist, and in the relationship between lay practitioners and the medical profession, the issues of gender and class interacted in complex ways. Class factors were clearly crucial in shaping the relationship between the aborting woman and her abortionist. While lay abortionists were generally recruited from the lower classes and attracted predomi-nantly women patients of their own social background, doctors were predominantly middle-class but were consulted by women of all classes. Socio-economic and cultural affinity between practitioner and patient was an important reason for the popularity of wise women and wise men. Conversely, cultural and social differences between doctors – whether male or female – and their patients made for a starkly hier-archical doctor–patient relationship.

However, the medical profession's attempt to outlaw all quack abortionists had implications for gender relations above and beyond the clash between professional/middle-class versus lay/lower-class practitioners. The marginalization of lay abortionists entailed a trans-fer of control from women to men as practitioners and a loss of con-trol for women as patients. A high percentage of lay abortionists were women, many of them midwives or de-registered midwives. More-over, such practitioners tended to co-operate with rather than dictate to the aborting woman. Thus the process of medicalization excluded many women from the practice of abortion and lessened the chances of women patients determining what happened in the abortion pro-cess.

Finally, the relationship between aborting women and male doctors was also shaped by the concept of women and their bodies as pollut-ing and dirty. As the sociologist Sophie Laws argues persuasively, pol-lution beliefs can be read as statements about power relations in society. They define, according to the dominant ideology, what is to be regarded as matter out of place and this in turn establishes who has control of such social definitions: "dirtiness" is ascribed by a domi-nant group to a weaker group.[92] Aborting women and their lay help-ers, "polluting" and powerless, offer a key example of such a group.

Notes

The research on which this chapter is based was made possible by a Research Leave Fellowship of the Wellcome Trust London, a travel grant by the German Academic Exchange Service and by support from the Arts Faculty Research Fund, Roehampton Institute. My special thanks to Willem de Blécourt for inspiring me to look at anthropological approaches to history.

1. Advertisement by A. R., cited in W. Köhler, *Das Delikt der Abtreibung im Bezirk des Landgerichts Gera in den Jahren 1896–1930* (Med. PhD thesis, University of Jena, Jena, 1935), pp. 44–5.
2. Paragraph 219, part of the abortion clause, prescribed a maximum of ten years' penal servitude for any person helping to procure an abortion for money. In 1926 the abortion clauses 218–20 were reformed into a single clause 218, reducing the penalty for the aborting woman but increasing that for the "commercial abortionist" to a maximum of 15 years' penal servitude. The police were reluctant to prosecute and preferred to turn a blind eye to such advertisements as long as they did not flout the law too blatantly.
3. Cited in H. Jahns, *Das Delikt der Abtreibung im Landgerichtsbezirk Duisburg in der Zeit von 1910 bis 1935* (Med. PhD thesis, University of Bonn, Düsseldorf, 1938), p. 65.
4. "Die Angst vor dem Kinde", *Vorwärts*, 21 May 1924.
5. Cf. U. Frevert, *Krankheit als politisches Problem 1770–1880: Soziale Unterschichten in Preussen zwischen medizinischer Polizei und staatlicher Sozialversicherung* (Göttingen: Vandenhoeck & Ruprecht, 1984); C. Huerkamp, *Der Aufstieg der Ärzte im 19. Jahrhundert* (Göttingen: Vandenhoeck & Ruprecht, 1985).
6. C. Usborne, *The politics of the body in Weimar Germany: women's reproductive rights and duties* (London: Macmillan and Ann Arbor, Mich.: University of Michigan Press, 1992). See also, e.g. A. Grossmann, *Reforming sex: the German movement for birth control and abortion reform 1920–1950* (New York & Oxford: Oxford University Press, 1995); A. Bergmann, *Die verhütete Sexualität: Die Anfänge der modernen Geburtenkontrolle* (Hamburg: Rasch & Röhring, 1992); C. von Soden, "Verwünschungen und Prophezeiungen: Die Befürwortung des Paragraphen 218 in der Weimarer Republik", in *Wir sind keine Mörderinnen!*, S. von Paczensky (ed.) (Reinbek near Hamburg: Rowohlt, 1984), pp. 127–37; J. Woycke, *Birth control in Germany 1871–1933* (London: Routledge, 1988); B. Brookes, *Abortion in England 1900–1967* (London: Croom Helm, 1988); J. F. Brodie, *Contraception and abortion in 19th-century America* (Ithaca, New York & London: Cornell University Press, 1994); C. Smith-Rosenberg, *Disorderly conduct: visions of gender in Victorian America* (New

York: Knopf, 1981). Exceptions are, e.g. G. Bock, *Zwangssterilisation im Nationalsozialismus: Studien zur Rassenpolitik und Frauenpolitik* (Opladen: Westdeutscher Verlag, 1986); G. Czarnowski, "Crime of women – crime of the state: abortion in Nazi Germany", paper delivered at Gender and crime in Britain and Europe Conference, Roehampton Institute, London, 1995; the contributions by L. Leibrock-Plehn and K. Stukenbrock in *Geschichte der Abtreibung: Von der Antike bis zur Gegenwart*, R. Jütte (ed.) (Munich: C. H. Beck, 1993) and P. Knight, "Women and abortion in Victorian and Edwardian England", *History Workshop Journal* 4, 1977, pp. 57–69..

7. For a fuller discussion see Usborne, *The politics of the body*, ch. 4.

8. Cf. C. Usborne, "Abortion for sale! The competition between quacks and doctors in Weimar Germany", in *Magic, faith, medicine: alternative healing traditions in Europe, 1500 to the present*, M. Gijwijt-Hofstra, H. Marland, H. de Waardt (eds) (London: Routledge, forthcoming).

9. *Ibid.*

10. Cf. R. P. Petchesky, *Abortion and woman's choice* (London: Verso, 1986), pp. 80–81.

11. The clearest evidence is leading gynaecologists' endeavour gradually to reduce the medical grounds on which abortion was deemed justified. It was argued that medical advances meant that illnesses that were formerly regarded as incurable could now be treated successfully: see G. Winter, *Der künstliche Abort: Indikationen, Methoden, Rechtspflege für den medizinischen Praktiker* (Stuttgart, 1926), pp. 8–10.

12. In March 1927 the German Supreme Court ruled that therapeutic abortion was to be permitted. Germany thereby became only the second country, after the Soviet Union, to legalize abortion on health grounds. Although the German decree did not exclude lay practitioners, doctors understood this to mean that legal termination was a prerogative of the medical profession.

13. Stadtarchiv Cologne, NL Wilhelm Marx, part III, Abt. 1070, no. 193, "Proposals to protect foetal life" by the Catholic hierarchy, 26 Feb. 1923.

14. For instance B. Duden, " 'Keine Nachsicht gegen das schöne Geschlecht': Wie sich Ärzte die Kontrolle über Gebärmütter aneigneten", in *Paragraph 218: Zu Lasten der Frauen*, S. von Paczensky & R. Sadrozinski (eds) (Hamburg: Rowohlt, 1988), pp. 114–33; Petchesky, *Abortion and woman's choice*; C. S. McClain (ed.), *Women as healers: cross-cultural perspectives* (New Brunswick & London: Rutgers University Press, 1989); Smith-Rosenberg, *Disorderly conduct*.

15. B. Duden, *The woman beneath the skin: a doctor's patients in eighteenth-century Germany* (Cambridge, Mass.: Harvard University Press, 1991); D. W. Sabean, *Power in the blood. Popular culture and village discourse in early modern Germany* (Cambridge: Cambridge University Press, 1984) and R. Schulte, "Infanticide in rural Bavaria in the nineteenth century", in *Interest and emotion: essays on the study of family and kinship*, H. Medick & D. W. Sabean (eds) (Cambridge: Cambridge University Press, 1984), pp.77–102.

16. Jahns, *Abtreibung in Duisburg*, pp. 64–5.

17. The preference for female abortionists is also mirrored by three of the four comprehensive legal studies of abortion cases in various *Landgerichte*. In the area of the *Landgericht* Duisburg there were 22 female abortionists (prosecuted and tried) and 15 men, in the area of the *Landgericht* Mönchen-Gladbach 9 women and 3 men, in Freiburg 4 women and 3 men (referring to the years 1925–30 only). Only the area of the *Landgericht* Gera was an exception with 5 women outnumbered by 8 men (Jahns, *Abtreibung in Duisburg*, p. 64 and footnote 92 about Gera; K. Inderheggen, *Das Delikt der Abtreibung im Landgerichtsbezirk M.-Gladbach in der Zeit von 1908 bis 1938* (Jena, 1940), pp. 106–12; W. Krieger, *Erscheinungsformen und Strafzumessung bei der Abtreibung dargestellt an Hand von Gerichtsakten des Landgerichts und Amtsgerichts Freiburg i. Br. aus den Jahren 1925–1951* (PhD dissertation, University of Freiburg i. Br., 1952), p. 42).

18. Jahns, *Die Abtreibung in Duisburg*, p. 68.

19. Landesarchiv Berlin (LAB), Rep. 58, 2137–9, 1918, vol. 1, p. 51, and midwife's advertisements included in letter of 15 Dec. 1920, letter Dr J. to *Landgericht*, 16 Oct. 1918 and letter of 17 Oct. 1918.

20. LAB, Rep. 58, 2137, Gutachten des Medizinalkollegiums, Province of East Prussia, 1 July 1920 and various letters by women 7 Oct. 1918.

21. LAB, Rep. 58, 416, vol. 1.

22. Staatsarchiv Munich (SAM), AG Mü, 16595, Anton Schn, engine driver and 13 others, 1926.

23. SAM, AG Mü, 16583, interview Maria Z. 18 June 1926.

24. SAM, AG Mü, 16583, interview 18 June 1926.

25. SAM, AG Mü, 16510, Maria St. and five others, abortion 1930, Bl. 18, 42R.

26. *Ibid.*, Bl. 48R, 31R, 32R.

27. LAB, Rep. 58, 2439, Frau Spr., 1929.

28. Inderheggen, *Die Abtreibung in M.-Gladbach*, case 7/8 p. 106, case 5/6 p. 105, cases 9 and 10/11 p. 107.

29. SAM, AG Mü, 16595, Bl. 34–5.

30. LAB, Rep. 58, 2064, Ferdinand St. 1928, case 1–3.

31. E.g. LAB, Rep. 58, 850, Dr Kurt M., 1926, concerning the 17-year-old dancer at the Berlin Komische Oper, Antonia M. When she found herself pregnant, her boyfriend, the actor Erich P., set out to find a doctor. He eventually found a young doctor prepared to terminate the pregnancy but he was unskilled and negligent and Antonia died of multiple internal injuries.

32. SAM, AG Mü, 16595, Bl. 66Rs ff.

33. SAM, AG Mü, 16727, August W., photographer, 1926.

34. SAM, AG Mü, 16727, Bl. 5Rs–8, 13Rs–14Rs.

35. SAM, AG Mü, 16727, Bl. 4, 65.

36. SAM, AG Mü, 16604, Sonntag, 1926.

37. Inderheggen, *Die Abtreibung in M.-Gladbach*, pp. 110–11: case no. 15.
38. See for example SAM, AG Mü, 16583, Mathilde B., seamstress, 1927, copy of original 13Rs–15Rs: Frau S. stated that her "husband knew of nothing" and that her mother knew of her pregnancy, but only heard about her abortion after the event. Interview 17 June 1926 Frau Therese S., mother of Anna W.
39. SAM, AG Mü, 16727, Bl. 5Rs. The woman's mother burnt the foetus.
40. SAM, AG Mü, 16595, Bl. 37.
41. SAM, AG Mü, 16595, Bl. 100, 105.
42. Smith-Rosenberg, *Disorderly conduct*, pp. 291–2.
43. Geheimes Staatsarchiv Preußischer Kulturbesitz, Berlin-Dahlem (GSAPK) Rep. 84a, 17109, Herr Ferdinand Adolf und Frau Hermine K. and 91 others, 1924.
44. GSAPK, Rep. 84a, 17109, case 1d, Bl. 19: both women became "slightly ill with peritonitis" but once treated by a doctor this soon cleared up.
45. GSAPK, Rep. 84a, 17109, e.g. Herr Sch., case 23, Bl. 15.
46. GSAPK, Rep. 84a, 17109, Bl. 14, case 8 paid with half a ton of wheat; another with a sack of oats; one husband ploughed K's potato field for free (case 18); Bl. 15: a jug of Schnapps, soap and malt coffee was paid in case 29 in 1923; one husband made a pair of shoes for Frau K. (case 53, Bl. 17).
47. GSAPK, Rep. 84a, 17109, case 15, Bl. 27; case 69, Bl. 28.
48. GSAPK, Rep. 84a, 17109, case 32, Bl. 25; case 55 Bl. 26.
49. GSAPK, Rep. 84a, 17109, case 41, Bl. 16.
50. Hauptstaatsarchiv Düsseldorf, Staatsanw. Kleve, Rep. 7, no. 896: this doctor was prosecuted for a large number of abortions as well as child abuse and incest, but interestingly not for rape.
51. H. Börner, "Zur Frage der Schwangerschaftsunterbrechung", *Die Ärztin* 6, 1930, p.77, commenting on the official guidelines on medical termination by Winter, *Der künstliche Abort*.
52. He remained anonymous for legal reasons but his medical case studies were published posthumously by the prominent professor of social hygiene Alfred Grotjahn as a monument to his courage; A. Grotjahn (ed.), *Eine Kartothek zu Paragraph 218: Ärztliche Berichte aus einer Kleinstadtpraxis über 426 künstliche Aborte in einem Jahr* (Berlin, 1932), introduction.
53. *Ibid.*, p. 17, case 19.
54. *Ibid.*, p. 15, case 3; pp. 136–7, case 433.
55. M. Kelchner, *Die Frau und der weibliche Arzt: Eine psychologische Untersuchung auf Grundlage einer Umfrage* (Berlin, 1934).
56. SAM, St.anw.Mü I, 1834, 1914: some of the sterilized women were as young as 23, 27 and 28; a butcher's wife with six children and several premature births said she did not know whether she had "a scraping" or a "cap inserted" (3 Apr. 1914).
57. E.g. Bundesarchiv Koblenz (BAK), R86, 2379, vol. 1, Reichsminister des Innern to president of the Reichsgesundheitsamt, 8 Nov. 1917, the case of Prof. Henkel of Jena University; GSAPK, Rep. 84a, 17153, Dr.med.St. of

Husum, 1930 who was found to have removed "the complete uterus in five cases including at least one healthy one".

58. L. Fink, "Schwangerschaftsunterbrechung und Erfahrung aus Ehe- und Sexualberatung", *Die Ärztin* 7, 1931, pp. 70–74.

59. L. Fink, "Die Tubensterilisation als Mittel der Geburtenregelung. Bericht über 375 Fälle der Ehe- und Sexualberatungsstelle Frankfurt a. M. (Mutterschutz)", *Medizinische Welt* 21, 1931, pp. 750–51: out of 375 analyzed cases of sterilized women, 270 were married to unskilled manual workers. Amongst the reasons featured such classic eugenic criteria as "nervous diseases" (90 women, 53 husbands), "morally defective" (20 women, 33 husbands), "alcoholism" (58 husbands), syphilis (18 women, 13 husbands), epilepsy (6 women, 3 husbands).

60. See Usborne, *The politics of the body*, pp. 151 ff.

61. Inderheggen, *Die Abtreibung in M.-Gladbach*, p. 111.

62. For more details see Usborne, "Abortion for sale!"; cf. also Jahns, *Die Abtreibung in Duisburg*, pp. 31–2: amongst the abortionists there were only 3 doctors compared to 37 lay practitioners (19 nature therapists, masseurs or homeopaths, 5 chemists, 9 midwives and masseurs and 4 others); in the majority of cases pregnancies were terminated by spouses, relatives, friends and neighbours.

63. For comparative prices see Usborne, "Abortion for sale!"; for gender distribution in the medical profession see Usborne, *Politics of the body*, pp. 191 ff.

64. One is the well-known case of Dr Else Kienle who faced prosecution in 1931 together with the communist doctor and playwright Friedrich Wolf, a case that unleashed the largest protest campaign against clause 218 of the criminal code: see Grossmann, *Reforming sex*, pp. 83 ff.; the other case concerned Dr Hope Bridges Adams-Lehmann, cf. Usborne, *Politics of the body*, pp. 7, 13, 154 and note 56.

65. Cf. Usborne, "Abortion for sale!"

66. S. Vollmann, "Die Bekämpfung der Abtreibungsseuche", *Ärztliches Vereinsblatt für Deutschland* 52, 1925, p. 45.

67. *Ärztliches Vereinsblatt* 53, 1925, p. 48; cf. F. Loenne, *Das Problem der Fruchtabtreibung vom medizinischen, juristischen und national-ökonomischen Standpunkt* (Berlin, 1924), p. 31.

68. Cf. Usborne, *Politics of the body*, pp. 181 ff.

69. E.g. the communist *Die Internationale* 4(20), 1922, pp. 464–5; the various etchings by Käthe Kollwitz used as posters for Carl Crede's play *Paragraph 218, Gequälte Menschen* and her etching for the poster *Down with the abortion clause!*, 1928. In the same vein is the role of Hete in Friedrich Wolf's famous abortion play, *Cyankali*, which shows Hete dying miserably after a bungled backstreet abortion.

70. Petchesky, *Abortion and woman's choice*, p. 27.

71. E.g. F. Loenne, *Das Problem der Fruchtabtreibung*, p. 11.

72. P. Shuttle & P. Redgrove, *The wise wound: menstruation and everywoman*

(London: HarperCollins, 1994), p. 21.

73. O. Moscucci, *The science of woman: gynaecology and gender in England 1800–1929* (Cambridge: Cambridge University Press, 1990), p. 102.

74. L. Bland, *Banishing the beast. English feminism and sexual morality 1885–1914* (London: Penguin, 1995), p. 197; Usborne, *Politics of the body*, pp. 92 ff.

75. A. Grotjahn, *Die Hygiene der menschlichen Fortpflanzung* (Berlin, 1926), pp. 75–6.

76. O. Moscucci, *The science of woman*, p. 56; cf. A. Oakley, "Wisewoman and medicine man: changes in the management of childbirth", in *The rights and wrongs of women*, J. Mitchell & A. Oakley (eds) (London: Penguin, 1976), pp. 17–58, 33–34; cf. D. Scully, *Men who control women's health: the miseducation of obstetricians-gynaecologists* (Boston: Houghton Mifflin, 1980), p. 25.

77. E.g. M. Douglas, *Purity and danger: an analysis of the concepts of pollution and taboo*, 2nd edn (London: Routledge, 1984); Oakley, "Wisewoman and medicine man", pp. 31 ff.; S. Laws, *Issues of blood: the politics of menstruation* (London: Macmillan, 1990); C. Shepherd McClain, "Reinterpreting women in healing roles", in *Women as healers: cross-cultural perspectives*, C. S. McClain (ed.) (New Brunswick & London: Rutgers University Press, 1989), pp. 1–19.

78. McClain, "Reinterpreting women in healing roles", p. 6.

79. Laws, *Issues of blood*, p. 139.

80. Douglas, *Purity and danger*, p. 36.

81. Oakley, "Wisewoman and medicine man", p. 32.

82. H. L. Moore, *Feminism and anthropology* (Cambridge: Polity, 1988), p. 19.

83. L. Fraenkel, "Physiologie der weiblichen Genitalorgane", in J. Halban & L. Seitz, *Biologie und Pathologie des Weibes*, [8 vols] (Berlin/Vienna 1924–9), vol. 1, 1924, pp. 517–634, 549–50, quoted in E. Fischer-Homberger, *Krankheit Frau* (Berne, Stuttgart, Vienna: Hans Huber, 1979) p. 60.

84. Cf. E. Shorter, *A history of women's bodies* (London: Allen Lane, 1982), pp. 179–207.

85. E.g. LAB, Rep. 58a, 850, case of Dr M. who fatally lacerated the uterus of a 17-year-old dancer.

86. G. Winter, "Strittige Punkte in der Bekämpfung des fieberhaften Aborts", *Medizinische Welt* (August 1927), p. 1041.

87. S. Peller, *Fehlgeburt und Bevölkerungsfrage* (Stuttgart & Leipzig, 1930), p. 135 alleged that a folk remedy (almost certainly the famous Heiser cream) was available on the open market and would induce a miscarriage after a few days without any mechanical intervention; if other "folk remedies achieve the same effect it is difficult to fathom since clinicians avoid these questions and leave the research in this area to the veterinary toxicology whose results are not always relevant to human pathology". M. Hirsch complained in *Fruchtabtreibung und Präventivverkehr im Zusammenhang mit dem Geburtenrückgang* (Würzburg, 1914) p. 171 that doctors showed

175

little interest in termination of pregnancy.
88. Cf. Usborne, *The politics of the body*, ch. 2.
89. LAB, Rep. 58a, 2442, Albertine L., seamstress, 1929–30.
90. Duden, *The woman beneath the skin*.
91. Cf. Usborne, "Abortion for sale!"
92. Laws, *Issues of blood*, p. 36.

Chapter Eight

ᴥᶋ

National Socialist policies towards female homosexuality

Claudia Schoppmann
Translated by Elizabeth Harvey

On 30 November 1940, Elli Smula and Margarete Rosenberg were brought to the women's concentration camp Ravensbrück north of Berlin. They were just 26 and 30 years old. The reason for their arrest was given on the camp's list of inmates as "lesbian". As in all concentration camps, the SS in Ravensbrück divided the inmates into different categories and marked them out by different coloured triangles on their clothing – a device that made it easier for the camp authorities to play one group of inmates off against another and prevent the organization of resistance. Elli Smula and Margarete Rosenberg were compelled to wear a red triangle; they were, in other words, assigned to the category of "politicals". The pink triangle, to identify actual or alleged homosexuality, was "reserved" for men; there was no separate category of inmates designated as lesbians. We know nothing of the two women's lives before their arrest, and we do not know whether or how they survived their imprisonment in Ravensbrück. Nor do we know the circumstances that led to their arrest. Had they come to the attention of the local block leader (*Blockwart*) in their neighbourhood and been denounced? Had they perhaps been arrested in a raid on a bar known to be a meeting-place for lesbians?

For too long such questions were never asked, and now they are nearly impossible to answer. Fifty years after the end of the Second World War, there are still "forgotten", suppressed pages in the most appalling chapter of German history. How did the life of lesbians change after the Nazi take-over? What happened to the hard-won freedom – limited though it was – enjoyed by lesbians during the Weimar Republic? What consequences did homophobic National Socialist ideology have for them? Up till now, National Socialist policy on female homosexuality has not been a topic addressed either by public debate or by historical scholarship. This silence reflects a reluctance, not only on the part of academic scholarship, to acknowledge homosexuality as a category that is as socially and historically determined as gender. If there has been any change in these attitudes over the last few years, it is only to the extent that historians have begun to examine the fate of homosexual men in the Third Reich.[1] Lesbians remain as invisible as ever. However, the historian who tries to reconstruct the experience of lesbians in Nazi Germany encounters major difficulties. Not only are there virtually no relevant files or documents on the subject (still) in existence; because of continuing discrimination, lesbians have left few personal accounts of their experiences in the Third Reich, and it is difficult to find any who are willing to be interviewed about it.

Homosexuality, as a form of sexual and social "deviance", was fundamentally condemned by National Socialism. By virtue of its very existence, homosexuality called into question Nazi norms of sexual behaviour, which were oriented towards the production of "hereditarily fit Aryans"; homosexuality therefore had to be eliminated. However, there was little that was specifically National Socialist about the regime's thinking on homosexuality: it simply built on the existing homophobia of the majority of the population, which was deeply rooted and influenced by the attitude of the churches. As far as attitudes to homosexuality were concerned, neither the Nazi takeover nor the end of the Second World War represented a fundamental break in continuity. What was specifically Nazi was thus not homophobic ideology but the way in which this ideology was ultimately put into practice.

Nazi policy towards homosexuals aimed at "deterrence through punishment", at some form of supposed "re-education". Its aim was not the physical destruction of all homosexuals. This was not merely because of the obvious practical difficulties of identifying and systematically registering homosexuals, although this was an important factor: it was much more difficult to stigmatize homosexual men and women and exclude them from the "national community" than it was to identify and persecute ethnic minorities and political opponents, who were already registered in some way (for instance in registers of births, deaths and marriages) or were identifiable through other records.

Although many slogans demanded the "elimination" of homosexuals, National Socialist policy towards homosexuals was in fact differentiated after the take-over of power in 1933. One example of this is the way in which homosexual men and women were treated differently. Apart from anything else, this distinction between the sexes made the Nazi persecution of homosexuals fundamentally different in kind from the racial war of destruction that the regime waged against the Jewish population and against Sinti and Roma. Even in the Nazi state, the "regime of injustice" (*Unrechtsstaat*) *par excellence*, no criminal prosecutions of lesbians took place. At the same time around fifty thousand men were convicted on the basis of Paragraph 175 of the Criminal Code, and between 10,000 and 15,000 were sent to concentration camps, of whom around two-thirds perished. How is this striking discrepancy between the treatment of homosexual men and women to be explained?

After January 1933, one of the most urgent tasks for Nazi policy on sexual matters was to destroy the organized public homosexual movement, which with its emancipatory demands and its infrastructure visibly flouted Nazi sexual morality. The major homosexual rights organizations, such as the Institute for Sexology founded by Magnus Hirschfeld, and the League for Human Rights, were dissolved or destroyed. Informal communication networks were smashed, pubs and bars closed or placed under surveillance. Raids and denunciations contributed to a climate of fear, and led many homosexuals to withdraw into the private sphere. Out of such fear some broke off all their contacts and moved away. The development of a collective lesbian lifestyle and identity, which had begun after the turn of the century and had gained momentum above all during the Weimar Republic, was brought to an abrupt halt. The impact of this destruction was profound, and its effects lasted well beyond the end of the Third Reich.

Some lesbians in Nazi Germany were at risk on the grounds of their ethnic identity, their political affiliation or for other reasons. However, for those who were not at risk on these grounds, the crucial factor defining the circumstances under which they lived was their status as women. The Nazi state, which sought to assert total control over reproductive behaviour, saw motherhood and marriage as the fundamental destiny of a woman who was "Aryan" and "hereditarily fit", while at the same time denying to those ethnic minorities defined as "inferior" the right to live at all. A population policy aimed at increasing the number of "desirable" births was the essential precondition for the National Socialist goal of conquest through war – particularly in view of a deficit of births that was estimated at 14 million for the years between 1915 and 1933. Under these circumstances, marriage and motherhood were political issues of prime importance. According to *Das Schwarze Korps*, the SS organ, a "real woman" suffered acutely if she was not married: however, it was argued, "it is not the absence of sexual intercourse which causes her suffering, but the lack of a child, the failure to fulfil her destiny to be a mother".[2]

The regime launched a fierce attack upon marriages that had remained childless. The prominent population policy expert Friedrich Burgdörfer labelled childless marriages as "racial desertion". While all this propaganda appears to have had little impact on the birthrate – the regime was able to achieve only a slight increase in the number of marriages and births – it had an impact on the lives of lesbians. The propaganda targeted at the single and childless woman was bound to affect lesbians particularly, since for obvious reasons they were more likely to remain unmarried than heterosexual women. After 1933, many of the estimated one million lesbians in Germany got married to escape social pressure and in some cases to avoid losing their jobs. The more fortunate were able to marry homosexual men, for whom marriage also offered some degree of protection from persecution, although such protection was by no means absolute. A Berlin fashion illustrator, for whom 1933 marked the beginning of a "life in disguise", described an example of this:

> I had already been living with my girlfriend for years. Sometimes people whispered among themselves: "Is there something going on between those two?" But when the Third Reich broke out, suddenly it was vicious: "There's definitely something going on between those two!" There were the *Hauswarte* and the *Blockwarte*, those who had the job of snooping into our private lives and reporting on anything. Our landlady was questioned about our "intimate affairs". One day the chief editor came to me in the studio and told me impatiently that I must get married or he could no longer employ me.

The fashion illustrator and her girlfriend decided to move in with two homosexual male friends.

But that was not enough to satisfy the new regime's commandments. Again it was the *Hauswart* with the party badge who said to us: "You can't live together without being married, that goes against what the Führer has ordered." And he wasn't even malicious, he was just an ordinary Berliner who was all right really. So if even he was talking like that . . . So we two women decided to marry our two male friends. But that plunged us into new conflicts. I certainly took a long time to get used to being asked about how my husband was. "What do you mean?", I would reply, and only then I would remember that being married was my disguise.[3]

The Nazi policy of "deterrence through punishment" was to be achieved through the radical tightening-up of Paragraph 175 of the Criminal Code which since 1871 had criminalized sexual acts between men. In the new version of June 1935, the paragraph read: "A male who indulges in indecent activities with another male or who allows himself to participate in such activities will be punished with imprisonment." Prison sentences of up to five years were envisaged, and the newly devised Paragraph 175a provided for sentences of hard labour of up to ten years (in so-called aggravated cases, for instance when the partner was under 21 years of age). The new law not only increased the penalties for homosexual offences; it also radically widened the definition of criminal homosexual activity by no longer restricting it to "acts simulating intercourse" (that is anal intercourse). As a result, the number of convictions under Paragraph 175 rose sharply between 1934 and the outbreak of war, from 800 per year to more than 8,000 per year.

While the criminalization of male homosexuality was never questioned, and the criminal law on male homosexuality was tightened up, the Criminal Law Commission of the Ministry of Justice, which was responsible for drafting new criminal legislation, decided in 1935 to reject proposals to extend Paragraph 175 to women. The discrepancy in the treatment of male and female homosexuality was justified with reference to socially defined gender roles. First, it was argued, the more emotional style of friendship between women would make it too difficult to draw the line clearly between behaviour that was permissible and behaviour that was forbidden; it would be impossible to determine when an offence had been committed. A change in the law could thus lead to baseless accusations. (This was admittedly all rather unconvincing given the way in which allegations of offences committed by men were accepted with little regard for evidence.) Secondly, it was pointed out that male homosexuality posed a greater menace than female homosexuality to public life and political institutions. Where men were concerned, it was feared that a "homosexual plague", threatening as it did the rigid sexual norms essential to the maintenance of order within the state, would lead to the "corruption of public life". Homosexuality among women, it was argued, in view of women's generally subordinate status and their exclusion from positions of power, posed no comparable risk. Furthermore, criminalizing female homosexuality was thought to be all the more superfluous since the threat posed by the feminist movement had been removed. Feminist organizations had been dissolved or brought into line with the new regime: the women's movement, assumed by the Nazis not only to have been a hotbed of "lesbian subversion" before 1933 but also to have been an active advocate of lesbian rights, was no longer a factor to be taken into account. A third argument against the criminalization of female homosexuality was derived on the one hand from assumptions about marital relationships and on the other from the stereotype of the lesbian who was only "pseudohomosexual" and thus "curable" – a notion reinforced by medical research into homosexuality since the turn of the century. According to Otto Thierack, the later Minister of Justice, writing in 1934, "A woman – in contrast to a man – is always capable of intercourse."[4] Most lawyers and population experts also took the view that the danger of women being "seduced" into homosexuality was less of a danger for the state than in the case of male homosexuals, since "a woman seduced in this way is not permanently withdrawn from normal sexual intercourse, but retains her utility for population policy purposes".[5]

All the same, some lawyers called for the extension of Paragraph 175 to women and denounced female homosexuality as "racially damaging" and a "threat to the *Volk*". Although this line of argument was very popular in the Third Reich, it did not ultimately prevail. A major advocate of the criminalization of lesbianism was the young lawyer and *SS-Scharführer* Rudolf Klare, who because of his writings on the subject has become the best-known representative of this view. Klare saw (female) homosexuality as "racial degeneration" and a symptom of "racial decline". "It is absolutely certain that homosexual activity is not an authentic feature of the German woman", observed Klare in his book *Homosexuality and the criminal law*, which appeared in 1937. "Homosexual activity is universally despised as immoral. Lesbianism (*Tribadie*) is by its nature contrary to the development of the valuable components of the race, and it cannot claim to be the repository of the German racial stock."[6] Although he admitted that "female homosexuality, as it presents itself to us at the moment, is *not a political problem*, as it is in the case of male homosexuality",[7] he called for the criminalization of lesbianism. His justification of this demand was the danger posed by female homosexuality to population policy, since lesbians "seduced" heterosexual women and prevented them from fulfilling their "racial duties" of bearing and raising children.

Although lesbianism was not criminalized, the Nazi regime went to some lengths to put pressure on lesbians to conform at least outwardly to the heterosexual norm. By propagating the traditional sexual norms that were threatened by homosexuality, Nazi ideologists sought to uphold the heterosexist social structure that underpinned the regime. Again and again warnings were issued against the "masculinization" of women which could manifest itself in clothing and hairstyles. For example, a book issued by the NS-*Frauenschaft* (the Nazi women's organization) in 1934 pointed out that

> Where one finds in women's clothing a tendency to blur the differences between the sexes, for instance an emphasis on narrow hips and broad shoulders in imitation of the male figure, these are signs of degeneration emanating from an alien race: they are inimical to reproduction and for this reason damaging to the *Volk*. Healthy races do not artificially blur sexual differences.[8]

Although these attempts to reinforce norms of femininity affected all women, heterosexual as well as lesbian, they were bound to be felt particularly acutely by lesbians. In order to avoid harassment in public, many lesbians adapted their appearance and their style of dress to fit a "feminine" image of womanhood and they were forced to lead a psychologically damaging double life.

This drive against the "masculinization" of women was given particular impetus by the interventions of Himmler, who on several occasions argued that the blurring of gender differences was one of the causes of homosexuality. Himmler's views on homosexuality were of course particularly significant given his position from 1936 onwards as *Reichsführer-SS* and Head of the German Police. This position gave him authority over the central bureaucratic apparatus that was set up to track down and register homosexuals, the "National Office for Combating Homosexuality and Abortion" (*Reichszentrale zur Bekämpfung der Homosexualität und Abtreibung*), as well as over regional and local police forces. In a speech to SS Group Leaders (*Gruppenführer*) in February 1937 he expressed the fear that in the "masculinized" state of the Third Reich, the decline or disappearance of "feminine charm" could encourage male homosexuality.

We must not allow the qualities of the masculine state (*Männerstaat*) and the virtues of the *Männerbund* (male-bonded group) to develop unchecked to the point where they cause problems. In my opinion we are currently witnessing an excessive masculinization of all spheres of life . . . I am always horrified to see girls and women – above all girls – marching around with expertly stuffed knapsacks on their backs. It is a nauseating sight. It will be catastrophic if we masculinize women to the extent that sexual differences and the polarity between the sexes vanish. From there it is only a short step to homosexuality.[9]

The local and central authorities attached to the Gestapo and the criminal police, which were set up after the murder of Sturmabteilung (SA) chief Ernst Röhm in June 1934 to hunt down and punish homosexuals, concentrated primarily on the homosexual male "enemy of the state". Male homosexuals were assumed to form an opposition capable of subverting the masculine state. Lesbianism, which was less politically threatening and was in any case not punishable by law, was less of a target for these authorities. Owing to the lack of sources it is impossible to make any quantitative assessment of the extent to which the party and state authorities in the Third Reich kept a formal register of lesbians whose identity became known to them, for instance through denunciation. There are some indications that the police authorities and other organizations such as the Racial Policy Office of the Nazi Party (NSDAP) collected information on lesbians. However, we do not know to what extent this happened or what consequences such collection and registration of information had for the women concerned.

There are only a few known cases in which women were persecuted because of their homosexuality, since officially they were usually accused of other "offences" such as "political unreliability" – as in the case of Elli Smula and Margarete Rosenberg, whom I mentioned at the beginning of this chapter – or "subversion of national defence"

(*Wehrkraftzersetzung*). A number of cases have come to light from the women's Labour Service (*Reichsarbeitsdienst für die weibliche Jugend*) where a so-called "dependent relationship" was alleged to exist, for instance between a superior and a subordinate, or between a tutor (*Erzieherin*) and a pupil, which could be punished under Paragraph 176 of the Criminal Code.

Lesbians were possibly threatened to a greater degree by the so-called "persecution of asocials". Himmler's decree of December 1937 on "preventive measures to combat crime" gave the police powers to take far-reaching measures in the struggle against the "enemy within" that threatened the *Volksgemeinschaft* (people's community). As a result, persons who had committed no criminal offence but who were in some way socially deviant were labelled "asocial" and taken by the police (without any judicial proceedings) into so-called "preventive custody" – which in effect meant concentration camp. "Asocial" was a conveniently flexible term. Anyone who failed to fulfil Nazi expectations of "performance" was liable to be so labelled, with deficiencies in working capacity, deviant reproductive behaviour patterns and symptoms of social deprivation being the main criteria used to judge this. The major targets of this drive against the "asocial" were homeless people, the unemployed, prostitutes, but also homosexuals and Sinti and Roma.

An individual case may serve to illustrate how lesbians were persecuted as part of the drive against "asocials". This case was recounted in the course of an interview with Erich Helbig, who was incarcerated on account of his homosexuality for ten years in a number of different concentration camps.[10] Born in 1917, Else – her surname is unknown – worked as a barmaid in Potsdam and lived there with her girlfriend. She was arrested, clearly because of her homosexuality, and sent to Ravensbrück as an "asocial". From there she was taken, for reasons that are unclear, to Flossenbürg concentration camp, whose inmates after 1938 were mainly men classified as "asocials" or "criminals". Erich Helbig met Else in the autumn of 1943 in Flossenbürg – in the camp brothel, which he was forced to visit as part of his supposed "re-education". Such camp brothels, neatly exemplifying Nazi double standards of morality, had been set up from October 1942 onwards by the SS in a number of concentration camps. Prostitutes, hunted down and persecuted by the Nazi regime in its campaign to "clean up" public morals, were from the beginning of the war systematically put to work in brothels servicing the armed forces, the SS and men's concentration camps. Himmler saw female prostitution both as an instrument with which – supposedly – male homosexuality could be combated, and as a means to boost the productivity of male concentration camp inmates forced to work in the munitions industry. Hundreds of female camp inmates, often bribed with false promises that after a fixed period of "service" they would be released, were made to work as prostitutes in camp brothels. Else worked in the Flossenbürg camp brothel for a number of months. For Erich Helbig, she was "the only person with whom I struck up a friendship in the whole of those ten years. The Nazis were particularly fond of putting lesbians in brothels. They thought that would soon bring them back up to scratch."[11] Else disappeared from the camp shortly afterwards and died some time later, probably before the end of the war: her fate cannot be precisely reconstructed. It is possible that she was deported to Auschwitz after working in Flossenbürg for the standard period of six months set by the SS for camp prostitutes, and perished there.

For the reasons I have mentioned, we cannot say for certain how many women endured the horrors of the concentration camps because of their homosexuality. All we can say is that there was no systematic persecution of lesbians comparable to the persecution of male homosexuals in the Third Reich. Most lesbians were spared the fate of the camps as long as they were not endangered for other reasons and were prepared to conform to the regime's norms. Some even accepted Nazi ideology and collaborated with the regime. One such case is that of the Austrian writer Grete von Urbanitzky (1891–1974), author of the popular lesbian novel *Der wilde Garten* (1927). Already in the 1920s she was propagating National Socialist ideas in her writing, and as co-founder and vice-president of the Austrian PEN Club she supported the Nazis actively. This, though, did not prevent her from becoming a target herself subsequently. She left Germany in 1936 and all of her books were banned five years later.[12] However, such prominent and active collaboration was unusual. The more typical reaction by the majority of lesbians was to try not to attract attention and to remain as inconspicuous as possible. This did not, however, prevent some from becoming involved in the resistance to Nazism. Either as a consequence of such activities, or because of their Jewish origins, many lesbians ended up being forced to leave their homeland and seek refuge abroad.

Notes

A longer version of this chapter appears in Claudia Schoppmann, *Days of masquerade: life stories of lesbians during the Third Reich* (New York: Columbia University Press, 1996). Copyright © 1996 by Columbia University Press. Reprinted with permission of the publisher.

1. The term "Third Reich" is used here in the text without inverted commas, following common practice in English-language publications, for the sake of readability: there is no intention to abandon the critical distance that inverted commas would signify.
2. "Zum neuen Ehescheidungsrecht", *Das Schwarze Korps* 3(42), 21 Oct. 1937, p. 5.
3. K. v. Sch., "Es begann die Zeit der Maskierung", in *Wir erlebten das Ende der Weimarer Republik*, R. Italiaander (ed.) (Düsseldorf: Droste, 1982), pp. 98–9.
4. Bundesarchiv Koblenz (BAK), R 22, 973. Bericht über die 45. Sitzung der Strafrechtskommission des Reichsjustizministeriums am 18. September 1934.
5. BAK, R 61, 127. Ministerialdirigent Schäfer auf einer Sitzung der Akademie für Deutsches Recht am 2. März 1936.
6. R. Klare, *Homosexualität und Strafrecht* (Hamburg: Hanseatische Verlagsanstalt, 1937), p. 122.
7. *Ibid.*, p. 131. Emphasis in the original.
8. *N. S. Frauenbuch* (Munich: J. F. Lehmann, 1934), cited in N. Westenrieder, *"Deutsche Frauen und Mädchen!" Vom Alltagsleben 1933–1945* (Düsseldorf: Droste, 1984), p. 47.
9. B. F. Smith & A. F. Peterson (eds), *Heinrich Himmler: Geheimreden 1933–1945 und andere Ansprachen* (Frankfurt am Main: Propyläen, 1974), pp. 93–104, here p. 99.
10. J. Lemke, *Ganz normal anders: Auskünfte schwuler Männer aus der DDR* (Frankfurt am Main: Luchterhand Literaturverlag, 1989), pp. 13–30.
11. *Ibid.*, p. 26. I have so far found no evidence to support this assumption. See C. Paul, *Zwangsprostitution: Staatlich errichtete Bordelle im Nationalsozialismus* (Berlin: Edition Hentrich, 1994).
12. U. Huber, "Grete von Urbanitzky – ungeliebte Parteigängerin der Nationalsozialisten", *L'Homme: Zeitschrift für Feministische Geschichtswissenschaft* 4(1), 1993, pp. 74–88.

Chapter Nine

Driving the message home: Nazi propaganda in the private sphere

Kate Lacey

Politics for the Nazis was a strictly male affair. According to the ideologues, the divide between public and private life was one that divided the sexes and on which the proper functioning of society and state had to rely. Women were expected to be aware and supportive of the political life of the nation, but were ascribed no active role in the public sphere of politics. Political propaganda, therefore, was ostensibly produced by men, for men, and about men. The official cultural news agency, for example, described the wartime newsreel as "an entirely masculine affair befitting a masculine age".[1] Yet despite the glut of images of male heroics and the posturing of male politicians, there is plenty of evidence to suggest that the propagandists were well aware of the vast numbers of women in the audience and the necessity to address and mobilize them. The various women's organizations were enlisted to this end, and the whole spectrum of media, from posters to public exhibitions, flysheets to film, were exploited in the dissemination of their propaganda.[2] This chapter will focus on just one aspect of that propaganda: their efforts to influence women's patterns of consumption in the interests of the *Volk*.

Of all these media, it was the radio that was identified as the key instrument by which propaganda messages could reach women in the home. The programmes produced by the Nazis have tended to be glossed over both in studies of "high" propaganda and in accounts of women's experience and organization in Nazi Germany, but they deserve closer attention, I would argue, not only to fill in something of a gap in the history books, but because a consideration of women's programming in this period draws out the implications for radio propaganda entering the private sphere as a gendered space and helps illuminate the way in which the radio contributed to the public assault on private life in the Third Reich.[3]

Politics and gender in Nazi Germany

In a speech to officials of the women's organizations in Berlin in 1934, the Minister of Popular Enlightenment and Propaganda, Joseph Goebbels, declared that "the National Socialist movement is by its nature a masculine movement". He claimed that the years of struggle had forged a new masculine ideal and that no true German woman would want to trespass on those areas of public life that were by rights the exclusive domain of men. Instead, German women should identify and pursue a new complementary feminine ideal, and win back the respect that was due to them and that had been lost by trying to compete in the masculine world.[4] In countless similar speeches, editorials and programmes, the message was drummed out that biology and instinct dictated that there were separate spheres of competence for men and women, but equal status within the racially pure, organic society of the *Volksgemeinschaft*. Men's heroic, intellectual natures fitted them for a life of work, politics and courageous struggle, while women's maternal, sentimental natures fitted them for motherhood and self-sacrifice in support of husband, family and people. National Socialism was avowedly anti-feminist in theory and practice, and this anti-feminism was closely bound up with the theory and practice of anti-Semitism and racism. While resources were poured into pro-natalist campaigns directed at the racially acceptable, some 200,000 other women were forcibly sterilized as a precursor to a policy of genocide.[5] Nevertheless, many women were either passively compliant in supporting the policies of the regime, or actively complicit, and certainly some were very enthusiastic in the production of its propaganda.

Although National Socialist women wanted to be "nationalist comrades of the people and not politicians", they did have political responsibilities within the new regime.[6] Women's political duty was defined in terms of their activity in the private sphere (and by extension to those activities in the public sphere of waged labour deemed to be expressions of feminine, maternal attributes). *Reichsfrauenführerin* Gertrud Scholtz-Klink, head of the women's organizations, asserted that women expressed their political contribution in entering into racially aware marriages, caring for their families and in following the guidelines for patriotic consumption dictated by the various state-run propaganda campaigns.[7] With two-thirds of the national income claimed to be passing through women's hands, the art of housekeeping was declared to be of national economic importance. Motherhood, too, was not only a personal responsibility, but a national one, with women bearing the responsibility for the future of the race and nation.

Despite the fact that within a year of its founding, one in ten of the members of the Nazi Party (NSDAP) were women, the "masculine character of the struggle" permitted no women to hold even minor office within the party or later within the government, but they were granted a certain degree of autonomy over their own organizations.[8] In 1931 the NS-*Frauenschaft* was declared to be the only women's organization officially affiliated to the party, achieving full party status in March 1933. After a protracted leadership crisis during 1933, in 1934 the organization began to be consolidated under the leadership of Gertrud Scholtz-Klink. It boasted 2 million members in 1936, although far from all members were actively engaged.[9] As an elite party organization headed by the *Reichsfrauenführung* (RFF), its primary task was the education of women as ideologically primed leaders for the *Deutsches Frauenwerk* (German Women's Bureau, DFW), the umbrella organization that was set up in September 1933 to absorb the various women's organizations in the process of *Gleichschaltung*. Left-wing and Jewish women's organizations were disbanded and many socialists and feminists either went into exile, or retreated from the public world of politics. The religious women's organizations, both Protestant and Catholic, broadly welcomed the new regime, although their willingness to integrate into the Nazi organizations varied.[10] The *Bund Deutscher Frauenvereine* (Federation of German Women's Associations, BDF) refused to undergo *Gleichschaltung* and dissolved, although some of its affiliated organizations continued to co-operate closely with the NSDAP, regarding the Nazi vision of separate but complementary spheres for men and women as a continuation of the ideas that had driven most of the civic, occupational and religious women's organizations during the Weimar Republic.[11] In July 1934, a woman's office was created within the *Deutsche Arbeitsfront* (German Labour Front, DAF), again under the nominal leadership of Scholtz-Klink, which, by recognizing women in the workforce, was an indication of the contradictory stances towards women within party doctrine. Its role was to reconcile the industrial working class to the new regime through propaganda and social welfare. The *Reichsmütterdienst* (National Mothers' Service, RMD) was set up on Mother's Day in 1934 by the RFF to train women in infant- and childcare and promote their "racial awareness". The other main section of the DFW was the home and national economics department based on the old *Reichsverband Deutscher Hausfrauen-vereine* (National Union of German Housewives' Associations), with the dual concerns of developing practical competence in housewifery and ensuring ideological commitment. Women were also targets for the propaganda of the *NS-Volkswohlfahrt* (welfare organization, NSV) and the *Reichsnährstand* (National Food Estate).[12] All of these organizations at some level turned to the radio to publicize their ideas. The resulting propaganda was therefore fundamentally political, while ostensibly maintaining an allegiance to the notion of separate spheres of competence for the sexes. As Claudia Koonz put it: "Whereas most conservative women viewed the family as an emotional 'space' and bulwark *against* the invasion of public life, Nazi women saw it as an invasion route that could give them access to every German's most personal values and decisions."[13]

The domestication of broadcast propaganda

By the time radio fell into the hands of the Nazis it was already established as a public medium, controlled by the state and designed to serve the national interest. It was also already firmly established as a medium situated in the private space of the home. Some moves were made to encourage collective listening in public places, in particular the workplace, but for the majority of people, for the majority of the time, listening remained a domestic affair. In October 1933, the then head of radio in the *Reichsministerium für Volksaufklärung und Propaganda* (Ministry for Popular Enlightenment and Propaganda, RMVP), Horst Dreßler-Andreß, announcing the availability of the new affordable *Volksempfänger*, declared his intention that no household in the country should be without a radio, taking part in the "communal reception" of the nation.[14] By 1939, some 3½ million sets had been sold, making Germany the country with the greatest penetration of radio sets in Europe. Efforts were also made to encourage effective listening practices, for example encouraging women to do their household chores to light entertainment programmes, leaving time to down dusters and devote all their attention to important political broadcasts, especially as radio provision neared saturation point.[15] The radio, then, was conceived as providing a link between the domestic and the national, between home and homeland, *Heim* and *Heimat*. Radio with its daily schedules provided a rhythm for the daily domestic routine, reflecting and reinforcing the preferred image of family life. It also broadcast the round of traditional and newly engineered national public events that punctuated the Nazi calendar. Radio seemed to be the ideal medium to forge a reinvented and re-imagined national community.

With an ideological schema that located the political squarely in the public sphere, the broadcasting of political programmes clearly threatened the sanctity of the private sphere and the secure demarcation of the public/private divide.[16] During much of the Weimar Republic, attempts had been made to overcome this contradiction (and to avoid controversy in a fractious political climate) by pursuing a policy of keeping party politics strictly off the air.[17] This was obviously not an option for the Nazi regime that, having long been banned from the airwaves, intended to exploit the propaganda potential of broadcasting to the full. Radio was celebrated as a modern, revolutionary medium well suited to serve in the ideological vanguard of the battle against the old system.[18]

Immediately, the airwaves were saturated with political speeches, reports from public rallies, military music. As a consequence, listening figures that had been rising consistently since public radio went on the air in 1923, began to fall.[19] The rhetoric and the bombast of public politics did not translate well into the domestic environment, and in order to win the audience back, the propagandists realized they had to take account of the conditions of reception in the private sphere.[20] Although important speeches and public events were still featured, there was a new premium on entertainment – particularly music – and, significantly, a transformation in talk-based programmes from public to private modes of address. In this respect, Gerhard Eckert of the official German news agency singled out the annual addresses at New Year and on Hitler's birthday as exemplary models for broadcasts that did not lecture the listener as if they were at a public rally, but spoke to them in an intimate, personal tone of voice.[21]Far from being an entirely masculine affair, radio in the Third Reich came to be infused with what a contemporary commentator called the "maternal spirit", located as it was in the home, appealing directly to the senses and drawing on feminine, privatized patterns of everyday speech.[22] The Nazis subscribed to a point of view that defined the masses as feminine, that is to say, emotional and suggestible.[23] Human interest stories, dialogues, drama, chat shows and conversations were thought most likely to "speak" to women and therefore also to the broader population. Many of these techniques had been pioneered by women's radio during the Weimar Republic, and now came to inform the practices of a great deal of the Nazis' broadcast propaganda, as I have argued more fully elsewhere.[24] To give just one example, in a move that owed something to the innovation of the soap opera on American commercial radio, the *Reichssender* Köln broadcast a regular series in 1938–9 called *Rund um den Familientisch* (Round the family table) which in a "humorous chatty manner" dramatized a whole range of propaganda issues from child-rearing to the proper celebration of national high days and holidays from the point of view of a familiar set of characters with which the listener was invited to identify and build a relationship.[25]

Since it was in the realm of presentational style that the "maternal spirit" was called upon to refresh radio output, women's voices were no rarity on the airwaves during the Third Reich, particularly when it came to announcing and presenting cultural, musical and entertainment programmes, especially during the war years.[26] However, they were not surprisingly deemed inappropriate for reading political reports and the news.

There were no such qualms about politics entering the private, female sphere. In fact, it was hoped that by bringing the voices of political leaders into the home, the radio made them into personalities who would then appeal to women on a personal, intimate level. One of the favourite slogans that was used to advertise the new National Socialist radio was *des Führers Wort in jeden Betrieb, in jedes Haus!* (The Führer's voice into every factory and home!), and indeed Hitler did make over fifty speeches in 1933 alone.[27] However, unlike Roosevelt, who made effective use of the radio with his "fireside chats", Hitler was a very poor studio performer, once stripped of the acclamation and ritual chanting of the crowd, and so efforts were made to improve the technical quality of recordings at public events.[28] These were then broadcast nationwide under the rubric of *Stunde der Nation* (Hour of the nation), when housewives in the home were expected to "down tools" with workers in factories and public institutions to participate in the synchronized ritual of the leadership cult and national community. There were other more effective broadcasters, of course, and that they did appeal as personalities to at least some women is suggested anecdotally by the kinds of letters sent to Hans Fritzsche, head of political programmes from 1942, whose regular programmes, *Es spricht Hans Fritzsche!*, made him one of the best known and consistently popular voices on German radio during the war. Many of these letters follow up their words of praise for the programme with a request for a photograph, one woman even writing to tell him that she always kept a vase of fresh flowers by the photograph she'd received (bluebells at the time of writing).[29]

It was not only politicians' and propagandists' voices that were heard on Nazi radio, but also "ordinary people's", albeit only those sympathetic to the regime. Under mottoes like *Heraus aus der Enge der Funkhäuser!* (Out of the confines of the radio stations!) and *Mit dem Mikrophon hinein ins Volk!* (With the microphone in among the people!), technological advances in outside broadcasting were exploited to bolster a propagandistic vision of a nation united in its diversity behind a common goal and sharing a common destiny. Very similar techniques were being developed in other countries like Great Britain to more democratic ends.[30] Again to take an example from the Cologne region in the winter of 1938–9, programmes came under titles like *Momentaufnahme* (Snapshot), *Griff ins Leben* (Reaching into life), *Stadt und Land Hand in Hand* (Town and country hand in hand), *Und was meinen Sie?* (And what do you think?) and the innocuous-sounding *Wir treiben Familienforschung* (We're researching our family) which was the rubric under which the regime's racial politics were propagated.[31] In programmes like these, patterns of everyday, mundane speech were translated into public talk, and represented another aspect of the domestication of political propaganda.

Propaganda for women, by women

A nationwide broadcasting system that could transcend regional and social barriers was, then, an ideal tool for the propagation of the idea of the *Volksgemeinschaft* that hoped to replace traditional loyalties based on locality or class by a loyalty to a national community based on the criterion of race.[32] For the most part, therefore, the Nazified schedules immediately abandoned the tradition of the Weimar period of speaking to a variety of constituencies in a mixed diet of programming across the day. Since German culture was theoretically indivisible, special interest programming gave way to a totalitarian construction of the audience. The one consistent exception was the continuation of separate programmes for women and children, a consequence of the ideological framework that understood women to be united in terms of their maternal spirit, regardless of age, financial or familial status, while men were differentiated by a variety of professional and other social functions. Women took responsibility for the production and presentation of those programmes, although even the female directors of the *Frauenfunk* departments did not hold senior positions within the stations' hierarchies.

The Nazi party had been refused access to the air until the reactionary radio reforms of June 1932 that had set the stage for the *Gleichschaltung* of the broadcasting system that followed the Nazi take-over.[33] Nevertheless, committed party members, men and women, had been preparing for the advent of Nazified radio by practising microphone techniques, drafting scripts and contriving mock transmissions.[34] There was some continuity of personnel across the divide of 1933, but all Jewish employees were hounded out of their jobs, and gradually other dismissals followed, with all contributors to the radio industry having to become card-carrying members of the newly established *Reichsrundfunkkammer*, a department of the national chamber of culture within the Ministry for Popular Enlightenment and Propaganda. Gradually, the responsibility for women's programming fell to the women's organizations, in particular the *Deutsches Frauenwerk*, which appointed a representative in the national broadcasting office, the *Reichssendeleitung* (National broadcasting headquarters, RSL) to oversee and direct the coverage of women's issues on the radio. The national and regional departments of the NS-*Frauenschaft* were also involved in collaboration with the regional stations in advising on and participating in the production of programmes for women. The *Bund deutscher Mädel* (League of German Girls) was also increasingly involved with the production of programmes for younger listeners under the auspices of the *Reichsjugendführung*.[35] From 1937, the women's office of the German Labour Front also had a radio representative who prepared regular reports on its work and achievements for the daily evening news service on the regional transmitters.[36] Thus the production of women's radio mirrored in microcosm other areas of public life in the "Hitler state", in being characterized by a complex of competing and overlapping institutions, each with its own internal hierarchy, which could lead to confusion and resentment, and threatened to undermine the coherence of the central ideological message.[37] It fell to the press and propaganda department of the RFF, under the leadership of Erika Fillies-Kirmsse, and to Gertrud Kappesser at the RSL to attempt some sort of co-ordination among the regional editors. The range of programmes targeted at women on Nazi radio was narrower in scope than had generally been the case during the Weimar Republic, not least because the cultural and literary items once explored from a female perspective were more often incorporated into the general schedules. The remaining output concentrated primarily on two broad areas, the first concerned "to nurture the idea of motherhood and the family", with advice on child-rearing, questions to do with the preservation of the national heritage, and the promotion of the health of the nation – an important plank of the regime's racial policies. The second, which was expanded to incorporate the demands of the war effort in later years, concentrated partly on promoting and explaining the "rational" deployment of female labour power according to feminine nature and the requirements of the *Volk*, but more particularly on influencing patterns of consumption. Trude Geißler, head of women's radio in Munich, for example, saw her task not so much in putting out a political programme as "anchoring programmes in the essential 'feminine politics' of a woman's responsibility towards her child and family".[38]

Broadcasting was only one of a whole variety of media available to the women's organizations, but time and again the propagandists applauded the fortuitous advantage of beaming their ideas straight into women's homes, to be imbibed without interfering in the domestic routine, even by those women who would be unlikely to attend regional meetings and exhibitions, or read the pamphlets and magazines, or participate in the courses laid on by the *Reichsmütterdienst* and so on.[39] It was also one of the most cost-effective, flexible and reliable means of disseminating information quickly and directly to a regional or a nationwide audience.

Propaganda and the domestic economy

Propaganda to consumers came in two main forms on the radio. One was in the shape of cookery programmes and market reports that attempted to influence the shopping habits of the nation's women. These were produced by the regional stations and were (at least, intended to be) sensitive to local variations in available produce. In fact, after the further round of centralization in the organization and production of broadcasting in 1940, almost the only programme material originating from the regional stations was information for farmers and the consumer advice for housewives.[40] The other type of programme came in the form of exhortations and suggestions to rationalize household chores in order to save valuable resources of energy and materials. These were primarily produced within the context of a series of major publicity campaigns, often of several years' duration, with titles like *Kampf dem Verderb* (Fight against wastage) and *Sachgemäßes Waschen: Wasche Wäsche Weise* (Proper washing: wash washing wisely). These *Verbrauchslenkung* and *Verbraucherziehung* campaigns (direction of consumption and education in consumption), which had their precedents in campaigns during the Weimar Republic, barraged housewives with information via every available means of communication about how, as customers and consumers, it lay in their power to have a direct and profound influence on the national economy and help meet the requirements laid down first of all by the Four Year Plans, and later by the war economy.[41] The Four Year Plans were concerned to make Germany as self-reliant on its own agricultural and manufacturing resources as possible – largely by means of strict wage and price controls, reducing imports and making synthetic materials out of domestic raw materials – and therefore independent of strategic imports in the event of war. In announcing the second Four Year Plan in 1936, Göring declared women to be the "trustees of the nation's wealth".[42] To this end, the government manipulated the media to encourage women to help realize its ambitions for economic autarky. From this point on, the consumer campaigns were co-ordinated by a privately owned organization affiliated to the RMVP, the *Reichsausschuß für Volkswirtschaftliche Aufklärung* (National Committee for Popular Economic Enlightenment, RVA), whose business it was to work in close co-operation with the women's organizations both to "sell" National Socialist economic policy to the people, and to persuade the people to co-operate with the implementation of individual policy strategies.[43]

These campaigns were readily upgraded to mobilize women's housecraft and consumption habits to serve the war economy.[44] In order to give some sort of flavour of these programmes, and to chart the transitional period during the latter part of 1939, we can take a closer look at the output of a representative station, such as the Reichssender Hamburg. Various programme styles were used, the most popular being the short play and conversational dialogue, but the majority of the RVA's material was incorporated into the station's *Frauenfunk* series called *Haushalt und Familie*. There were five instalments of this series broadcast in June 1939, including tips on making the most of an allotment, preparing pickles and preserves and darning stockings, but there was also a special programme on women's role during airraids and a play that dealt with themes from the *Kampf dem Verderb* campaign. A sequel to this play was broadcast on the 14th of the following month, alongside another two *Kampf dem Verderb* programmes, *Vorratswirtschaft im Juli* (Stocking up in July) and *Schädlinge im Haushalt* (Pests in the home). The remaining programmes broadcast in July were concerned largely with urging women to accept plainer goods (such as black bread or fresh herrings) or going without certain goods altogether, as in *Das Morgenfrühstück schmeckt auch ohne Kaffee* (Breakfast tastes just as good without coffee). August brought only an RVA-sponsored series based on the *Reichsnährstand*'s brochure about nutritional policy and schools. While other stations like Leipzig, apart from a brief lull during the latter part of August and early September, managed to keep a full schedule of *Verbrauchslenkung* programmes going out during the autumn months, albeit largely made up of recipes and kitchen tips, Hamburg's output dried up during these months of uncertainty, and even when it got going again in November, very few of the programmes dealt specifically with wartime conditions. Exceptions to the rule of recipes and refreshers were a play about the blackout, and a discussion on the morality of eating cake at a time of national need. December brought only an address on the subject of women and the national economy as a whole.[45]

A few of the programme scripts have survived, particularly those associated with the wartime *Sachgemäßes Waschen* campaign, and are held in the files of the RVA at the Bundesarchiv in Potsdam. Most of them take the form of short conversational scenes, with titles like *Wir werfen nichts weg!* (We don't throw anything away!), *Falsche Sparsamkeit* (False economies) and *Die gute Kundin* (The good customer). The following extract is taken from a three-minute programme broadcast from the Danzig station on 25 June 1940, and is an interesting example of how the most banal propaganda was exploited to reconfirm the gender ideology of separate spheres of competence. It features a mildly cantankerous exchange between a wife and her husband, and is entitled *Wenn Männer Hausfrauenverstand haben* . . . (When men have a housewife's common sense . . .).[46]

> She: But Männe, that's really unbelievable – look, I'm always telling you . . .
>
> He: My God, Clara, now what's the matter this time? Don't get so excited, you'll raise your blood pressure! You're practically speechless with indignation . . .
>
> She: Yes I'm speechless, because it's simply incredible that you don't see reason. And there you are imagining yourself to be in possession of a housewife's common sense, and think you know better than me when it comes to my personal household affairs.
>
> He: Don't you say anything against my housewifely common sense! Who stopped you with your endless cleaning and polishing from soaping down the doors and window frames . . .
>
> She: . . . and told me to use a special commercial product instead, oh my dear, you are so clever – when you get your information from the newspaper . . .

The conversation continues in this tone as he tries to persuade her that he knows about looking after materials in the home, and she persuades him that he still has a lot to learn, as in this final exchange:

> He: No, Clara, if I'm honest, I wouldn't have thought of that myself.
>
> She: Yes it is asking a bit too much of a man. I won't trouble you with all the other tips for saving soap and caring for the laundry.

Otherwise I'll just provoke your husbandly wrath (*eheherrlicher Zorn*).

A staggering range of resources and organizations were employed in the service of this propaganda at a cost of millions of marks. Much more than the fictional images portrayed at the movies that worked at a subtle suggestive level, these campaigns were overtly designed to influence and change actual behaviour, and to leave women in no doubt as to their function and status in Nazi society. The wartime campaigns were considered more effective than those that ran in concert with the Four Year Plan in the mid-1930s, because of the greater incentives for thrift and patriotic consumption, although efforts to mobilize women in other forms of war work were rather half-hearted and ineffectual.[47] Private and public spheres merged in the propaganda for the home front as each measure to save resources was directly translated into resources freed for the war effort.

The priority given to these campaigns can be gauged by some of the battles waged over female labour during the war. The Armaments Commission of the Four Year Plan, for example, wanted to know if any of the large number of women engaged in the propaganda work for the RVA could be spared for the armaments industry. In its reply, the RVA reiterated its view that enlightening the nation's women in matters of economy was just as essential to the war effort as producing arms, and that the personnel carrying out this important work had already been pared down to the minimum.[48] The RVA view won through over the Commission, although the campaign budget for 1943, while still substantial, was considerably down, 25 per cent on the 10 million marks spent the previous year.[49] It is difficult to assess the impact of these programmes, and it is not my purpose here to engage in that discussion. Suffice it to say that it has been argued that for so much investment of time and money, the return was hardly impressive.[50] Nevertheless, there can have been few women who were not aware of this propaganda or what was expected of them, regardless of whether they followed or resisted the role models provided for them.

These consumer-orientated programmes reassured women of their personal economic agency in words that obscured the limitations of their function as economic actors. But more than just alerting women to their potential power, the propaganda insisted it was their patriotic duty to ensure they acted in the best interests of the *Volk*, the welfare of which, as always, was to come before that of the individual or even of the family. Moreover, as Dr Emmy Wagner argued in the *Völkischer Beobachter* in 1936, the housewife needed to learn to see the household economy in a "racial-political light", in order to play her part in "making the economy serve racial objectives".[51] Clearly there was a link between anti-Semitic propaganda and the propaganda attempts to direct or influence patterns of consumption. Patriotic consumption meant not only supporting the German farmer by buying home-grown produce wherever possible, but also refusing to frequent Jewish shops and businesses. It was not a link that was made very explicit in the *Verbrauchslenkung* programmes on women's radio, but it is a theme that is always there at a subtextual level when the exhortations to participate in the regeneration of the national community were clearly understood to exclude the Jewish population. The absence of explicit anti-Semitic propaganda from the programmes on women's radio does not mean that the question of racism was removed from the concerns of the *Frauenfunk*; but rather that much of the rhetoric was constructed in terms of this exclusion.

In a recent essay on consumption as "the vanguard of history", Daniel Miller invokes the housewife as the archetypal image of consumer decision-making and consequently identifies her as the unrecognized fulcrum of modernity, going so far as to characterize the housewife as the aggregate "global dictator".[52] In so doing, he claims to highlight the contradictions of the modern First World consumer. Far from conforming to the consumer of economic theory who independently makes choices based on rational self-interest, or the stereotype of the superficial status-seeking shopaholic, the "flesh and blood housewife emerges as one of the least individualistic of the social beings of the First World". Her own interests are subsumed under the interests generated by "the moral economy of the home", in which one of the housewife's key skills is thrift. At the same time, the exercise of power through consumption is not experienced as empowering. Miller puts this down to a historical contingency by which production-centred political movements superseded those based on consumption. His essay points to ways in which a shift in emphasis would be fruitful for consumption studies, but the similarities to the rhetoric discussed in this chapter are unsettling.[53]

Within the context of the Third Reich, the problems involved in reading political power off the practices of consumption are evident.

Nazi propaganda had nothing to fear in alerting the nation's wo.
to the "power" they wielded with their shopping bags and their housewifely competence. It fitted in with the ideology of separate spheres
divided by function but not by status, by telling women that there was
a space for them to make decisions that could affect the life of the
nation, where they were needed and would be respected. That space,
of course, was the home. Excluded from positions of any real power,
they were fed the myth of an alternative power, one based on the permanent sacrifice of public and political agency. The law of nature was
invoked to justify the regime's insistence that women's economic
power, however great, was ultimately defined in terms of maternal
duty and that the willingness to perform that duty defined a woman's
political position. Thus a woman's reluctance to engage wholeheartedly in the state-run campaigns could be read, by the initiators
of those campaigns, as an expression of dissent. Deprived of a vote or
a voice in the political life of the nation, women were told their political opinions were expressed by their behaviour as housewives and
mothers. They were expected to believe their motherly devotion was
an expression of devotion to the state, which left very little room for
resistance. Such an indicator of political opinion was always bound to
be favourable to the government, and drew the boundaries of political
expression open to women still tighter in.

The contradictions of women's programming

If the private condition of the reception of radio broadcasts gave rise
to the feminization of at least some of the propaganda output, then it
also contributed to an ongoing politicization of the private sphere,
and underscored the contradictions already inherent in Nazi policies
and rhetoric about the family.[54] The radio spearheaded the state's
intrusion into the home even while exalting the family as the basic
building block of the nation. It represented an authoritative voice in
the home that undermined the sole authority of the head of the household, even while preaching the integrity of the family. There was necessarily a structural tension between the atomized experience of radio
listening as individuals or family groups and the message of national
unity emanating from the loudspeakers. Women were exhorted to
draw their families together around the wireless set, even while the

203

family members were being encouraged to participate in political activities outside the home. Meanwhile, women's political support was measured by the extent to which they subordinated their individual and familial interests to the interests of the national community. In short, the most modern apparatus of communication was seized on by the Nazis to advocate a nostalgic and reactionary return to a vision of womanhood expressed in terms of nature, spirit, instinct and biology.

Underpinning this discussion is the recognition that a female *public* was addressed by a medium that was organized according to, and that was designed to serve, ideological principles that sought to exclude women from the public sphere and confine them to the *private*. Friendly chats and lightweight dramas about home-making, shopping and childcare might seem fairly harmless in contrast to the most virulent fascist propaganda; but their value to the regime should be measured not simply in terms of their content but also in terms of their structural function within the whole. The concentration within women's radio on traditional domestic and familial concerns promoted the impression of tradition, continuity, stability and normality that helped disguise the radical changes that were taking place. The contradictory phenomenon of female contributors to women's radio insisting on women's retreat into a separate *Lebensraum* remote from public politics and power while themselves maintaining a disarming semblance of participation in the public sphere, was indispensable in enabling the easy acceptance of the Nazi regime, and by extension, the success of racist and expansionist policies in pursuit of that wider *Lebensraum*.[55] Fatefully, the space that women had carved out within the broadcast public sphere became exclusively devoted to reinforcing women's exclusion from the public sphere more generally.

Nazi propaganda has in many ways come to stand as the benchmark for what we understand by propaganda as a genre – that blatant, dishonest manipulation of public opinion associated with the passionate demagoguery and mass spectacle of the Nuremberg rallies. Nazi propaganda was not, however, so monolithic, nor were the propagandists so insensitive to the tastes and opinions of their "captive public". Certainly, a gendered analysis of the "domestic propaganda" of Nazi radio and the transitional space between the public and the private spheres that it occupied allows a more differentiated understanding of the everyday techniques of propaganda and draws attention to the shades of grey where those techniques manifest similarities with less pernicious attempts at persuasion in contemporary promotional media cultures.[56]

Notes

1. *Deutscher Kulturdienst* 83, 8 Apr. 1943. Bundesarchiv Koblenz (BAK) R34, 284.
2. G. Scholtz-Klink, *Die Frau im dritten Reich* (Tübingen: Grabert, 1978); L. J. Rupp, *Mobilising women for war: German and American propaganda 1939–1945* (Princeton, NJ: Princeton University Press, 1978); J. Stephenson, "Propaganda, autarky and the German housewife", in *Nazi propaganda: the power and the limitations*, D. Welch (ed.) (London: Croom Helm, 1983), pp. 117–42.
3. This chapter is concerned only with characterizing the organization, output and propagandistic intent of the domestic broadcast propaganda of the period. It does not, therefore, attempt to measure the effect of these programmes retrospectively, either on individual listeners or on the audience as a whole. Clearly, there was a discrepancy between the propaganda images and reality, both social and even political, but working from the hypothesis that the media reflect and influence change in society and ideology, an examination of the prevailing discourses can give a useful indication of the boundaries within which meanings and experiences were negotiated. These issues are dealt with in more detail in my forthcoming book, *Feminine frequencies: gender, German radio and the public sphere, 1923–45* (Ann Arbor: University of Michigan Press, 1996). A research group at the University of Hanover, led by Adelheid von Saldern and Inge Marßolek, are currently working on a project about gender relations in German radio of the Third Reich and the GDR in the 1950s: *Zuhören und Gehörtwerden: Radiogeschichte und Geschlechterordnung im Dritten Reich und der DDR der fünfziger Jahre* (Ein Zwischenbericht, Historisches Seminar, Universität Hannover, 1995).
4. [n.a.], "Pflichten und Rechte der deutschen Frau im nationalsozialistischen Deutschland: Rede von Minister Dr. Goebbels auf der Amtswalterinnentagung des Gaues Groß-Berlin", *Amtliche Frauenkorrespondenz* 8, 15 Feb. 1934, p. 533.
5. G. Bock, "Racism and sexism in Nazi Germany: motherhood, compulsory sterilization, and the state", in *When biology became destiny: women in Weimar and Nazi Germany*, R. Bridenthal, A. Grossmann, M. Kaplan (eds), (New York: Monthly Review Press, 1984), pp. 271–96; A. Kuhn, "Der Antifeminismus als verborgene Theoriebasis des deutschen Faschismus", in *Frauen und Faschismus in Europa: Der faschistische Körper*, L. Siegele-Wenschkewitz & G. Stuchlik (eds) (Pfaffenweiler: Centaurus, 1990), pp. 39–50.

6. [n.a.], "Weshalb sind wir Nationalsozialisten? Frauen sprechen über ihren Weg zur deutschen Volksgemeinschaft", *Der Angriff* 89, 15 Apr. 1933.

7. Speech to members of the Austrian women's organizations reported by Edith Hessig of the Reichsfrauenführung in *Frauenstunde: Zeitungsdienst des Reichsnährstandes* 19, 19 May 1938, p. 76. Despite her grand title, Scholtz-Klink had a very low profile within the party hierarchy, and had very little say in policy decisions affecting women: see C. Koonz, *Mothers in the fatherland: women, the family and Nazi politics* (London: Jonathan Cape, 1987), pp. 181–2.

8. D. Klinksiek, *Die Frau im NS Staat* (Stuttgart: Deutsche Verlags-Anstalt, 1982), p. 20.

9. M. Lück, *Die Frau im Männerstaat. Die gesellschaftliche Stellung der Frau im Nationalsozialismus: Eine Analyse aus pädagogischer Sicht* (Frankfurt am Main: Peter Lang, 1979), p. 102; J. Stephenson, *The Nazi organisation of women* (London: Croom Helm, 1981), pp. 148–50.

10. Koonz, *Mothers in the fatherland*, chs 7 and 8.

11. Indeed, much of Nazi propaganda was concerned with the reinforcement and sharpening of existing beliefs, not least in the propaganda aimed at women.

12. Other Nazi organizations for women formed in 1933, the *Deutsche Frauen-Front* led by Lydia Gottschewski and the National Federation led by Paula Siber, were subsequently incorporated into the newly created DFW. As its base broadened and its political limitations became more clearly defined, the firebrands of the *Kampfzeit* found themselves expelled or marginalized from their own organizations as more "respectable" women like Gertrud Scholtz-Klink took over the helm.

13. C. Koonz, *Mothers in the fatherland*, p. 14.

14. Text of a speech broadcast on 23 October 1933, reproduced in G. Aberle, "Rundfunk und Rundfunkhören im Dritten Reich", unpublished programme script (Bayerischer Rundfunk, Munich, broadcast 3 May 1982), p. 8.

15. See E. Rodt, "Rundfunk-Hörkultur", *Amtliche Frauenkorrespondenz* 13, 1933, pp. 924–5.

16. Newspapers, too, entered the home, of course, bridging the divide between public and private, but there was not the same concern as with radio because of the greater control and selectivity over what was read on the part of the household and the individual. Nevertheless, the *Reichsfrauenführung* did publish guidelines and hold seminars for women on *how* to read a daily paper so that they could furnish themselves as efficiently as possible with all the information relevant to leading a properly politicized everyday life. See E. Anderson, "Wie liest man eine Tageszeitung?", *Nachrichtendienst der Reichsfrauenführung* (July 1939), pp. 304–5.

17. For more details of the policy of non-political radio during the Weimar Republic, see H. Bausch, *Der Rundfunk im politischen Kräftespiel der Weimarer Republik 1923–1933* (Tübingen: J. C. B. Mohr, 1956); W. B.

Lerg, *Rundfunk in der Weimarer Republik*, vol. 1 of *Rundfunk in Deutschland*, H. Bausch (ed.) (Munich: dtv, 1980). In the latter years of the republic, the guidelines concerning the exclusion of political programmes were interpreted rather more loosely, and the debate about the politicization of radio was couched in terms of a *Kampf um die Parität*, a struggle for parity of representation and access (although the Communist Party (KPD) and NSDAP remained excluded). The gradual politicization of the airwaves meant that radio did play a role in the elections of 1930, for example, and government ministers increasingly came to use the radio to speak directly to the people.

18. E. Hadamovsky, *Der Rundfunk im Dienste der Volksführung* (Leipzig: [n.publ.], 1934), pp. 11–13; J. Wulf, *Presse und Funk im Dritten Reich: Eine Dokumentation* (Frankfurt am Main: Ullstein, 1983), pp. 330–46.

19. W. Hagemann, *Handbuch des deutschen Rundfunks* (Heidelberg & Berlin: [n. publ.] 1938) p. 46.

Official listening figures in Germany 1924–1943:

1 Jan. 24   1,580
1 Jan. 25   548,749
1 Jan. 26   1,022,299
1 Jan. 27   1,376,564
1 Jan. 28   2,009,842
1 Jan. 29   2,635,567
1 Jan. 30   3,066,682
1 Jan. 31   3,509,509
1 Jan. 32   3,981,000
1 Jan. 33   4,307,722
1 Jan. 34   5,052,607
1 Jan. 35   4,142,921
1 Jan. 36   7,192,000
1 Jan. 37   8,167,957
1 Jan. 38   9,087,454
1 Jan. 41   14,882,496
1 Jan. 43   16,000,000

Figures compiled from information in E. Fischer, *Dokumente zur Geschichte des deutschen Rundfunks und Fernsehens* (Göttingen: Muster-Schmidt, 1957), pp. 14–37 and the statistics published by the Reichs-kulturkammer (RKK), BAK R56I, 115, p. 165. Note that the 1941–3 figures are for the whole of the extended territory of the German Reich.

20. R. Kolb & H. Stiekmeier (eds), *Rundfunk und Film im Dienste Nationaler Kultur* (Düsseldorf: Friedrich Floeder, 1933), p. 11.

21. G. Eckert, *Der Rundfunk als Führungsmittel* (Heidelberg: Vowinckel, 1941), pp. 243–7.

22. L. Peck, "Die Frau und der Rundfunk!", *Rufer und Hörer* 3, 1933/4, pp. 243–5.

23. In *Mein Kampf*, Hitler had written that: "an immense majority of the people are so feminine in nature and point of view, that their thoughts and

actions are governed more by feeling and sentiment than by reasoned consideration". And furthermore, "the receptive ability of the masses is very limited, their understanding small; on the other hand, they have a great power of forgetting. This being so, all effective propaganda must be confined to very few points . . ." See A. Hitler, *My struggle* (London: Hurst & Blackett, 1938), pp. 81–2.

24. K. Lacey, "From *Plauderei* to propaganda: on women's radio in Germany 1924–35", *Media, Culture and Society* 16, 1994, pp. 589–607. There had been programmes targeted at women from as early as 1924, inspired by the *feuilleton* pages for women in some of the metropolitan newspapers. There was a great variety of programming styles across the regions, from recipes and household advice by representatives of the housewives' unions, to information about leading women in cultural and political life by women from the bourgeois feminist movement who were concerned to take advantage of speaking directly to newly enfranchised women and to broaden their horizons. Other programmes spoke to women as consumers, either by advertising household goods and gadgets, or by appealing to women to buy German. They tended to be broadcast during the day, to represent a distinctly middle-class perspective, and to avoid the really controversial women's issues, such as the debate about Paragraph 218. The one thing they all had in common was the conviction that broadcasting could change and improve women's experience in the transitional space between public and private life.

25. Reichssender Köln – Winterplan 1938/9. BAK, NS15, 139. See also, L. Peck, "Der Zyklus im Frauenfunk?", *Rufer und Hörer* 4, 1934/5, pp. 231–7.

26. See G. Eckert, "Männerstimmen – Frauenstimmen", *Deutscher Kulturdienst* 123(1941) [n.p.]. BAK, R34, 237; "Noch mehr die Ansage durch Frauen forcieren!" minutes of a meeting chaired by Hans Hinkel, head of the RKK, 21 Jan. 1943: Bundesarchiv Potsdam (BAP) 50.01, 624: 7.

27. Eckert, *Der Rundfunk als Führungsmittel*, p. 242.

28. Z. A. B. Zeman, *Nazi propaganda*, 2nd edn (London & New York: Oxford University Press, 1973), pp. 48–9.

29. BAK, R55, 532. RMVP. Hörerzuschriften (letter quoted from Elisabeth Habo, Budapest, 13 May 1944, p. 57).

30. D. Cardiff, "The serious and the popular: aspects of the evolution of style in the radio talk 1928–1939", in *Media, culture and society: a critical reader*, R. Collins (ed.) (London: Sage, 1986), pp. 228–46; P. Scannell, "Public service broadcasting and modern public life", *Media, Culture and Society* 11, 1989, pp. 135–66.

31. Reichssender Köln – Winterplan 1938/9. BAK, NS15, 139.

32. There was, of course, a discrepancy between the propagandists' claims about the achievement of such a community, and its reality. For an assessment of the current state of research on this matter, see D. Welch, *The Third Reich: politics and propaganda* (London: Routledge, 1993), pp. 50–65.

Welch argues that while the *Volksgemeinschaft* did not overcome existing social divisions, it was widely accepted as a concept that helped lend at least passive support to the regime.

33. In these reforms, drafted by Erich Scholz at the Ministry of the Interior, private capital was withdrawn from all radio concerns, giving the national and regional governments total financial control. The *Reichsrundfunkgesellschaft* became the central radio authority and was given new powers to pursue the interests of the state in broadcasting according to a new set of guidelines drawn up by the Ministry of the Interior. Supervision of programming was carried out by state officials.

34. G. von Bremen-Hirschkendt, "Frauenschulung für den Rundfunk", *Die Deutsche Frauenfront* 1, 1933, p. 119.

35. H. Freytag, "Unsere Rundfunkarbeit", in *Mädel im Dritten Reich*, H. Munske (ed.) (Berlin: Freiheitsverlag, 1935), pp. 39–42.

36. [n.a.], "Frauenamt der DAF: Rundfunk-Meldungen des Frauenamtes", *Nachrichtendienst der Reichsfrauenführung* (February 1937), p. 61.

37. M. Broszat, *The Hitler state: the foundation and development of the internal structure of the Third Reich* (London: Longman, 1981).

38. F. Hallenberger, "Hier arbeitet Reichssender München!", *Völkischer Beobachter*, 8 Sept. 1934 (a special report marking ten years of broadcasting in Bavaria).

39. E.g. "Wozu bringt der Rundfunk besondere Frauensendungen?", *Pressedienst des Deutschen Frauen-Werkes* **30**, 19 Dec. 1935.

40. [n.a.], "Zusammenarbeit mit dem Reichssender", *Nachrichtendienst der Reichsfrauenführung* (March 1941), p. 137. In the 12 months up to March 1941, the Reichssender Stuttgart, for example, in addition to its regular scripted women's hours, broadcast more than 40 reports with contributions from both local and national women's leaders, from each of the various departments within the women's organizations, including the *Reichsmütterdienst* and the *Volkswirtschaft-Hauswirtschaft* departments and from the *Rassenpolitisches Amt* of the NSDAP.

41. Hjalmar Schacht, the minister responsible for economic affairs from July 1934, who announced the first Four Year Plan, was charged with the economic preparation for war, to which everything else was to be subordinated, although the economy was not put on a full war footing until well into the war. See R. Overy, "Hitler's war and the German economy: a reinterpretation", in *War, peace and social change in twentieth century Europe*, C. Emsley, A. Marwick, W. Simpson (eds) (Milton Keynes: Open University Press, 1989), pp. 208–25.

42. Klinksiek, *Die Frau im NS Staat*, p. 110.

43. "Das Aufgabengebiet des RVA", BAP 50.02, 18, pp. 30–41.

44. It is interesting to note that this training in the jargon of consumer power, not to mention the techniques of thrift and good home management, were taken up again in the reconstruction and consumer-orientated society of the post-war period. See Katherine Pence's contribution to this volume .

45. BAP 50.02, 12, pp. 206–13.
46. BAP 50.02, 26, p. 117.
47. T. Mason, "Women in Germany, 1925–1940: family, welfare and work", *History Workshop* 2, 1976, pp. 5–32; U. von Gersdorff, *Frauen im Kriegs-dienst* (Stuttgart: Deutsche Verlags-Anstalt, 1969); L. J. Rupp, *Mobilising women for war: German and American propaganda 1939–1945* (Princeton, NJ: Princeton University Press, 1978).
48. Letter dated 8 June 1943, BAP 50.02, 40, p. 304.
49. Figures for the advertising campaign 1942/3, BAP 50.02, 17, p. 43.
50. Stephenson, "Propaganda, autarky and the German housewife", pp. 117–42, esp. p. 119.
51. E. Wagner, "Auf die Hausfrau kommt es an: Die wirtschaftspolitische Bedeutung der Konsumgewohnheiten der Frauen", *Völkischer Beobachter*, 16 February 1936.
52. D. Miller, "Consumption as the vanguard of history", in *Acknowledging consumption: a review of new studies*, D. Miller (ed.) (London: Routledge, 1995), pp. 1–57.
53. Miller is careful, however, to reassure his readers that the image of the housewife is taken as an image to illustrate a polemic against conventional conceptualizations of economic actors in classic economic theory, rather than as a normative model.
54. J. P. Stern, *Hitler, the Führer and the people* (Berkeley: University of California Press, 1975), p. 172; Mason, "Women in Germany, 1925–1940", pp. 5–32, esp. p. 24; Lück, *Die Frau im Männerstaat*, p. 91; D. Welch, *Propaganda and the German cinema 1933–45* (Oxford: Clarendon Press, 1983), pp. 64–5; Koonz, *Mothers in the fatherland*, pp. 177–80.
55. An analysis of women's participation in the broadcast propaganda of this period therefore highlights the ambiguities identified in the debate between two different approaches to the role of women in the Nazi state, as represented by Gisela Bock and Claudia Koonz. In Bock's view, National Socialism was particularly pernicious for women precisely because of the sexist and racist invasion of the private, maternal sphere. Koonz, on the other hand, regards women's defence of and retreat into a separate sphere, a separate *Lebensraum*, as having been fundamental to the maintenance of the Nazi state, and has provided a wealth of evidence describing women's support for and active participation in that state. For commentaries on these positions, see K. Windäus-Walser, "Gnade der weiblichen Geburt? Zum Umgang der Frauenforschung mit Nationalsozialismus und Anti-semitismus", *Feministische Studien* 6(1), 1988, pp. 102–15; A. Grossmann, "Feminist debates about women and National Socialism", *Gender and History* 3, 1991, pp. 350–58.
56. T. J. Smith (ed.), *Propaganda: a pluralistic perspective* (London: Praeger, 1989); A. Wernick, *Promotional culture* (London: Sage, 1990); R. Jackall (ed.), *Propaganda* (London: Macmillan, 1995).

Chapter Ten

Labours of consumption: gendered consumers in post-war East and West German reconstruction

Katherine Pence

After the Second World War, the renegotiation of gender roles and identities became an integral aspect of German national reconstruction. The effort to leave National Socialism in the past and the progression towards the future Cold War division of Germany into two opposing socialist and capitalist states formed the economic and political context for the development of gender identities. Since the end of the war brought a breakdown of the economy, grim shortages and widespread hunger, a central issue of the post-war period was the regulation of consumption and the need to increase productivity to restore abundance. As the Soviet-guided East and the Allied-supported West followed their own paths to prosperity, Germans and occupiers negotiated definitions of female and male labour to fit these paths. This negotiation involved confrontation with traditional norms of the nuclear family encapsulating a division of labour between a male breadwinner and a female housewife. Owing to shortages the redefinition of gendered wage-earners and consumers became a crucial aspect of this confrontation. While the traditional division of labour constructed wage-earning as typically male, the labour of consumption, which involved shopping, budgeting and studying the marketplace, was left to women as part of their housework. This division of labour remained largely intact in the transition to the new German economies, but the meaning of the consumer role shifted in different phases of economic reconstruction.

This chapter will examine the shifts in the meaning of consumption as primarily female labour in its relationship to wage labour, which was largely cast as masculine, during three phases of post-war economic reconstruction: the period of extreme shortages from 1945 to 1948, the 1948 dual currency reforms and reappearance of un-rationed goods in East and West that marked a transition to the normalization of separate economies, and the prosperity that Germans increasingly felt in the early 1950s. An array of sources suggests ways that popular discourses and societal structures which shaped gender roles represented continuities with the past as well as commonalities between the two German states undergoing conflicting but parallel developments.

Rations and alternative economies in the four zones: conflicts over labour in a period of scarcity

When the Nazi regime was defeated and Allied bombs stopped falling, the German population was left to find food, clothing and shelter in badly destroyed cities. Since so many men had died in the war or were caught in prisoner-of-war camps, these often back-breaking tasks usually fell to the women who had stayed at the home front. Under severe circumstances in which transportation and markets had largely broken down, consumers seeking goods had to resort to such tactics as trading illegally on the black market, stealing or walking long distances carrying wood, food or coal. When goods were available in stores, long queues kept shoppers waiting for hours. Therefore, the task of consumption became an even more strenuous form of labour than the usual daily chore of shopping and often it was actually dangerous. This labour of consumption became a crucial part of reconstruction since it enabled the basic survival of the population in the most difficult periods of shortage.

As Germans and the Allied occupiers took the rubble that had been collected and began making long-term plans to rebuild, the heavy labour of construction, industry and especially coalmining began to take priority. Official systems of rationing were instituted that were meant to distribute food to the whole population but also reflected the goal of providing food to workers involved in the labour of production in order to eliminate the strenuous work of attaining food outside the regular market. The labour that would have gone towards scrounging, carrying food and so on, was to be channelled into getting the economy back on its feet.

However, owing to the continuing shortages and the inefficacy of the rationing systems in providing sufficiently for the whole population, these official systems for regulating consumption continued to coexist with frequently illegal forms of consumption outside the official market. In this period of extreme shortage, consumption took place between the strict regulation of official rationing systems, designed to promote higher productivity, and unofficial strategies for acquiring goods, which themselves required inordinate amounts of uncompensated labour. Inherent in the tension between these co-existing economies of labour and provision was the negotiation of gendered definitions of labour. While the strict rationing systems reinstated hierarchical, patriarchal structures based on a gender-specific division of labour, the black market and other strategies offered opportunities for alternative definitions of labour and gender roles. Separate rationing systems were established by the victorious French, British, American and Soviet Allies as part of their post-war administration of Germany, which they divided into four occupation zones. Alongside ideological and political goals for democratization, denazification and demilitarization, the concrete tasks of physically rebuilding the country and of providing for the hungry German population became pressing issues central to reconstruction. Management of food shortages was fundamental to the effort to rebuild infra-structure and industry, since undernourished workers exhibited low production levels. At the same time, regulating consumption was connected to the loftier task of legitimizing Allied projects of democratization, since the population would lose faith in an administration unable to ensure basic provisions. Thus, the difficult task of controlling consumption was crucial not only to keep the population from starving but in conjunction with broader goals of garnering support for each Allied reconstruction programme, especially as the rift grew between the Soviet administration and the Western powers and as competition stiffened for the population's loyalties.

By privileging certain types of labourers, which the occupiers viewed as crucial to these goals, the ration systems established hier-archical categorizations of consumers based on economic priorities. Inscribed in these hierarchical systems were gendered definitions of labour, which cast "heavy labour" as industrial work performed pri-marily by men for wages, and privileged this labour over the house-work performed mainly by women. In all zones women were recruited for and sometimes forced into typically male labour, especially in construction work, in order to fill gaps left in the workforce by the absence of men. However, even in the Soviet zone where the administration's long-term plans for socialist reforms included incorporating women into the workforce, prejudices and stereotypes continued to demarcate distinctions between male and female jobs.[1] In the West, female work in traditionally male jobs was largely viewed as a temporary necessity in a time of emergency rather than as a lasting structural change.[2] Despite an influx of women into many areas of the workforce, heavy industry remained a male-dominated sector and women stayed overwhelmingly in lower-paid jobs and as unpaid housewives. Although the rationing systems in each occupation zone were set up on different principles coincident with their plans for societal reconstruction, they shared hierarchical gender-based prioritization of certain types of labour.

The rationing system in the Soviet Occupation Zone (SBZ) most blatantly reproduced a hierarchy of labour with women's unpaid housework at the bottom. It particularly emphasized differential values of labour by categorizing ration recipients in six levels according to "consideration of economic or societal meaning of the work of the individual consumer".[3] The highest level consisted of heavy labourers, such as workers in mines or at smelting furnaces, and of leading members of the administration.[4] This and the next category of semi-heavy labourers represented jobs requiring either great strength or qualification, which have been traditionally considered "male" jobs. The third, fourth and fifth categories were for normal workers, white-collar workers and children. The sixth and final category (for "others" – *die Sonstigen*) included not only the unemployed, retirees, disabled persons and Nazi-party members, but also primarily "unemployed housewives".[5] This last category was popularly called the "hunger card" or the "graveyard card" since it barely provided enough food to survive. The categorization of unemployed housewives as "others" not only failed to recognize and reward their labour but also discursively positioned them as societal outsiders.

The Western occupiers designed rationing systems in their zones that based the basic categorization schemes on age differences rather than on the type of labour performed by the consumers. Most adults were categorized as "average consumers" (*Normalverbraucher*) and allotted rations based on minimum calorie levels. However, certain categories of workers, especially coalminers, were still privileged through a series of extra rations and higher calorie allotments to prevent undernourishment and fatigue. As a further incentive, Ruhr area mine-workers were issued "point cards" that allowed them to obtain scarce goods beyond regular rations.[6] Housewives formed the majority of the *Normalverbraucher* without any bonus allotments, a category that also came to be known as the "hunger card".[7]

The SBZ and Western rationing systems defined categories of labour to be compensated directly with food and goods based on earlier conceptions of labour rewarded with wages. Industrial and professional work was the most highly compensated labour, despite the acknowledgement of some critics and planners that housework, including shopping, was itself labour requiring proper nourishment. In November 1945, for example, the Berlin municipal administration discussed the difficulties for women in the lowest category of the Soviet system, who remained uncompensated for their heavy burden of housework. One member of the group cited a study claiming that housework required 50 hours of labour per week, not including the time required to stand in queues for food.[8] Despite this early criticism of categorical discrimination against housewives, however, the "hunger card" was not eliminated until 1947, when housewives were placed in category III. Another study from a West German institute suggested that female housework entailed "medium-heavy labour" and required enough calories to perform this work.[9] Such acknowledgement of the labour performed by housewives effected some changes, as in the eventual elimination of the final Soviet category, but did little to reorganize food distribution priorities to compensate housewives for their labour.

The Allied rationing systems, then, created hierarchies of gender that aimed to regulate who had access to consumption within these structures based on definitions of labour. These structures set conditions for reinstatement of traditional gender roles and ideals of masculinity and femininity. First, the distribution of food had concrete effects on male and female bodies. While most of the population faced weakness and undernourishment, according to the ration categorization, bodies involved in a primarily male definition of heavy labour and production were to be strengthened by consuming greater amounts of food. Programmes in the East and West instituted factory meals for workers to be eaten on the premises, specifically in order to raise productivity. Such programmes may have benefited employed women, but housewives had no access to such additional food.[10] The low calorie allotments for housewives surely affected the health and strength of women's bodies. One contemporary commentator drew attention to the effects of undernourishment on women in his observation that "with daily sustenance of 1,150 calories [women] suffer the loss of feminine grace."[11] This comment suggests both the physical effects of hunger on women and points to the conception that what women had to lose was not the strength required to do labour but their beauty.

Although extra rations for heavy labourers were meant to strengthen them specifically, they could also bring home their food supplements to help feed family members. This dynamic was recognized by contemporaries such as a West German union women's representative who stated, "The family father distributes extra rations to his family."[12] The higher rations for typically male jobs possibly enforced patriarchal nuclear family structures in which a primary provider supported his family.[13] The generally lower wages for women and the reinforcement of this wage structure through the ration systems created difficulties for single women who did not have an additional means of support and made unemployed housewives more dependent on a male wage-earner.

However, at the same time that the rationing systems enforced gender norms and hierarchies, the actual strategies for survival used by the population often bypassed these systems and offered alternative sets of values, which often led to a more fluid division of labour between producers and consumers. The continuing shortages and the weak currency set the conditions for an economy of barter and subsistence that did not rely only on wages to purchase goods. The inability of the ration systems to provide sufficiently for even the most privileged workers lowered the incentive for them to work for rations rather than to acquire goods through other means. The insufficiency of ration allotments increased reliance on other sources such as the black market, which was frequented by over half the population.[14] However, low wages, frozen by decree at the level of 1939, usually did not provide workers with enough cash to purchase goods on the black market for the inflated prices there.[15] To compensate for the low wages, workers demanded payment in goods, which they could use themselves or barter, or they would steal from their workplaces.

...s take a "hamstering" trip to the country to barter with ...telle, Berlin).

...ional year of 1948, goods reappeared in stores ...ould be purchased for wages, but were still too ...he population to afford. This situation in which ...ut broadly unattainable cast the consumer in a ...cal role as workers protested against the inequi-

...money in your hands!": the West German ...the construction of wage-earners and ...s

...ency reform on 20 June 1948 has been estab-
...ory as the crucial turning-point in the course of
...ajor step towards solidifying the economic and
...ermany.[18] These important political develop-
...nt with developments that restructured gender
...new valuable currency tightened the labour

Still, worker
and then le
male and fe
sanctioned
itself: stand
trade with
goods in o
market. Th
important,
goods in thi
system the
housework
broke dow
labour of c

For wom
meant that
ration syst
wages, lack
cally "femi
goods coul
poorer wo
the Reich,
such as cle
vasiveness
from the
made the a
rather thai
other labo

Part of tl
was the el
Steps to "n
included a
stop the b
vancemen
black marl
acquire go
cies in Eas
in stores s
of German

Figure 10.1   Berlin citize
farmers, 1946 (Landesbilc

societies. In the trans
in East and West that
expensive for most of
goods were available
more prominent polit
ties of the new system

"You have valuable
currency reform an
housewife-consume

The West German cu
lished in popular men
reconstruction and a
political division of C
ments were concomit
roles. Demand for th

218

Still, workers would often work only long enough to get such bonuses and then leave. Absenteeism became a daily occurrence.[16] Hence, male and female workers participated in a combination of officially sanctioned work for wages and rations and the work of consumption itself: standing in queues, taking "hamstering" trips to the country to trade with farmers, planting crops in municipal parks, bartering goods in official "free markets", stealing, and trading on the black market. The lower value of wages meant that, while they were still important, they represented only one of a variety of means to acquire goods in this shortage economy. Therefore, while within the rationing system the division of labour between male breadwinning and female housework was reinforced, the actual functioning of the economy broke down these divisions and made all citizens participate in the labour of consumption.

For women, this multiplicity of available consumption strategies meant that they did not necessarily have to rely on the wage-earning/ration system in which they were disadvantaged through lower wages, lack of qualification and frequent prejudicial slotting into typically "feminine" jobs. Wealthier women who had access to valuable goods could best take advantage of the opportunities to barter, while poorer women, especially refugees from former eastern territories of the Reich, had fewer options and often had to take low-paid jobs such as clearing the rubble of destroyed buildings.[17] Still, the pervasiveness of the alternative barter economy partly freed women from the dependence on a gender-biased wage-based system and made the act of consumption itself a direct route to attaining goods rather than only a means to buy goods using wages earned through other labour.

Part of the task of reconstruction in the occupation zones, however, was the elimination of these alternatives, such as the black market. Steps to "normalize" the economy and society in the West and the East included attempts to end shortages and strengthen the currency to stop the black market and to give the impression of economic advancement and the advent of better times. The attempt to abolish the black market reinforced the importance of wage-earning as a means to acquire goods. The context created by the introduction of new currencies in East and West in 1948 and the reappearance of available goods in stores symbolized the growing differences between the two halves of Germany and made consumption a central aspect of the diverging

Figure 10.1 Berlin citizens take a "hamstering" trip to the country to barter with farmers, 1946 (Landesbildstelle, Berlin).

societies. In the transitional year of 1948, goods reappeared in stores in East and West that could be purchased for wages, but were still too expensive for most of the population to afford. This situation in which goods were available but broadly unattainable cast the consumer in a more prominent political role as workers protested against the inequities of the new systems.

"You have valuable money in your hands!": the West German currency reform and the construction of wage-earners and housewife-consumers

The West German currency reform on 20 June 1948 has been established in popular memory as the crucial turning-point in the course of reconstruction and a major step towards solidifying the economic and political division of Germany.[18] These important political developments were concomitant with developments that restructured gender roles. Demand for the new valuable currency tightened the labour

Figure 10.2   Women trade on the black market in the Zehlendorf district of Berlin, 1948 (Landesbildstelle, Berlin).

market at the same time that desire for newly available goods caused inflation and revealed social inequalities. In this transitional period, shifting employment patterns reinforced the nuclear family with a male breadwinner, and conflicts around consumption made house-wife-shoppers central figures in mediating this transition. At the same time that the women had less access to wages, their role as consumers took on greater political significance.

Consumption became a central issue of conflict when the currency reform precipitated a disjuncture between apparent affluence and actual continuing inequalities and hardship. Eyewitnesses remembered with awe the "miracle" of sudden abundance in formerly empty shop windows: "Suddenly everything was there. Stuff that one could only dream of . . . Overnight as if it had flown in."[19] Such stories of awe were often accompanied by anger at shopkeepers who had kept their wares from the hungry population while waiting for the impending "Day X", when the new currency would arrive. This hoarding was illegal but tolerated. Perhaps it was even promoted by the director of the Economic Administration and future economics minister, Ludwig Erhard, in order to enhance the appearance of abundance on the day of the reform.[20] The spectacle of plenty was designed to convince the population not only of the new currency's stability but also of the progress of West German reconstruction and even of the efficacy of Erhard's liberal economic programme. The spectacle of full windows may have offered promises for future consumer satisfaction making this event a central founding myth of West Germany's 1950s "economic miracle". However, most of the population recognized that behind this opulent display lay continuing inequalities. The new abundance reminded hungry workers of the hardship caused by shopkeepers who had kept goods from them prior to the reform and by the rising prices thereafter. The demand for previously unavailable goods caused prices to rise rapidly, while wages remained frozen at 1938 levels.

The distribution of the new marks itself reflected this tension between the appearance of equally available wealth and the reinstatement of social hierarchies. On the day of the reform, each citizen was issued a sum of 40 new marks traded at a 1:1 basis for old Reichsmarks, thereby creating an initial illusion of economic equality and levelling. However, individual cash savings were deflated at a rate of 10:1 while property kept its value. Thus, many suffered from the virtual loss of their cash savings and ultimately the population was stratified with those who retained fixed capital on top. Plans for redistributing financial burdens (*Lastenausgleich*) were actualized only partly in 1949 and more thoroughly only in 1952, but by then it was too little too late and most social inequalities were never eradicated.

Reinforced class hierarchies were accompanied by codification of gender hierarchies, owing to changes in the job market and in the

Figure 10.3 Berlin shoppers stare at sudden abundance in a shop window after the lifting of the Berlin blockade in 1949 (Landesbildstelle, Berlin).

means of consumption. Elimination of the barter economy meant a greater reliance on wage-earning, and high prices necessitated higher wage levels, but greater general unemployment meant women were often first to be fired. Competition for women's jobs became particularly intense when more women began registering for employment. Some women had formerly avoided wage work prior to the currency reform since available jobs such as those clearing rubble were unpleasant and tiring, some women had to care for children, and alternatives were available to attain goods without wages. Now, many women needed wages, since the currency reform eliminated not only their savings but also alternative channels to attain goods, such as the black market.[21] In addition, since the high prices made it harder for families to survive on a single male wage, wives who had previously remained unemployed registered to work because they "now had to contribute to supporting the family".[22] At the same time, however, it was often "double earners" along with unskilled women and women in "male" professions who were the first to be fired.[23]

Women who managed to stay employed remained at a disadvantage in this period of inflation since many of them were stuck with low

221

wages frozen from the National Socialist period. Despite the Allied Control Council's introduction of a minimum wage of 50 pfennigs per hour in 1947, which improved wages for underpaid women, this wage often was still too low to afford goods at the new prices.[24] In addition, wages for men and women remained generally unequal. A trade union report from September 1948 illustrated that the average hourly wage for men was 116.2 pfennigs whereas the same for women was only 72.2 pfennigs. The gross weekly male wage averaged DM 51.46 while for women it totalled DM 29.34.[25] These difficulties for women seeking employment created conditions that increased women's dependency on a male wage-earner, a development particularly troublesome for the numerous single women heading post-war German households.

While the tight labour market restructured wage labour as a primarily male domain and gave women less access to this form of work, women's labour in the arena of consumption gained political significance. As the aftermath of the currency reform highlighted social inequalities and concentrated workers' anger around the discrepancy between low wages and outrageous prices, women were called upon to protest against this injustice through their role as consumers. Workers called for not only a general work stoppage in November 1948 but also a series of consumer boycotts (*Käuferstreiks*) that year. A report of a boycott in Münster in July 1948 reveals the perception of male and female roles in such actions:

> On 28 July 1948 a handful of men went to the weekly market and engaged in unprecedented propaganda activity. First they demanded that the salespeople lower their prices to a tolerable level. At the same time, housewives were asked not to pay the high prices and above all not to buy thoughtlessly everything that was offered.[26]

This passage suggests that male workers, and presumably primary household wage-earners, took part in the shopping strikes not mainly as shoppers themselves but as instructors enlightening housewives who took the real responsibility for family consumption. The remark that women would otherwise "thoughtlessly" buy everything on the market reintroduced an older discourse on women as irrational, uncontrollable consumers seduced into buying. A flyer distributed at another shoppers' strike similarly reflected didactic attempts to control reckless female buying behaviour: "German Housewife!

Boycott! You have valuable money in your hands! Your husband worked hard for it with his own sweat! You sin against your family when you pay exorbitant prices! If you don't buy, the prices must fall! German housewife, recognize your power! Take part in the boycott!"[27] This leaflet illustrates the assumed division of labour between a male breadwinner and a female housewife-consumer. The reference to the husband's sweat also reiterates the image of labour as masculine and physical, an image that recalls the earlier discussed archetype of the worker as a male heavy labourer. Especially interesting is the type of appeal aimed at the housewife-shopper. The flyer urges women to exercise power through their role as consumer and imbues this role with both moral and nationalist responsibility, by claiming that a misplaced purchase is a "sin against your family" and by referring to the housewife as specifically "German". This strategy constructed the housewife as a member of the national community and of a patriarchal family specifically through consumption.

Some housewives themselves rose to the challenge to master the conditions of the new market through their expertise as consumers. One of several women's organizations established after the war, the Berlin Housewives' Organization, used its newspaper to tackle the problems of the post-currency reform situation:

> Every purchase must be preceded by an exact study of costs and the urgency of the acquisition. The currency reform presents the housewife with new tasks. And the Berlin housewife will master these tasks with proper consideration of the conditions created by the currency reform, since she has proven her flexibility in the post-war years time and again.[28]

This passage echoes the exhortations of the union boycott organizers and claims power for housewives as consumers but also recognizes the dangers of unstudied consumption. The discourses that both cast women in a housewife-shopper role and that opened the possibility for women to have power as consumers placed women consumers at the centre of the discussion of problems in consumption after the currency reform and set the stage for the construction of housewife-consumers as expert contributors to the prosperity of the "economic miracle". The newly available goods and hard currency offered new promise for fulfilment of desires but also presented difficulties and challenges with gender-specific implications for the West German population in general and workers in particular.

"The fifth wheel on the cart": the HO, labour, consumption and housework in the Soviet zone

While the West German developments in the transitional period of the currency reform reinforced the division between male wage-earners and female consumers, East German events that same year worked to construct ideal socialist labourers and consumers as alternatives to the Western model. Like the engineers of the Western currency reform, planners in the SBZ sought to eliminate the black market and to create the image of restored abundance in order to legitimize Soviet reconstruction and spur productivity. Their specifically socialist answer to these problems was the creation of state-run stores that came to be known as the *Handelsorganisation* (HO).

These stores were meant to form a third retailing branch alongside consumer co-operatives and privately owned stores, which had previously offered both rationed goods and unrationed goods when they were available. Technically, HO sales would return money directly to the state to be funnelled back into production. Symbolically, in the context of building socialism in the Soviet zone, the HO was to form a potential alternative to Western displays of affluence and to provide the context for the construction of an ideal socialist consumer. Th discussion that took place around the opening of the HO offers possi ble insight into idealized gender roles for consumers.

After the currency reform the East German press attacked the "shop-window politics in the West"[29] and attempted to dim the allure of the "Golden West"[30] with the argument that "the full shop windows are just the expression of the fact that people can't buy as much [in the West] but not an expression of greater production".[31] This spectre of Western affluence put a degree of pressure on the Soviet administration to strengthen its position as a valid alternative for consumers.

The HO was meant to meet this challenge by offering quality goods outside of ration allotments for inflated prices and to give the impression of a socialist version of a consumer paradise. At one of the HO planning meetings the proposed merchandise for the new stores was described in opulent, if perhaps optimistic, terms: "excellent baked goods, candied fruit, jams, coffee, tea, chocolate and cocoa, high-quality spirits (especially brand-name liqueurs), outstanding tinned fish . . . first-class lingerie, textiles, shoes, as well as accordions, cameras and radios too".[32] The atmosphere of the stores themselves were to enhance the image of the HO as a quality establishment:

> The HO firms should not be average stores or restaurants but especially cultivated establishments representing the highest standards. That demands besides the most tasteful decoration and furnishings, effective advertising, meticulous cleanliness everywhere, knowledgeable, tactful and polite personnel, impeccable quality, highest standards, satisfactory goods and a general atmosphere in which the customer is at ease.[33]

Eventually the goods were to become more accessible through successive planned price reductions, but initially few people could afford HO offerings.

The propaganda for the HO implied that it was meant to satisfy the demand of workers earning higher wages as a part of new productivity-based wage programmes known as the progressive piece wage (*progressiver Leistungslohn*). This new higher wage was an extension of earlier material incentives to increase productivity that divided workers into "normal workers" and "*Aktivisten*", those who achieved rates of production above the norm, ideally through technical innovation and rationalization. Since recipients of higher wages needed merchandise to buy in order to make the new wage a real incentive, the HO was introduced. As one planner stated in an early meeting about the HO:

> The introduction of the free shops [later called the "HO"] in Berlin and the Soviet zone is in my opinion inextricably connected to the problem of the *Leistungslohn* . . . if we want to create an incentive for raised productivity among the workers, the workers [must] have the opportunity to buy something additionally above their rations.[34]

To what extent were the *Aktivisten* or recipients of the *Leistungslohn* who were cast in propaganda as the ideal HO customers constructed along gender lines? Indeed, all members of the population were encouraged to raise productivity and to become *Aktivisten*. Women were explicitly included in this general effort. For example, Luise Ermisch (a textile worker) became an *Aktivistin* and was lauded as the first female "Work Hero".[35] As compared with the Western zones, the Soviet zone made a more concerted effort to bring women into the workplace and offer them equal pay for equal work. However, women's wages remained generally lower than men's owing to women's lower levels of qualification and the slow implementation of wage equalization.[36] In addition, it is not clear that women would have had equal access to the higher-paying *progressiver Leistungslohn*, because it was primarily introduced in certain key industries that were prioritized by the Soviet occupiers and that had the capacity to achieve rates of higher production, such as coalmining, a male-dominated industry. Indeed, the main propaganda campaign accompanying the introduction of the *progressiver Leistungslohn* centred on the figure of a coalminer, who lent the ideal *Aktivist* a decidedly masculine image.

The *Aktivist* "movement" found a spokesperson a month before the opening of the first HO store. Modelled on the figure of Stachanov in the Soviet Union, a miner named Adolf Hennecke was used to symbolize this movement when, through some prior orchestration, he exceeded his daily production norm in the coalmines by 387 per cent. His name became synonymous with that of the *Aktivist* as the movement took the name "Hennecke-movement". A staged photo of Hennecke, shirtless, sweaty and covered with coal dust, muscles straining with the labour of drilling into the side of a mine shaft, was reproduced ubiquitously. This masculine image, emphasizing the physical effort of male labour, epitomized the continuing perseverance of traditional gendered ideas of true labour and productivity.[37]

If the HO was meant, then, to cater to the extra high wage-earner, that is the *Aktivist* receiving a progressive piece wage, the masculinized quality of that movement suggests that the HO potentially meant to appeal to male shoppers. This would make sense if the HO aimed to provide a direct reward to individual male workers in privileged industries in the same way that other incentives had hoped to spur workers on to greater productivity by rewarding them personally. It is plausible that planners hoped to appeal to individual workers since the goods offered in the HO were meant to be high-quality semi-luxuries, perhaps to be enjoyed as a treat for the working individual. This type of shopping experience is described by a participant in the discussions to plan the HO, Frau Loessner of the Socialist Unity Party (*Sozialistische Einheitspartei Deutschlands*, SED), who presented an image of a female consumer treating herself with her extra wages: "I can well imagine that when a working woman can for once buy coffee or chocolate, that it is not just coffee or chocolate for her, but that it really means something for this woman."[38] Since HO

Figure 10.4   Adolf Hennecke, the coalminer whose image exemplified the archetype of the masculine heavy labourer (*Neue Berliner Illustrierte*/Verlag die Wirtschaft).

prices were too high for people to purchase its wares daily, it seems more likely that HO customers would follow this scenario of pleasurable, perhaps individual consumption on a rare and special occasion in their free time. In fact, the HO limitations caused by high prices worked to define HO's shoppers almost through the exclusion of those who needed to purchase goods for daily use.

A representative of the mass women's organization, the *Demokratischer Frauenbund Deutschlands* (DFD) already noted the HO's limitations for daily shopping requirements in one of the stores' initial planning meetings:

> If you ask a woman what gets bought when the man brings a little more money home, the answer is: first of all foodstuffs, potatoes, bread and soap. These four most important items . . . will probably not be offered for sale in the free stores [i.e. the HO] . . . . Women will hardly be able to do without these items, so that we will continue to have the black market beside the free stores and a differentiation will simply set in, in which these important foodstuffs will be channelled through the black market and certain luxury items and additional items will be available in the free stores.[39]

This mention of the husband's pay-packet points to the continuing ideal of the male breadwinner, despite the aforementioned introduction of the ideal working woman enjoying the fruits of her own wages, and the female housewife, responsible for daily shopping and budgeting. The initial proposition of relegating luxury items to the HO suggests, as in this comment, that the housewife's work of shopping was meant to be done elsewhere, implying that the HO would remain a site of pleasure or luxury shoppers. Whereas the housewife/consumer, as in the West, was taken for granted as a female figure, it may be that the occasional pleasure shopper, ideally an *Aktivist* reaping the benefits of high achievement, was a more gender-neutral figure. However, given the fact that male wages remained generally higher than women's, especially in jobs like coalmining, it may have been more likely that the HO shopper was either male or a woman at least partially supported by a male breadwinner.

The establishment of the HO stores created a hierarchy of prices and of consumption that paralleled other hierarchies in East Germany and embodied the contradictions internal to its version of socialism. Reactions to the HO collected by the state party revealed acute awareness among the population of the unjust hierarchies it created. Many comments shared the view of a worker in Dresden who, according to the report, stated that the HO was "just a concern of the *Aktivisten*; the average worker can't buy anything. So 'one throws everything in the mouths of the *Aktivisten*'. The *progressiver Leistungslohn* can't be introduced into every factory." However, another commentator doubted that even the propaganda's target for HO consumption, the *Aktivisten*, could afford the HO goods: "in the papers, the 'Free Stores' and the *progressiver Leistungslohn* are always coupled", but he believed, "that even with the *progressiver Leistungslohn* one doesn't earn enough to pay these [HO] prices".[40] This opinion that *Aktivisten* would not, in fact, be able to shop at the HO was supported by an observation elsewhere that stated, "a large portion of the shoppers is not *Aktivisten* as we had predicted, but workers from other levels, who laboriously saved their money in order to purchase this or that article in the free stores".[41]

Other commentators believed that HO shoppers would be the same black marketeers that the HO was fighting against. Perhaps the real hierarchy is hidden in the statement by a woman from Gera: "These privileges only ever benefit a certain class. The simple worker only keeps getting the slogan: First produce more, then live better! In practice, however, it looks very different."[42] This vague statement could be posing the contrast between the "classes" of the "simple worker" and the *Aktivist*. However, hidden in this reference to continuing class structures in socialist East Germany could be a reference to the privileged position of party functionaries, who were perhaps the real primary customers of the HO. In any case it is clear from these statements that workers, according to the report, acknowledged and were bitter about the construction of both a hierarchy of consumers and a hierarchy within wage work, set up by the *Leistungslohn* and the *Aktivisten* movement.

This inequality exposed by the HO also paralleled a gender-specific hierarchy between work outside the home and housework. Besides this supposed hierarchy among wage-earners themselves, then, the reconstruction of work culture in the Soviet zone reinforced a traditional devaluation of the housework performed mostly by women. As discussed above, the rationing system in the SBZ already failed to acknowledge the work of women performing the household tasks of daily survival. The HO reinforced a new hierarchy between the ideal wage-earning woman and the "just-housewife". This new system of value for women's roles surfaced in a letter written by a housewife to a female *Aktivistin* at a nearby factory to express her concerns that housewives faced discrimination:

Not everyone can be employed, whether as a result of sickness or having to take care of a sick person at home, or just because there are children to care for (because without children then no youth and without youth then no future) or some other reason . . . It's my opinion that every single person is needed for reconstruction and that no one should be shut out. A housewife can't be everything at once. She would surely rather be in the workplace enjoying all the privileges such as communal kitchens, bonus cards, etc., than always just slaving over the housekeeping and food and figuring out where to get it. That's why I ask you what you would do for the housewife, who is already the fifth wheel on the cart and now is even to be shut out from shopping in the free stores.[43]

Government authorities took this woman's appeal as a sign to prioritize the plan to erect more day-care centres so that women could work outside the home.[44] But it could also be viewed as an acknowledgement of the dilemma of the housewife who saw herself unappreciated for the difficult work she had to perform and who felt shut out from the rewards provided by the new socialist state for wage-earning participants in the reconstruction (communal kitchens, bonus cards, free stores). While the author of this letter used rhetoric that signalled a desire to participate in work outside the home, the reasons she presented were not those of wanting to participate more fully in rebuilding the economy because she indicated that she already considered her work as a housewife important for this reconstruction ("every single person is needed for reconstruction"). Nor did she state any desire for fulfilment through work outside the home but rather referred to the material rewards of wage work from which she was excluded as someone participating only in housework. This appeal to acknowledge the work of housewives exemplifies the contradictions of women's role in the developing socialist system.

The contradictions of the consumer economy exemplified by the HO extended to the complicated construction of gender roles in the Soviet zone and the German Democratic Republic (GDR). While women were urged to seek employment and were rewarded for this labour, they could not always do so owing to domestic responsibilities. In a system that valorized wage labour as the primary contribution to society, women were caught in the pressure to seek employment while still maintaining responsibility for household labour, such as daily domestic shopping. Whereas housewives in the West could seize authority and power as consumers in the transitional period after the currency reform, the centrally planned price structure of the HO may have partly eliminated this source of consumer power for women and instead exposed their position at the bottom of the socialist system.

"The housewife as an economic factor": domestic consumption in the two new German states

The double currency reforms set the stage economically for the political division of the country into separate states in 1949. After the spectacle of full shop windows in the West and the creation of the state-run HO in the East symbolized the heightened political and economic competition between the two systems, consumption continued to be a conspicuous terrain of Cold War rivalries.

Ideals of male and female roles as producers and consumers also continued to be reshaped to fit into the political contexts of the newly founded western Federal Republic (FRG) and the eastern GDR and their growing economies. Just as women had borne the major burden of standing in queues and scavenging for goods during the years of extreme post-war shortages and had carried responsibility for dealing with changing market situations after the currency reforms and the founding of the HO, women remained primary household shoppers into the 1950s. However, after the worst shortages had been mostly relieved and standards of living began to improve, household shoppers gained increasing political recognition as agents for fuelling the two economies. Both popular discourses and employment and wage patterns reinforced an idealized nuclear family with a male primary breadwinner and a female housewife-shopper. Even in East Germany where women were more encouraged to enter the labour force, traditional gender roles were reconstructed in the nuclear family because women maintained the primary burden of housework. As consumers became more central to economic growth, politicians valorized housewife-shoppers as "experts" and women themselves seized opportunities to enhance their power as consumers. A variety of sources from government ministries and from women's organizations in both East and West Germany in the 1950s explicated ways that women as expert household consumers should play a vital role in the two state economies and could strengthen the two political systems through their consumer activity.

As a means to raise the standard of living and help the economy, propaganda from the West German economics ministry in the early 1950s aimed to promote consumption of durable commodities such as refrigerators and electric ovens. Such initiatives as the 1953 programme "Erhard helps the housewife", named after its founder, the economics minister, specifically targeted female consumers as the primary expert shoppers in their households and advised and encouraged those planning to purchase major household appliances. For example, radio shows for women sponsored by the ministry for economics offered tips on how to compare prices and models to help with major purchases. These didactic radio skits presented normative ideals of how housewife-shoppers were to take part in their families as well as in the political economy as consumers.

Two such plays suggested patterns for negotiating family consumption in which housewives from various classes exercised power in the family as shopping experts. Two women discussed different refrigerator models in one play written in a thick dialect, perhaps to appeal to an average working-class audience. The first woman, Gisela, asked her friend, Frau Brandl, "So what does Herr Brandl think [about the refrigerators]"? Frau Brandl replied, "I haven't talked to him about it yet. I want to know everything myself – all the ins and outs – before I do. I already collected all the brochures myself, so I could see what's out there."[45] This interchange suggests that although the process of purchasing such durable goods would ideally involve discussion among married couples, the wife was to be the expert.

The interactions between a male breadwinner and a female expert consumer in the ideal household were explicated further in a radio play called "The forgotten consumer", about a husband who decided to discover what it would be like to be an "active consumer" for the purpose of writing a book. To do this he ordered his wife to leave for a week so that he would be forced for a change to do the shopping. When the man announced to his wife that he would write a book about the consumer, this interchange took place:

> Woman: About the consumer? – Well, that'll be easy. Look at me, write about me. That's all you need.
> Author: Why about you? Look at me! Aren't I a consumer?

Woman: At the most a passive one! – You eat what I put on the
table, put on what I buy for you, and complain that I can't make
do with the household budget, because the prices are so high.
The active consumer – that's me, the housewife and shopper.[46]
This excerpt reiterated a division of labour between the husband as
wage-earner and the wife as consumer and showed the terrain for
intra-familial negotiation of power relationships between these two
roles. While the wage-earning male, in this case probably a member of
the middle class since he was a writer or journalist, may have had ultimate financial authority as the primary family provider, according to
the depiction in this government-sponsored play, housewife-shoppers
had the option of claiming an alternate base of authority in the family
as expert consumers.

Women's organizations themselves emphasized this consumer role
for women as a means of contributing to the economy and strengthening the political system in each opposing German state. In the FRG,
for example, the German Housewives' Union, which worked with
federally sponsored consumer advocacy groups, held a conference in
1954 entitled "The housewife as an economic factor". The keynote
speech by the Union's chair, Fini Pfannes, outlined the importance
of housewife-consumers in the West German economy and framed
her discussion of consumption in political terms. Pfannes connected
the behaviour of consumers to the maintenance of West German
democracy in the statement, "It is in [the economy's] interest to help
develop conscious consumers as partners in the market, so that they
don't – like fledgelings – practise their sovereignty dictatorially, but
democratically."[47] The parallel Pfannes drew between democratic
political activity and "conscious consumption" suggests possible ways
that consumption took on political significance at a time when the
Federal Republic sought to maintain a reconstructed political culture,
especially in the shadow of the ever-present reference-point of what
they viewed as the "dictatorial" alternatives: the National Socialist
regime as well as Sovietized East Germany. Thus, housewives were to
fit into the so-called "economic miracle" as consumers, not only to
aid the market but also to bolster democratic political culture against
the threats of reliving the Nazi past or falling to the FRG's socialist
competitor.

Confronted with the economic successes of its western neighbour,
the East German government also aimed to improve its economy and

raise the standard of living of the population. In this context the role of consuming housewives also gained significance in propaganda and in the programmes of the central women's organization, the DFD. The DFD in particular sponsored activities that called on women to contribute to the economy as expert consumers. For example, DFD housewives were recruited to serve on HO-councils where they were to improve the "selling culture" of the state stores by offering suggestions based on their expertise in domestic shopping.[48] In fact, the DFD used the assumption that shopping would be a major concern for women as a lure to recruit them to join the organization. The DFD planned educational meetings for women focused on issues of consumption to encourage them to harness their power as consumers to improve the economy within the context of this state-sponsored group. For example, a 1956 plan for housewife education and propaganda programmes suggested a session dedicated to consumption with the justification, "Every woman likes to buy good wares. Women as the main shoppers in the family have a great influence on the development of the market."[49]

A pamphlet from the same year to be used for similar educational programmes entitled, "Beautiful shop windows, good products, satisfied women" urged women to work towards improving the socialist marketplace as an extension of their "natural" interest in consumption:

> We women value the ability to set a nice table and present our families with varied, good and tasty fare. In a friendly, comfortable environment we feel well; nice, fashionable clothes give us new productive energy. We also know, however, that this can only be achieved when we actively support our socialist trade.[50]

These texts suggest that, like women in West Germany, East German women were expected to maintain primary responsibility for household consumption and, at least within the context of the women's organization, some seized the opportunity to turn this task into a source of authority and influence in society. Just as Fini Pfannes placed consumption in the political context of rebuilding democracy in West Germany, these pamphlets from the DFD connected consumption in East Germany to the task of buttressing the socialist political and economic system. Consumption was one crucial element of women's part in the ideal family in the GDR, as these quotes suggest. Unlike in the West, the relationship of the female consumer to employment and wage-earning was more ambiguous. The reference to the "productive energy" gleaned from satisfaction with consumer goods ("fashionable clothes") connotes a possible connection between women's productive labour and their ability to consume products of that labour, perhaps with their own wages.

Therefore, East and West Germany shared a common vocabulary that defined ideal female consumers of the 1950s as family experts who contributed to the political economy using this authority. However, the GDR's emphasis on recruiting women into the workforce joined women's consumer role more explicitly with their role as producers, while discourses in the FRG reinforced an ideal in which husbands brought home a family wage that their wives were left to budget.

Conclusion

The progression from a period of shortages to increasing abundance in the post-war era was a central dynamic in German reconstruction. Ideals of male and female labour were reproduced and redefined during various stages in this process. Due to the crucial problem of regulating scarce goods and strengthening the two opposing economies and political systems, the world of goods and consumption became a terrain for the negotiation of East and West German gendered identities as the two states progressed towards parallel modernizations and reconstructions. The role of the male breadwinner was reconstructed around images of the heavy labourer literally rebuilding German cities that set the context for a reification of the male producer at the base of the two German economies. Women's place as employed labour was more ambiguous, but throughout the period of reconstruction they performed the labour of consumption. In this sense, "woman's place was reasserted and reified"[51] as a primary housekeeper to be supported largely by a male wage, but the shifting conditions of the economy led to varying meanings for woman's place as a consumer. While domestic consumption was always labour for women, at some junctures in the reconstruction of the two economies this labour was cast as a source of authority and power and an important role for women in the reconstruction of the two societies.

Notes

1. W. Zank, *Wirtschaft und Arbeit in Ostdeutschland 1945–1949: Probleme des Wiederaufbaus in der Sowjetischen Besatzungszone Deutschlands* (Munich: Oldenbourg, 1987), p. 39.
2. C. von Oertzen & A. Rietzschel, "Neuer Wein in alten Schläuchen: Geschlechterpolitik und Frauenerwerbsarbeit im besetzten Deutschland zwischen Kriegsende und Währungsreform", *Ariadne* 27 (May 1995), pp. 28–35.
3. R. Gries, *Die Rationen-Gesellschaft: Versorgungskampf und Vergleichs-mentalität: Leipzig, München und Köln nach dem Kriege* (Münster: Westfälisches Dampfboot, 1990), p. 95.
4. Archiv des Deutschen Gewerkschaftsbund-Bundesvorstandes (DGB), Gewerkschaftlicher Zonenbeirat–Britische Besatzungszone (BBZ) 11/223.
5. Gries, *Die Rationen-Gesellschaft*, p. 94.
6. M. Roseman, *Recasting the Ruhr 1945–1958: manpower, economic recovery and labour relations* (New York & Oxford: Berg, 1992), pp. 65 ff.
7. Gries, *Die Rationen-Gesellschaft*, pp. 195 ff.
8. Landesarchiv Berlin (LAB), Zeitgeschichtliche Sammlung (LAZ), 8500/25. Magistratssitzung 26 Nov. 1945, comment by Schwenk.
9. DGB, BBZ 11/220. Max-Planck-Institut für Arbeitsphysiologie, "Vereinheitlichung und Umrechnung von techn. Einheiten und Kalorienwerten", Dortmund, July 1948.
10. DGB, BBZ 11/225. Memo to Bipartite Control Office, Food and Agriculture Group, betr. Industrie-Speisung. Frankfurt, 6 Mar. 1948.
11. Quoted in Gries, *Die Rationen-Gesellschaft*, p. 297.
12. DGB, Gewerkschaftsrat der vereinten Zonen (GVZ) 13/93. Sitzung des ernährungspolitischen Ausschusses am 13.–14. Feb. 1948 in Frankfurt am Main.
13. DGB, BBZ 11/224. Stellungnahme der Gewerkschaften zur Frage der gewerblichen Lebensmittelzulagen. 18 Oct. 1949.
14. K.-J. Ruhl (ed.), *Frauen in der Nachkriegszeit 1945–1963* (Munich: dtv, 1988), p. 297. Ruhl cites a study of working-class households in Lower Saxony from 1946 that puts the number of participants in the black market at 63.9 per cent.
15. DGB, BBZ 11/91. Länderrat Abt. Sozialpolitik, Entwurf zu einem Vorschlag der Arbeitsminister an OMGUS über ein Programm der Leistungssteigerung, 1 Dec. 1947, written by Dr Preller.
16. P. Erker, "Solidarität und Selbsthilfe: Die Arbeiterschaft in der Ernährungskrise", in *Neuanfang in Bayern 1945–1949: Politik und Gesellschaft in der Nachkriegszeit*, W. Benz (ed.) (Munich: C. H. Beck, 1988), p. 87; J. Diskant, "Scarcity, survival and local activism: miners and steelworkers, Dortmund 1945–8", *Journal of Contemporary History* 24, 1989, pp. 547–74, here p. 562.
17. Von Oertzen & Rietzschel, "Neuer Wein", p. 29.

18. L. Niethammer, "Privat-Wirtschaft: Erinnerungsfragmente einer anderen Umerziehung", in *"Hinterher merkt man, daß es richtig war, daß es schiefgegangen ist." Nachkriegserfahrungen im Ruhrgebiet: Lebensgeschichte und Sozialkultur im Ruhrgebiet 1930 bis 1960*, vol. 2, L. Niethammer (ed.) (Berlin: Dietz, 1983), p. 82; C. Buchheim, "Die Währungsreform 1948 in Westdeutschland", *Vierteljahreshefte für Zeitgeschichte* 36(1), 1988, pp. 222 ff.

19. Niethammer, "Privat-Wirtschaft", p. 81.

20. M. Wildt, *Am Beginn der "Konsumgesellschaft": Mangelerfahrung, Lebenshaltung, Wohlstandshoffnung in Westdeutschland in den fünfziger Jahren* (Hamburg: Ergebnisse, 1994), p. 33.

21. DGB, BBZ 11/33. Aussprache mit weiblichen englischen Parlamentsmitgliedern, 20 June 1948 in Hanover.

22. DGB, BBZ 11/33 (as previous note).

23. Ruhl (ed.), *Frauen in den Nachkriegszeit*, p. 72.

24. DGB, GVZ 13/12. Denkschrift der KPD-Fraktion im Wirtschaftsrat über die Rolle und Bedeutung der Frauen und Jugendlichen im Produktionsprozess, 6. Aug. 1948.

25. DGB, GVZ 13/17. "Wichtigste Ergebrisse der Lohnerhebung Sept. 1948 (Brit. Zone)".

26. DGB, BBZ 11/93. "Bericht über die Protestkundgebung des DGB-Kreisausschusses Münster am 11. August auf dem Servatiplatz".

27. DGB, BBZ 11/93. DGB Kreisausschuß Recklinghausen, Aug. 1948.

28. A. Heinicke, "Währungsumstellung – eine Studie für Hausfrauen", *Wir Hausfrauen* 1(4), 1949, p. 1.

29. *Neues Deutschland* (ND) 8 Oct. 1948, p. 3.

30. ND 13 Oct. 1948, no. 239, p. 4.

31. ND 28 Oct. 1948, no. 252, p. 5.

32. Bundesarchiv Potsdam (BAP) DA–1/186. Volksrat Wirtschaftsausschuß Sitzung 15 Oct. 1948, commentary by Erich Freund.

33. Stiftung Archiv der Partei und Massenorganisationen der DDR im Bundesarchiv (SAPMO BArch), Zentralkomitee der Sozialistischen Einheitspartei Deutschlands (SED ZK), Abteilung Wirtschaftspolitik DY 30–IV 2/6.02/76. 2 Dec. 1948: Deutsche Wirtschaftskommission (DWK) für die Sowjetische Besatzungszone (SBZ) Hauptverwaltung für Handel und Versorgung (HVHV) provisional guidelines for the stores from 3 Nov. 1948.

34. BAP, DA–1/186. Deutscher Volksrat Economic Committee on 15 Oct. 1948.

35. G. Dittrich, *Die Anfänge der Aktivistenbewegung* (Berlin [East]: Dietz, 1987), p. 159.

36. Zank, *Wirtschaft und Arbeit*, p. 135.

37. I. Merkel, ". . . *und Du, Frau an der Werkbank": Die DDR in den 50er Jahren* (Berlin: Elefanten Press, 1990), pp. 111 ff.

38. BAP, DA–1/186.

39. BAP, DA–1/186. Comment by Frau Schmidt-Wagemann.

40. SAPMO BArch, SED ZK, DY 30–IV 2/6.02/76. Information über die Reaktion der Bevölkerung zur Eröffnung der "Freien Läden" 1 Dec. 1948.

41. SAPMO BArch, Freier Deutscher Gewerkschaftsbund Bundesvorstand (FDGB Buvo) 0462–Landesvorstand Brandenburg report to the Buvo Zöllner, 18 Dec. 1948.

42. SAPMO BArch, SED ZK, DY 30–IV 2/6.02/76.

43. BAP, DA–1/140. Petition 19 Oct. 1948.

44. BAP, DA–1/140. Letter 4 Nov. 1948, Zeichen Jo/Dz Abt. 3.

45. Bundesarchiv Koblenz (BAK), B102/35963. "Der Haushaltslehrling". *Frauenfunk* 14 June 1953.

46. BAK, B102/35963. "Der vergessene Verbraucher". *Nordwestdeutscher Runkfunk* Köln, Abt. Politik 10 June 1953.

47. BAK, B211/27–18 Sept. 1954. Vortrag von Fini Pfannes in Bad Honnef.

48. SAPMO BArch, Demokratischer Frauenbund Deutschlands (DFD) Bundesvorstand Buvo–317, 22 Feb. 1955.

49. SAPMO BArch, DFD Buvo–324, 23 Oct. 1956.

50. Demokratischer Frauenbund Deutschlands, *Schöne Schaufenster gute Waren zufriedene Frauen* (DDR: Demokratischer Frauenbund Deutschlands, April 1956), p. 2.

51. R. G. Moeller, *Protecting motherhood: women and the family in the politics of postwar West Germany* (Berkeley, New York, Los Angeles, London: University of California Press, 1993), p. 228.

Bibliography

Abrams, L. Martyrs or matriarchs? Working-class women's experience of marriage in Germany before the First World War. *Women's History Review* 1, 1992, pp. 81–100.

Abrams, L. Concubinage, cohabitation and the law: class and gender relations in nineteenth-century Germany. *Gender and History* 5, 1993, pp. 81–100.

Ahrendt-Schulte, I. Schadenzauber und Konflikte: Sozialgeschichte von Frauen im Spiegel der Hexenprozesse des 16. Jahrhunderts in der Grafschaft Lippe. See Wunder & Vanja (eds), 1991, pp. 198–228.

Ahrendt-Schulte, I. *Weise Frauen – böse Weiber: Die Geschichte der Hexen in der Frühen Neuzeit* (Freiburg, Basel, Vienna: Herder, 1994).

Albisetti, J. C. *Schooling German girls and women: secondary and higher education in the nineteenth century* (Princeton, NJ: Princeton University Press, 1988).

Allen, A. Taylor *Feminism and motherhood in Germany, 1800–1914* (New Brunswick, NJ: Rutgers University Press, 1991).

Amussen, S. D. *An ordered society: gender and class in early modern England* (Oxford & New York: Basil Blackwell, 1988).

Baumann, U. *Protestantismus und Frauenemanzipation in Deutschland 1850 bis 1920* (Frankfurt am Main & New York: Campus, 1992).

Bausch, H. *Der Rundfunk im politischen Kräftespiel der Weimarer Republik 1923–1933* (Tübingen: J. C. B. Mohr, 1956).

Benn, S. I. & G. F. Gaus (eds). *Public and private in social life* (London: Croom Helm, 1983).

Bennett, J. M. Feminism and history. *Gender and History* 1, 1989, pp. 251–72.

Benz, W. (ed.). *Neuanfang in Bayern 1945–1949: Politik und Gesellschaft in der Nachkriegszeit* (Munich: C. H. Beck, 1988).

Bergmann, A. *Die verhütete Sexualität: Die Anfänge der modernen Geburtenkontrolle* (Hamburg: Rasch & Röhring, 1992).

Bessel, R. J. *Germany after the First World War* (Oxford: Clarendon Press, 1993).

Bischoff, C. Krankenpflege als Frauenberuf. *Jahrbuch für Kritische Medizin* 8, Argument Sonderband 86, 1982.

Bland, L. *Banishing the beast. English feminism and sexual morality 1885–1914* (London: Penguin, 1995).

Bischoff, C. *Frauen in der Krankenpflege: Zur Entwicklung von Frauenrolle und Frauenberufstätigkeit im 19. und 20. Jahrhundert*, rev. edn (Frankfurt am Main & New York: Campus, 1992).

Blasius, D. Bürgerliche Rechtsgleichheit und die Ungleichheit der Geschlechter. See Frevert (ed.), 1988, pp. 67–84.

Bleker, J. & H.–P. Schmiedebach (eds). *Medizin und Krieg: Vom Dilemma der Heilberufe 1865–1985* (Frankfurt am Main: Fischer, 1987).

Boak, H. Women in Weimar Germany: the Frauenfrage and the female vote. In *Social change and political development in Weimar Germany*, R. Bessel & E. J. Feuchtwanger (eds) (London: Croom Helm, 1981), pp. 155–73.

Bock, G. Racism and sexism in Nazi Germany: motherhood, compulsory sterilization, and the state. *Signs* 8, pp. 400–421, 1983.

Bock, G. *Zwangssterilisation im Nationalsozialismus: Studien zur Rassenpolitik und Frauenpolitik* (Opladen: Westdeutscher Verlag, 1986).

Bock, G. Antinatalism, maternity and paternity in National Socialist racism. In *Maternity and gender policies: women and the rise of the European welfare states, 1880s–1950s*, G. Bock & P. Thane (eds) (London & New York: Routledge, 1991), pp. 233–55.

Bock, G. Challenging dichotomies: perspectives on women's history. In *Writing women's history: international perspectives*, K. Offen, R. R. Pierson, J. Rendall (eds) (Bloomington, Indiana & Indianapolis: Indiana University Press, 1991), pp. 1–23.

Braun, L. *Selected writings on feminism and socialism* (Bloomington, Indiana & Indianapolis: Indiana University Press, 1987).

Brewer, J. This, that and the other: public, social and private in the seventeenth and eighteenth centuries. See Castiglione & Sharpe (eds), 1995, pp. 1–21.

Bridenthal, R. & C. Koonz. Beyond Kinder, Küche, Kirche: Weimar women in politics and work. In *When biology became destiny: women in Weimar and Nazi Germany*, R. Bridenthal, A. Grossmann, M. Kaplan (eds) (New York: Monthly Review Press, 1984), pp. 33–65.

Brodie, J. F. *Contraception and abortion in 19th-century America* (Ithaca, New York & London: Cornell University Press, 1994).

Brookes, B. *Abortion in England 1900–1967* (London: Croom Helm, 1988).

Broszat, M. *The Hitler state: the foundation and development of the internal structure of the Third Reich* (London: Longman, 1981).

Brückner, W. Neues zur "Geistlichen Hausmagd". *Volkskunst* 2, 1981, pp. 71–8.

Brunner, O. Das ganze Haus und die alteuropäische Ökonomik. In O. Brunner, *Neue Wege der Sozialgeschichte* (Göttingen: Vandenhoeck & Ruprecht, 1956), pp. 33–61.

Burghartz, S. Ehen vor Gericht: Die Basler Ehegerichtsprotokolle im 16. Jahrhundert. In *Eine Stadt der Frauen*, H. Wunder (ed.) together with S. Burghartz, D. Rippmann, K. Simon-Muscheid (Basel & Frankfurt am Main: Helbing & Lichtenhahn, 1995), pp. 167–214.

Bussemer, H.-U. *Frauenemanzipation und Bildungsbürgertum: Sozialgeschichte der Frauenbewegung in der Reichsgründungszeit* (Weinheim & Basel: Beltz, 1985).

Canning, K. Gender and the politics of class formation: rethinking German labor history. *American Historical Review* 97, 1992, pp. 736–68.

Canning, K. Feminist history after the linguistic turn: historicizing discourse and experience. *Signs* 19, 1994, pp. 368–404.

Cardiff, D. The serious and the popular: aspects of the evolution of style in the radio talk 1928–1939. In *Media, culture and society: a critical reader*, R. Collins (ed.) (London: Sage, 1986), pp. 228–46.

Carter, E. Alice in the consumer wonderland: West German case studies in gender and consumer culture. In *Gender and generation*, A. McRobbie & M. Nava (eds) (London: Macmillan, 1984), pp. 185–214.

Castiglione, D. & L. Sharpe (eds). *Shifting the boundaries: transformation of the languages of public and private in the eighteenth century* (Exeter: Exeter University Press, 1995).

Clark, A. *The struggle for the breeches: gender and the making of the British working class* (London: Rivers Oram Press, 1995).

Clemens, B. *"Menschenrechte haben kein Geschlecht!": Zum Politikverständnis der bürgerlichen Frauenbewegung* (Pfaffenweiler: Centaurus, 1988).

Conrad, A. *Zwischen Kloster und Welt: Ursulinen und Jesuitinnen in der katholischen Reformbewegung des 16./17. Jahrhunderts* (Mainz: Philipp von Zabern, 1991).

Crips, L. Modeschöpfung und Frauenbild am Beispiel von zwei nationalsozialistischen Zeitschriften: Deutsche Mutter versus Dame von Welt. In *Frauen und Faschismus in Europa: Der faschistische Körper*, L. Siegele-Wenschkewitz & G. Stuchlik (eds) (Pfaffenweiler: Centaurus, 1990), pp. 228–35.

Czarnowski, G. *Das kontrollierte Paar: Ehe- und Sexualpolitik im Nationalsozialismus* (Weinheim: Deutscher Studienverlag, 1991).

Czarnowski, G. & E. Meyer-Renschhausen. Geschlechterdualismen in der Wohlfahrtspflege: "Soziale Mütterlichkeit" zwischen Professionalisierung und Medikalisierung, Deutschland 1890–1930. *L'Homme: Zeitschrift für Feministische Geschichtswissenschaft* 5(2), 1994, pp. 121–40.

Daniel, U. *Arbeiterfrauen in der Kriegsgesellschaft: Beruf, Familie und Politik im Ersten Weltkrieg* (Göttingen: Vandenhoeck & Ruprecht, 1989).

Davidoff, L. "Alte Hüte": Öffentlichkeit und Privatheit in der feministischen Geschichtsschreibung. *L'Homme: Zeitschrift für Feministische Geschichtswissenschaft* 4(2), 1993, pp. 7–36.

Davidoff, L. *Worlds between: historical perspectives on gender and class* (Cambridge: Polity, 1995).

Davis, N. Z. "Women's history" in transition: the European case. *Feminist Studies* 3, 1975/6, pp. 83–103.

Dekker, R. & L. C. van de Pohl. *The tradition of female transvestism in early modern Europe*, trans. J. Marcure & L. C. van de Pohl (London: Macmillan, 1989).

241

BIBLIOGRAPHY

Diller, A. *Rundfunkpolitik im Dritten Reich* (Munich: dtv, 1980).

Dinges, M. Frühneuzeitliche Armenfürsorge als Sozialdisziplinierung: Probleme mit einem Konzept. *Geschichte und Gesellschaft* 17, 1991, pp. 5–29.

Diskant, J. Scarcity, survival and local activism: miners and steelworkers, Dortmund 1945–8. *Journal of Contemporary History* 24, 1989, pp. 547–74.

Dittrich, G. *Die Anfänge der Aktivistenbewegung* (Berlin [East]: Dietz, 1987).

Domansky, E. Der erste Weltkrieg. In *Bürgerliche Gesellschaft in Deutschland: Historische Einblicke, Fragen, Perspektiven*, L. Niethammer et al. (eds) (Frankfurt am Main: Fischer, 1990), pp. 285–319.

Dörner, H. *Industrialisierung und Familienrecht: Die Auswirkungen des sozialen Wandels dargestellt an den Familienmodellen des ALR, BGB und des französischen Code civil* (Berlin: Duncker & Humblot, 1974).

Douglas, M. *Purity and danger: an analysis of the concepts of pollution and taboo*, 2nd edn (London: Routledge, 1984).

Dülmen, R. van (ed.). *Körper-Geschichten: Studien zur historischen Kulturforschung V* (Frankfurt am Main: Fischer, 1996).

Duden, B. *The woman beneath the skin: a doctor's patients in eighteenth century Germany* (London & Cambridge, Mass.: Harvard University Press, 1991).

Duden, B. *Disembodying women: perspectives on pregnancy and the unborn*, trans. L. Hoinacki (Cambridge, Mass.: Harvard University Press, 1993).

Dürr, R. *Mägde in der Stadt: Das Beispiel Schwäbisch Hall in der Frühen Neuzeit* (Frankfurt am Main & New York: Campus, 1995).

Eifert, C. et al. (eds). *Was sind Männer, was sind Frauen? Geschlechterkonstruktionen im historischen Wandel* (Frankfurt am Main: Suhrkamp, 1996).

Elshtain, J. B. *Public man, private woman: women in social and political thought* (Oxford: Martin Robertson, 1981).

Evans, R. J. *The feminist movement in Germany 1894–1933* (London: Sage, 1976).

Evans, R. J. Family and class in the Hamburg grand bourgeoisie 1815–1914. In *The German bourgeoisie: essays on the social history of the German middle class from the late eighteenth to the early twentieth century*, R. J. Evans & D. Blackbourn (eds) (London & New York: Routledge, 1991), pp. 115–39.

Fasolt, C. Visions of order in the canonists and civilians. In *Handbook of European history 1400–1600: Late Middle Ages, Renaissance and Reformation*, vol. 2: *Visions, programs and outcomes*, T. A. Brady, jun., H. A. Oberman, J. D. Tracy (eds) (Leiden, New York, Cologne: Brill, 1995), pp. 31–59.

Fietze, K. *Spiegel der Vernunft: Theorien zum Menschsein der Frau in der Anthropologie des 15. Jahrhunderts* (Paderborn, Munich, Vienna, Zurich: Schöningh, 1991).

Finch, J. & A. P. Summerfield. Social reconstruction and the emergence of companionate marriage, 1945–59. In *Marriage, domestic life and social change*, D. Clark (ed.) (London: Routledge, 1991), pp. 7–32.

Fischer, E. *Dokumente zur Geschichte des deutschen Rundfunks und Fernsehens* (Göttingen: Muster-Schmidt, 1957).

Fischer, E. *Aimée & Jaguar: Eine Frauenliebe, Berlin 1943* (Cologne: Kiepenheuer & Witsch, 1994).

242

Fischer-Homberger, E. *Krankheit Frau* (Berne, Stuttgart, Vienna: Hans Huber, 1979).

Fischer-Homberger, E. *Medizin vor Gericht: Zur Sozialgeschichte der Gerichtsmedizin* (Darmstadt: Luchterhand, 1983).

Fletcher, A. *Gender, sex and subordination in England, 1500–1800* (New Haven, Connecticut & London: Yale University Press, 1995).

Foucault, M. *Discipline and punish: the birth of the prison* (Harmondsworth: Penguin, 1977).

Foucault, M. *The history of sexuality: an introduction* (Harmondsworth: Penguin, 1978).

Fout, J. C. (ed.). *German women in the nineteenth century: a social history* (New York & London: Holmes & Meier, 1984).

Fout, J. C. Sexual politics in Wilhelmine Germany: the male gender crisis, moral purity, and homophobia. In *Forbidden history: the state, society, and the regulation of sexuality in modern Europe*, J. C. Fout (ed.) (Chicago & London: University of Chicago Press, 1992), pp. 259–92.

Frevert, U. (ed.). *Bürgerinnen und Bürger: Geschlechterverhältnisse im 19. Jahrhundert* (Göttingen: Vandenhoeck & Ruprecht, 1988).

Frevert, U. *Women in German history* (Leamington Spa: Berg, 1989).

Frevert, U. *"Mann und Weib, und Weib und Mann": Geschlechter-Differenzen in der Moderne* (Munich: C. H. Beck, 1995).

Frevert, U. *Men of honour* (Cambridge: Polity, 1995).

Frühsorge, G. (ed.). *Gesinde im 18. Jahrhundert* (Hamburg: Meiner, 1995).

Fussell, P. *The Great War and modern memory* (New York & Oxford: Oxford University Press, 1975).

Gerhard, U. *Verhältnisse und Verhinderungen: Frauenarbeit, Familie und Rechte der Frauen im 19. Jahrhundert. Mit Dokumenten* (Frankfurt am Main: Suhrkamp, 1981).

Gersdorff, U. von. *Frauen im Kriegsdienst* (Stuttgart: Deutsche Verlags-Anstalt, 1969).

Gijwijt-Hofstra, M., H. Marland, H. de Waardt (eds). *Magic, faith, medicine: alternative healing traditions in Europe, 1500 to the present* (London: Routledge, forthcoming).

Gleixner, U. *"Das Mensch" und "der Kerl": Die Konstruktion von Geschlecht in Unzuchtsverfahren der Frühen Neuzeit (1700–1760)* (Frankfurt am Main & New York: Campus, 1994).

Gordon, L. *Heroes of their own lives: the politics and history of family violence* (London: Virago, 1989).

Gössmann, E. Anthropologie und soziale Stellung der Frau nach Summen und Sentenzenkommentaren des 13. Jahrhunderts. *Miscellania Medievalia* 12, 1979, pp. 281–97.

Gössmann, E. (ed.). *Das wohlgelahrte Frauenzimmer* (Munich: iudicium, 1984).

Gössmann, E. (ed.). *Eva Gottes Meisterwerk* (Munich: iudicium, 1985).

Gössmann, E. (ed.). *Ob die Weyber Menschen seyn, oder nicht?* (Munich: iudicium, 1988).

Gössmann, E. (ed.). *Kennt der Geist kein Geschlecht?* (Munich: iudicium, 1994).

Gowing, L. Gender and the language of insult in early modern London. *History Workshop Journal* 35, 1993, pp. 1–21.

Grau, G. (ed.). *Homosexualität in der NS-Zeit: Dokumente einer Diskriminierung und Verfolgung* (Frankfurt am Main: Fischer Taschenbuch, 1993).

Grau, G. (ed.). *Hidden Holocaust? Lesbian and gay persecution in Nazi Germany* (London: Cassell, 1995).

Greven-Aschoff, B. *Die bürgerliche Frauenbewegung in Deutschland 1894–1933* (Göttingen: Vandenhoeck & Ruprecht, 1981).

Gries, R. *Die Rationen-Gesellschaft: Versorgungskampf und Vergleichsmentalität: Leipzig, München und Köln nach dem Kriege* (Münster: Westfälisches Dampfboot, 1990).

Griswold, R. *Family and divorce in California, 1850–1900: Victorian illusions and everyday realities* (Albany: State University of New York Press, 1982).

Groebner, V. Außer Haus: Otto Brunner und die "alteuropäische Ökonomik". *Geschichte in Wissenschaft und Unterricht* 46, 1995, pp. 69–80.

Grossmann, A. The new woman and the rationalization of sexuality in Weimar Germany. In *Powers of desire: the politics of sexuality*, A. Snitow, C. Stansell, S. Thompson (eds) (New York: Monthly Review Press, 1983), pp. 153–76.

Grossmann, A. Feminist debates about women and National Socialism. *Gender and History* 3, 1991, pp. 350–58.

Grossmann, A. *Reforming sex: the German movement for birth control and abortion reform 1920–1950* (New York & Oxford: Oxford University Press, 1995).

Hammerton, A. J. *Cruelty and companionship: conflict in nineteenth-century married life* (London: Routledge, 1992).

Harrington, J. F. *Reordering marriage and society in Reformation Germany* (Cambridge: Cambridge University Press, 1995).

Hausen, K. Die Polarisierung der "Geschlechtscharaktere": Eine Spiegelung der Dissoziation von Erwerbs- und Familienleben. In *Sozialgeschichte der Familie in der Neuzeit Europas: Neue Forschungen*, W. Conze (ed.) (Stuttgart: Klett-Cotta, 1976), pp. 363–93.

Hausen, K. Family and role-division: the polarisation of sexual stereotypes in the nineteenth century – an aspect of the dissociation of work and family life. In *The German family: essays on the social history of the family in nineteenth- and twentieth-century Germany*, R. J. Evans & W. R. Lee (eds) (London: Croom Helm, 1981), pp. 51–83.

Hausen, K. The German nation's obligations to the heroes' widows of World War I. In *Behind the lines: gender and the two world wars*, M. R. Higonnet et al. (eds) (New Haven, Connecticut & London: Yale University Press, 1987), pp. 126–40.

Hausen, K. Öffentlichkeit und Privatheit, gesellschaftspolitische Konstruktionen und die Geschichte der Geschlechterbeziehungen. See Hausen & Wunder (eds), 1992, pp. 81–8.

Hausen, K. & H. Wunder (eds). *Frauengeschichte – Geschlechtergeschichte*

(Frankfurt am Main & New York: Campus, 1992).

Heißler, S. & P. Blastenbrei. *Frauen in der italienischen Renaissance: Heilige – Kriegerinnen – Opfer* (Pfaffenweiler: Centaurus, 1990).

Herzog, D. Liberalism, religious dissent, and women's rights: Louise Dittmar's writings from the 1840s. In *In search of a liberal Germany: studies in the history of German liberalism from 1789 to the present*, K. H. Jarausch & L. E. Jones (eds) (New York, Oxford, Munich: Berg, 1990), pp. 55–85.

Herzog, D. *Intimacy and exclusion: religious politics in pre-revolutionary Baden* (Princeton, NJ: Princeton University Press, 1996).

Herzog, U. *Geistliche Wohlredenheit: Die katholische Barockpredigt* (Munich: C. H. Beck, 1991).

Hess, U. Lateinischer Dialog und gelehrte Partnerschaft: Frauen als humanistische Leitbilder in Deutschland (1500–1550). In *Deutsche Literatur von Frauen*, vol. 1, G. Brinker-Gabler (ed.) Munich: C. H. Beck, 1988), pp. 113–48.

Heymann, L. & A. Augspurg. *Erlebtes – Erschautes: Deutsche Frauen kämpfen für Freiheit, Recht und Frieden 1850–1940* (Meisenheim am Glan: Anton Hain, 1977).

Hirschfeld, G., G. Krumeich, I. Renz (eds). *Keiner fühlt sich hier mehr als Mensch . . .: Erlebnis und Wirkung des Ersten Weltkrieges* (Essen: Klartext, 1993).

Höhn, M. Frau im Haus und Girl im *Spiegel*: discourse on women in the interregnum period of 1945–1949 and the question of German identity. *Central European History* 26(1), 1993, pp. 57–90.

Honegger, C. *Die Ordnung der Geschlechter: Die Wissenschaften vom Menschen und das Weib, 1750–1850*, 2nd edn (Frankfurt am Main & New York: Campus, 1991).

Hong, Y. S. Femininity as a vocation: gender and class conflict in the professionalization of German social work. In *German professions 1800–1950*, G. Cocks & K. H. Jarausch (eds) (New York & Oxford: Oxford University Press, 1990), pp. 232–51.

Huerkamp, C. *Der Aufstieg der Ärzte im 19. Jahrhundert* (Göttingen: Vandenhoeck & Ruprecht, 1985).

Hull, S. W. *Chaste, silent and obedient: English books for women* (San Marino: Huntington Library, 1982).

Jackall, R. (ed.). *Propaganda* (London: Macmillan, 1995).

Jeffreys, S. (ed.). *The sexuality debates* (London: Routledge & Kegan Paul, 1987).

Jerouschek, G. *Lebensschutz und Lebensbeginn: Kulturgeschichte des Abtreibungsverbots* (Stuttgart: Enke, 1988).

Jordan, C. *Renaissance feminism: literary texts and political models* (Ithaca, New York & London: Cornell University Press, 1990).

Jordanova, L. *Sexual visions: images of gender in science and medicine between the eighteenth and the twentieth centuries* (London: Harvester Wheatsheaf, 1989).

Jütte, R. Die Persistenz des Verhütungswissens in der Volkskultur: Sozial- und medizinhistorische Anmerkungen zur These von der "Vernichtung weiser Frauen". *Medizinhistorisches Journal* 24, 1989, pp. 214–31.

Jütte, R. (ed.). *Geschichte der Abtreibung: Von der Antike bis zur Gegenwart* (Munich: C. H. Beck, 1993).

Kerber, L. K. Separate spheres, female worlds, woman's place: the rhetoric of women's history. *Journal of American History* 75(1), 1988, pp. 9–39.

Kermode, J. & G. Walker (eds). *Women, crime and the courts in early modern England* (London: UCL Press, 1994).

Klinksiek, D. *Die Frau im NS Staat* (Stuttgart: Deutsche Verlags-Anstalt, 1982).

Kloke, I. E., Die gesellschaftliche Situation der Frauen in der Frühen Neuzeit im Spiegel der Leichenpredigten. In *Die Familie als sozialer und historischer Verband: Untersuchungen zum Spätmittelalter und zur Frühen Neuzeit*, P.-J. Schuler (ed.) (Sigmaringen: Thorbecke, 1987), pp. 147–63.

Knight, P. Women and abortion in Victorian and Edwardian England. *History Workshop Journal* 4, 1977, pp. 57–69.

Koch, E. *Maior dignitas est in sexu virili: Das weibliche Geschlecht im Normensystem des 16. Jahrhunderts* (Frankfurt am Main: Klostermann, 1991).

Könneker, B. Die Ehemoral in den Fastnachtsspielen von Hans Sachs. In *Hans Sachs und Nürnberg*, H. Brunner et al. (eds) (Nuremberg: Verein für Geschichte der Stadt Nürnberg, 1976), pp. 219–44.

Koonz, C. *Mothers in the fatherland: women, the family and Nazi politics* (London: Jonathan Cape, 1987).

Kramer, K.-S. *Grundriß einer rechtlichen Volkskunde* (Göttingen: Schwartz, 1974).

Kuhn, A. Die vergessene Frauenarbeit in der deutschen Nachkriegszeit. In *"Das Schicksal Deutschlands liegt in der Hand seiner Frauen": Frauen in der deutschen Nachkriegszeit*, A. Kuhn (ed.) (Düsseldorf: Schwann, 1984), pp. 170–201.

Kuhn, A. Power and powerlessness: women after 1945, or the continuity of the ideology of femininity. *German History* 7, 1989, pp. 35–46.

Kuhn, A. Der Antifeminismus als verborgene Theoriebasis des deutschen Faschismus. In *Frauen und Faschismus in Europa: Der faschistische Körper*, L. Siegele-Wenschkewitz & G. Stuchlik (eds) (Pfaffenweiler: Centaurus, 1990), pp. 39–50.

Lacey, K. From *Plauderei* to propaganda: on women's radio in Germany 1924–35. *Media, Culture and Society* 16, 1994, pp. 589–607.

Lacey, K. *Feminine frequencies: gender, German radio and the public sphere, 1923–1945* (Ann Arbor: University of Michigan Press, forthcoming).

Laqueur, T. *Making sex: body and gender from the Greeks to Freud* (Cambridge, Mass.: Harvard University Press, 1990).

Laws, S. *Issues of blood: the politics of menstruation* (London: Macmillan, 1990).

Leed, E. *No man's land: combat and identity in World War I* (Cambridge: Cambridge University Press, 1979).

Leibrock-Plehn, L. *Hexenkräuter oder Arznei: Die Abtreibungsmittel im 16. und 17. Jahrhundert* (Stuttgart: Steiner, 1992).

Lenz, R. (ed.). *Leichenpredigten als Quelle historischer Wissenschaften*, [3 vols], vol. 1 (Cologne & Vienna: Böhlau, 1975), vols 2 and 3 (Marburg a.d. Lahn:

Schwarz, 1979 and 1984 respectively).

Lerg, W. B. *Rundfunk in der Weimarer Republik* (Munich: dtv, 1980).

Lindemann, M. Jungfer Heinrich: Transvestitin, Bigamistin, Lesbierin, Diebin, Mörderin. In *Von Huren und Rabenmüttern: Weibliche Kriminalität in der Frühen Neuzeit*, O. Ulbricht (ed.) (Cologne, Weimar, Vienna: Böhlau, 1995), pp. 259–79.

Lipp, C. (ed.). *Schimpfende Weiber und patriotische Jungfrauen: Frauen im Vormärz und in der Revolution 1848/49* (Moos & Baden-Baden: Elster, 1986).

Lipp, C. Das Private im Öffentlichen: Geschlechterbeziehungen im symbolischen Diskurs der Revolution 1848–49. See Hausen & Wunder (eds), 1992, pp. 99–116.

Lück, M. *Die Frau im Männerstaat: Die gesellschaftliche Stellung der Frau im Nationalsozialismus: Eine Analyse aus pädagogischer Sicht* (Frankfurt am Main: Peter Lang, 1979).

McClain, C. S. (ed.). *Women as healers: cross-cultural perspectives* (New Brunswick & London: Rutgers University Press, 1989).

McLaren, A. *Reproductive rituals: the perception of fertility in England from the sixteenth century to the nineteenth century* (London & New York: Methuen, 1984).

Maclean, I. *The Renaissance notion of woman: a study in the fortunes of scholasticism and medical science in European intellectual life*, repr. (Cambridge: Cambridge University Press, 1985).

McNay, L. *Foucault and feminism: power, gender and the self* (Cambridge: Polity, 1992).

Maier, H. *Die ältere deutsche Staats- und Verwaltungslehre*, 2nd edn (Munich: C. H. Beck, 1980).

Maisch, A. *Notdürftiger Unterhalt und gehörige Schranken: Lebensbedingungen und Lebensstile in württembergischen Dörfern der frühen Neuzeit* (Stuttgart: Gustav Fischer Verlag, 1992).

Mangan, J. A. & J. Walvin (eds). *Manliness and morality: middle-class masculinity in Britain and America 1800–1940* (Manchester: Manchester University Press, 1987).

Marland, H. (ed.). *The art of midwifery: early modern midwives in Europe* (London: Routledge, 1994).

Mason, T. Women in Germany, 1925–1940: family, welfare and work. In *Nazism, Fascism and the working class: essays by Tim Mason*, J. Caplan (ed.) (Cambridge: Cambridge University Press, 1995), pp. 131–211.

Merkel, I. *". . . und Du, Frau an der Werkbank": Die DDR in den 50er Jahren* (Berlin: Elefanten Press, 1990).

Meyer, S. & E. Schulze. Von Wirtschaftswunder keine Spur. In *Perlonzeit: Wie die Frauen ihr Wirtschaftswunder erlebten*, A. Delille & A. Grohn (eds) (Berlin: Elefanten Press, 1985), pp. 92–9.

Meyer-Renschhausen, E. *Weibliche Kultur und soziale Arbeit: Eine Geschichte der Frauenbewegung am Beispiel Bremens 1810–1927* (Cologne & Vienna: Böhlau, 1989).

BIBLIOGRAPHY

Miller, D. Consumption as the vanguard of history. In *Acknowledging consumption: a review of new studies*, D. Miller (ed.) (London: Routledge, 1995), pp. 1–57.

Mitchell, J. & A. Oakley (eds). *The rights and wrongs of women* (London: Penguin, 1976).

Moeller, B. Die Brautwerbung Martin Bucers für Wolfgang Capito: Zur Sozialgeschichte des evangelischen Pfarrerstandes. In *Philologie als Kulturwissenschaft. Studien zur Literatur und Geschichte des Mittelalters: Festschrift für K. Stackmann zum 65. Geburtstag*, L. Grenzmann (ed.) (Göttingen: Vandenhoeck & Ruprecht, 1987), pp. 306–25.

Moeller, R. G. *Protecting motherhood: women and the family in the politics of postwar West Germany* (Berkeley, New York, Los Angeles, London: University of California Press, 1993).

Möhrmann, R. (ed.). *Frauenemanzipation im deutschen Vormärz* (Stuttgart: Reclam, 1978).

Moore, C. N. Mein Kindt, nimm diß in acht. *Pietismus und Neuzeit* 6, pp. 164–85, 1980.

Moore, C. N. Die adelige Mutter als Erzieherin: Erbauungsliteratur adeliger Mütter für ihre Kinder. In *Europäische Hofkultur im 16. und 17. Jahrhundert*, A. Buck et al. (eds) (Hamburg: Hauswedell, 1981), vol. 3, pp. 505–10.

Moore, C. N. Mädchenlektüre im 17. Jahrhundert. In *Literatur und Volk im 17. Jahrhundert: Probleme populärer Kultur in Deutschland*, W. Brückner et al. (eds), pt 2 (Wiesbaden: Harrassowitz, 1985), pp. 489–97.

Moore, C. N. *The maiden's mirror: reading material for German girls in the sixteenth and seventeenth centuries* (Wiesbaden: Harrassowitz, 1987).

Moscucci, O. *The science of woman: gynaecology and gender in England 1800–1929* (Cambridge: Cambridge University Press, 1990).

Moser, D.-R. Exempel – Paraphrase – Märchen: Zum Gattungswandel christlicher Volkserzählungen im 17. und 18. Jahrhundert am Beispiel einiger "Kinder- und Hausmärchen" der Brüder Grimm. In *Sozialer und kultureller Wandel in der ländlichen Welt des 18. Jahrhunderts*, E. Hinrichs & G. Wiegelmann (eds) (Wolfenbüttel: Herzog August Bibliothek, 1982), pp. 117–48.

Moser-Rath, E. *Predigtmärlein der Barockzeit* (Berlin: de Gruyter, 1964).

Moser-Rath, E. *Dem Kirchenvolk die Leviten gelesen . . .* (Stuttgart: Metzler, 1991).

Müller, M. E. Naturwesen Mann: Zur Dialektik von Herrschaft und Knechtschaft in Ehelehren der Frühen Neuzeit. See Wunder & Vanja (eds), 1991, pp. 43–68.

Münch, P. Die Obrigkeit im Vaterstand – Zu Definition und Kritik des "Landesvaters" während der Frühen Neuzeit. *Daphnis* 11, 1982, pp. 16–40.

Münch, P. (ed.). *Ordnung, Fleiß und Sparsamkeit: Texte und Dokumente zur Entstehung der "bürgerlichen Tugenden"* (Munich: dtv, 1984).

Münch, P. Parsimonia summum est vectigal – Sparen ist ein ryche gült: Sparsamkeit als Haus-, Frauen- und Bürgertugend. In *Ethische Perspektiven: "Wandel der Tugenden"*, H.-J. Braun (ed.) (Zurich: Chronos, 1989), pp. 169–87.

Nienhaus, U. *Vater Staat und seine Gehilfinnen: Die Politik mit der Frauenarbeit bei der deutschen Post (1864–1945)* (Frankfurt am Main: Campus, 1995).

Niethammer, L. Privat-Wirtschaft: Erinnerungsfragmente einer anderen Umerziehung. In *"Hinterher merkt man, daß es richtig war, daß es schiefgegangen ist." Nachkriegserfahrungen im Ruhrgebiet: Lebensgeschichte und Sozialkultur im Ruhrgebiet 1930 bis 1960*, vol. 2, L. Niethammer (ed.) (Berlin: Verlag J. H. W. Dietz, 1983), pp. 17–106.

Noonan, J. T., jun. *Contraception: a history of its treatment by the Catholic theologians and canonists*, 2nd edn (Cambridge, Mass.: Belknap Press of Harvard University Press, 1986).

Oakley, A. *The captured womb: a history of medical care of pregnant women* (Oxford: Basil Blackwell, 1984).

Oertzen, C. von & A. Rietzschel. Neuer Wein in alten Schläuchen: Geschlechterpolitik und Frauenerwerbsarbeit im besetzten Deutschland zwischen Kriegsende und Währungsreform. *Ariadne* 27 (May 1995), pp. 28–35.

Oestreich, G. Strukturprobleme des europäischen Absolutismus. *Vierteljahresschrift für Sozial- und Wirtschaftsgeschichte* 55, 1968, pp. 329–47.

Offen, K. Defining feminism: a comparative historical approach. *Signs* 14, 1988, pp. 119–57.

Opitz, C. Neue Wege der Sozialgeschichte? Ein kritischer Blick auf Otto Brunners Konzept des "ganzen Hauses". *Geschichte und Gesellschaft* 20, 1994, pp. 88–98.

Overy, R. J. Hitler's war and the German economy: a reinterpretation. In *War, peace and social change in twentieth century Europe*, C. Emsley, A. Marwick, W. Simpson (eds) (Milton Keynes: Open University Press, 1989), pp. 208–25.

Paczensky, S. von. (ed.). *Wir sind keine Mörderinnen!* (Reinbek near Hamburg: Rowohlt, 1984).

Paletschek, S. *Frauen und Dissens* (Göttingen: Vandenhoeck & Ruprecht, 1990).

Pateman, C. *The sexual contract* (Cambridge: Polity, 1994).

Petchesky, R. P. *Abortion and woman's choice* (London: Verso, 1986).

Porter, R. & M. Teich (eds.). *Sexual knowledge, sexual science: the history of attitudes towards sexuality* (Cambridge: Cambridge University Press, 1994).

Prelinger, C. M. *Charity, challenge and change: religious dimensions of the mid-nineteenth-century women's movement in Germany* (New York: Greenwood, 1987).

Riddle, J. M. *Contraception and abortion from the ancient world to the Renaissance* (Cambridge, Mass. & London: Harvard University Press, 1992).

Riesenberger, D. *Das Internationale Rote Kreuz 1863–1977: Für Humanität in Krieg und Frieden* (Göttingen: Vandenhoeck & Ruprecht, 1992).

Roberts, E. *Women and families: an oral history, 1940–1970* (Oxford: Basil Blackwell, 1995).

Roberts, M. L. *Civilization without sexes: reconstructing gender in postwar France, 1917–1927* (Chicago: University of Chicago Press, 1994).

Roper, L. Discipline and respectability: prostitution and the Reformation in

Augsburg. *History Workshop Journal* 19, 1985, pp. 3–28.

Roper, L. *The holy household: women and morals in Reformation Augsburg* (Oxford: Clarendon Press, 1989).

Roper, L. Will and honor: sex, words and power in Augsburg criminal trials. *Radical History Review* 43, 1989, pp. 45–71.

Roper, L. Männlichkeit und männliche Ehre. See Hausen & Wunder (eds), 1992, pp. 151–72.

Roper, L. *Oedipus and the devil: witchcraft, sexuality and religion in early modern Europe* (London & New York: Routledge, 1994).

Roper, M. & J. Tosh (eds). *Manful assertions: masculinity in Britain since 1800* (London: Routledge, 1991).

Roseman, M. *Recasting the Ruhr 1945–1958: manpower, economic recovery and labour relations* (New York & Oxford: Berg, 1992).

Rosenhaft, E. Women, gender, and the limits of political history in the age of "mass" politics. In *Elections, mass politics, and social change in modern Germany: new perspectives*, L. E. Jones & J. Retallack (eds) (Cambridge: Cambridge University Press, 1992), pp. 149–73.

Rosenhaft, E. Women in modern Germany. In *Modern Germany reconsidered 1870–1945*, G. Martel (ed.) (London: Routledge, 1992), pp. 140–58.

Rosenhaft, E. Aufklärung und Geschlecht: Bürgerlichkeit, Weiblichkeit, Subjektivität. In *Rationale Beziehungen? Geschlechterverhältnisse im Rationalisierungsprozeß*, D. Reese et al. (eds) (Frankfurt am Main: Suhrkamp, 1993), pp. 19–37.

Ross, E. Fierce questions and taunts: married life in working-class London. *Feminist Studies* 8, pp. 575–602, 1982.

Ross, E. *Love and toil: motherhood in outcast London, 1870–1918* (New York & Oxford: Oxford University Press, 1993).

Rouette, S. *Sozialpolitik als Geschlechterpolitik: Die Regulierung der Frauenarbeit nach dem Ersten Weltkrieg* (Frankfurt am Main & New York: Campus, 1993).

Rowlands, A. To wear a virgin's wreath: gender and problems of conformity in early modern Germany. *European Review of History – Revue européenne d'Histoire* 1, 1994, pp. 227–32.

Rublack, U. Pregnancy, childbirth and the female body in early modern Germany. *Past and Present* 105, 1996, pp. 84–108.

Ruhl, K.-J. (ed.). *Frauen in der Nachkriegszeit 1945–1963* (Munich: dtv, 1988).

Rupp, L. J. *Mobilising women for war: German and American propaganda 1939–1945* (Princeton, NJ: Princeton University Press, 1978).

Rupp, L. J. "I don't call that *Volksgemeinschaft*": women, class, and war in Nazi Germany. In *Women, war and revolution*, C. R. Berkin & C. M. Lovett (eds) (New York & London: Holmes & Meier, 1980), pp. 37–53.

Sabean, D. W. *Property, production and family in Neckarhausen, 1700–1870* (Cambridge: Cambridge University Press, 1990).

Sachße, C. *Mütterlichkeit als Beruf: Sozialarbeit, Sozialreform und Frauenbewegung, 1871–1929* (Frankfurt am Main: Suhrkamp, 1986).

Sachße, C. Social mothers: the bourgeois women's movement and German welfare-state formation, 1890–1929. In *Mothers of a new world: maternalist politics and the origins of welfare states*, S. Koven & S. Michel (eds) (New York & London: Routledge, 1993), pp. 136–58.

Safley, T. M. *Let no man put asunder. The control of marriage in the German southwest: a comparative study, 1550–1600* (Kirksville, Mo.: Sixteenth Century Journal Publishers, 1984).

Scannell, P. Public service broadcasting and modern public life. *Media, Culture and Society* 11, 1989, pp. 135–66.

Schiebinger, L. *Nature's body: gender in the making of modern science* (Boston: Beacon Press, 1993).

Schlumbohm, J. "Wilde Ehen": Zusammenleben angesichts kirchlicher Sanktionen und staatlicher Sittenpolizei (Osnabrücker Land, c. 1790–1870). In *Familie und Familienlosigkeit: Fallstudien aus Niedersachsen und Bremen vom 15. bis 20. Jahrhundert*, J. Schlumbohm (ed.) (Hanover: Hahnsche Buchhandlung, 1993), pp. 63–80.

Schmitt, S. *Der Arbeiterinnenschutz im deutschen Kaiserreich: Zur Konstruktion der schutzbedürftigen Arbeiterin* (Stuttgart: J. B. Metzler, 1995).

Schoppmann, C. *Nationalsozialistische Sexualpolitik und weibliche Homosexualität* (Pfaffenweiler: Centaurus, 1991).

Schoppmann, C. *Zeit der Maskierung: Lebensgeschichten lesbischer Frauen im "Dritten Reich"* (Berlin: Orlanda Frauenverlag, 1993).

Schoppmann, C. *Days of masquerade: life stories of lesbians during the Third Reich* (New York: Columbia University Press, 1996).

Schorn-Schütte, L. "Gefährtin" und "Mitregentin": Zur Sozialgeschichte der evangelischen Pfarrfrau in der Frühen Neuzeit. See Wunder & Vanja (eds), 1991, pp. 109–53.

Schreiner, K. & Schwerhoff, G. (eds). *Verletzte Ehre: Ehrkonflikte in Gesellschaften des Mittelalters und der Frühen Neuzeit* (Cologne, Weimar, Vienna: Böhlau, 1995).

Schulte, R. Dienstmädchen im herrschaftlichen Haushalt: zur Genese ihrer Sozialpsychologie. *Zeitschrift für bayerische Landesgeschichte* 41, 1978, pp. 879–920.

Schulte, R. *The village in court: arson, infanticide, and poaching in the court records of Upper Bavaria* (Cambridge: Cambridge University Press, 1994).

Schüngel-Straumann, H. *Die Frau am Anfang: Eva und die Folgen* (Freiburg im Breisgau: Herder, 1989).

Schuster, B. *Die freien Frauen: Dirnen und Frauenhäuser im 15. und 16. Jahrhundert* (Frankfurt am Main & New York: Campus, 1995).

Scott, J. W. Gender: a useful category of historical analysis. *American Historical Review* 91, 1986, pp. 1053–75.

Scott, J. W. *Gender and the politics of history* (New York: Columbia University Press, 1988).

Scribner, B. (ed.). *Germany: a new social and economic history*, vol. 1: *1450–1630*. (London: Arnold, 1996).

Scribner, R. Reformation, Karneval and the world turned upside-down. *Social*

History 3, 1978, pp. 303–29.

Scully, D. *Men who control women's health: the miseducation of obstetricians-gynaecologists* (Boston: Houghton Mifflin, 1980).

Sharpe, L. Theodor Gottlieb von Hippel: argumentative strategies in the debate on the rights of women. See Castiglione & Sharpe (eds), 1995, pp. 89–104.

Shorter, E. *Women's bodies: a social history of women's encounter with health, ill-health and medicine* (London: Transaction, 1991).

Shuttle, P. & P. Redgrove. *The wise wound: menstruation and everywoman* (London: HarperCollins, 1994).

Simon-Muscheid, K. Geschlecht, Identität und soziale Rolle: Weiblicher Transvestismus vor Gericht, 15./16. Jahrhundert. In *Weiblich – männlich. Geschlechterverhältnisse in der Schweiz: Rechtsprechung, Diskurs, Praktiken. Féminin – masculin. Rapports sociaux de sexes en Suisse: législation, discours, pratiques*, R. Jaun & B. Studer (eds) (Zurich: Chronos, 1995), pp. 45–57.

Smart, C. Disruptive bodies and unruly sex: the regulation of reproduction and sexuality in the nineteenth century. In *Regulating womanhood: historical essays on marriage, motherhood and sexuality*, C. Smart (ed.) (London: Routledge, 1992), pp. 7–32.

Smith, T. J. (ed.). *Propaganda: a pluralistic perspective* (London: Praeger, 1989).

Smith-Rosenberg, C. *Disorderly conduct: visions of gender in Victorian America* (New York: Knopf, 1981).

Spamer, A. *Bilderbogen von der "Geistlichen Hausmagd": Ein Beitrag zur Geschichte des religiösen Bilderbogens und der Erbauungsliteratur im populären Verlagswesen Mitteleuropas* (Göttingen: Schwartz, 1970).

Stahr, H. Liebesgaben für den Ernstfall: Das Rote Kreuz in Deutschland zu Beginn des Ersten Weltkrieges. In *August 1914: Ein Volk zieht in den Krieg*, Berliner Geschichtswerkstatt (ed.) (Berlin: Nishen, 1989).

Steakley, J. D. Iconography of a scandal: political cartoons and the Eulenburg affair in Wilhelmine Germany. In *Hidden from history: reclaiming the gay and lesbian past*, M. B. Duberman, M. Vicinus, G. Chauncey, jun. (eds) (London: Penguin, 1989), pp. 233–57.

Steinbrügge, L. *Das moralische Geschlecht: Theorien und literarische Entwürfe über die Natur der Frau in der französischen Aufklärung* (Weinheim: Beltz, 1987).

Stephenson, J. *Women in Nazi society* (London: Croom Helm, 1975).

Stephenson, J. *The Nazi organisation of women* (London: Croom Helm, 1981).

Stephenson, J. Propaganda, autarky and the German housewife. In *Nazi propaganda: the power and the limitations*, D. Welch (ed.) (London: Croom Helm, 1983), pp. 117–42.

Stoehr, I. *Emanzipation zum Staat? Der Allgemeine Deutsche Frauenverein – Deutscher Staatsbürgerinnenverband (1893–1933)* (Pfaffenweiler: Centaurus, 1990).

Stoehr, I. Housework and motherhood: debates and policies in the women's movement in Imperial Germany and the Weimar Republic. In *Maternity and gender policies: women and the rise of the European welfare states, 1880s–*

1950s, G. Bock & P. Thane (eds) (London & New York: Routledge, 1991), pp. 213–32.

Stolleis, M. *Geschichte des öffentlichen Rechts in Deutschland*, vol. 1. (Munich: C. H. Beck, 1988).

Stone, L. *The family, sex and marriage in England, 1500–1800* (London: Weidenfeld & Nicolson, 1977).

Summers, A. *Angels and citizens: British women as military nurses, 1854–1914* (London: Routledge, 1988).

Theweleit, K. *Male fantasies*, vol. 1: *Women, floods, bodies, history*; vol. 2: *Male bodies: psychoanalysing the white terror* (Cambridge: Polity, 1987 (vol. 1) and 1989 (vol. 2)).

Thomas, G. *Life on all fronts: women in the First World War* (Cambridge: Cambridge University Press, 1989).

Tomes, N. "A torrent of abuse": crimes of violence between working-class men and women in London, 1840–1875. *Journal of Social History* 11, 1978, pp. 328–45.

Tröger, A. German women's memories of World War II. In *Behind the lines: gender and the two world wars*, M. Higonnet et al. (eds) (New Haven, Connecticut & London: Yale University Press, 1987), pp. 285–99.

Troßbach, W. Das "ganze Haus" – Basiskategorie für das Verständnis der ländlichen Gesellschaft in der frühen Neuzeit? *Blätter für deutsche Landesgeschichte* 129, 1993, pp. 277–314.

Twellmann, M. (ed.). *Die deutsche Frauenbewegung: Ihre Anfänge und erste Entwicklung: Quellen 1843–1889* (Meisenheim am Glan: Anton Hain, 1972).

Ulbrich, C. Unartige Weiber: Präsenz und Renitenz von Frauen im frühneuzeitlichen Deutschland. In *Arbeit, Frömmigkeit und Eigensinn*, R. van Dülmen (ed.) (Frankfurt am Main: Fischer, 1990), pp. 13–42.

Ulbricht, O. Infanticide in eighteenth-century Germany. In *The German underworld: deviants and outcasts in German history*, R. J. Evans (ed.) (London: Routledge, 1988), pp. 108–40.

Ulbricht, O. (ed.). *Von Huren und Rabenmüttern: Weibliche Kriminalität in der Frühen Neuzeit* (Cologne: Böhlau, 1995).

Usborne, C. "Pregnancy is the woman's active service": pronatalism in Germany during the First World War. In *The upheaval of war: family, work and welfare in Europe, 1914–1918*, R. Wall & J. Winter (eds) (Cambridge: Cambridge University Press, 1988), pp. 192–236.

Usborne, C. *The politics of the body in Weimar Germany: women's reproductive rights and duties* (London: Macmillan and Ann Arbor, Mich.: University of Michigan Press, 1992).

Vanja, C. "Verkehrte Welt": Das Weibergericht zu Breitenbach, einem hessischen Dorf des 17. Jahrhunderts. *Journal für Geschichte* 5, 1986, pp. 22–9.

Vickery, A. Golden age to separate spheres? A review of the categories and chronology of English women's history. *Historical Journal* 36, 1993, pp. 383–414.

Vogel, U. Property rights and the status of women in Germany and England. In *Bourgeois society in nineteenth-century Europe*, J. Kocka & A. Mitchell (eds)

(Oxford & Providence: Berg, 1992), pp. 241–69.

Vogel, U. The fear of public disorder: marriage between revolution and reaction. See Castiglione & Sharpe (eds), 1995, pp. 71–88.

Völger, G. & K. von Welck (eds). *Männerbande, Männerbünde: Zur Rolle des Mannes im Kulturvergleich*, [2 vols] (Cologne: Rautenstrauth-Joest-Museum, 1990).

Watt, J. R. *The making of modern marriage: matrimonial control and the rise of sentiment in Neuchâtel, 1550–1800* (Ithaca, New York: Cornell University Press, 1992).

Weber, M. *Ehefrau und Mutter in der Rechtsentwicklung* (Tübingen: J. C. B. Mohr, 1907).

Weber, M. *Frauenfragen und Frauengedanken* (Tübingen: J. C. B. Mohr, 1919).

Weedon, C. *Feminist practice and poststructuralist theory* (Oxford: Basil Blackwell, 1987).

Wehler, H.-U. *Deutsche Gesellschaftsgeschichte*, vol. 1 (Munich: C. H. Beck, 1987).

Weigand, R. Zur mittelalterlichen kirchlichen Ehegerichtsbarkeit. *Zeitschrift für Rechtsgeschichte, Kanonistische Abteilung* 67, 1981, pp. 213–47.

Welch D. *Propaganda and the German cinema 1933–1945* (Oxford: Clarendon Press, 1983).

Welch, D. *The Third Reich: politics and propaganda* (London: Routledge, 1993).

Wernick, A. *Promotional culture* (London: Sage, 1990).

Whalen, R. W. *Bitter wounds: German victims of the Great War 1914–1939* (Ithaca, New York & London: Cornell University Press, 1984).

Wiesner, M. E. *Working women in Renaissance Germany* (New Brunswick, NJ: Rutgers University Press, 1986).

Wiesner, M. E. Frail, weak and helpless: women's legal position in theory and reality. In *Regnum, religio et ratio: essays presented to R. M. Kingdon*, J. Friedman (ed.) (Kirksville, Mo.: Sixteenth Century Journal Publishers, 1987), pp. 161–9.

Wiesner, M. E. Guilds, male-bonding and women's work in early modern Germany. *Gender and History* 1, 1989, pp. 125–37.

Wiesner, M. E. The midwives of south Germany and the public/private dichotomy. In *The art of midwifery: early modern midwives in Europe*, H. Marland (ed.) (London: Routledge, 1993), pp. 77–94.

Wiesner, M. E. *Women and gender in early modern Europe* (Cambridge: Cambridge University Press, 1993).

Wildt, M. *Am Beginn der "Konsumgesellschaft": Mangelerfahrung, Lebenshaltung, Wohlstandshoffnung in Westdeutschland in den fünfziger Jahren* (Hamburg: Ergebnisse, 1994).

Wiltenburg, J. *Disorderly women and female power in the street literature of early modern England and Germany* (Charlottesville, Va. & London: University Press of Virginia, 1992).

Windäus-Walser, K. Gnade der weiblichen Geburt? Zum Umgang der Frauenforschung mit Nationalsozialismus und Antisemitismus. *Feministische Studien* 6(1), 1988, pp. 102–15.

Winkler, D. *Frauenarbeit im Dritten Reich* (Hamburg: Hoffmann & Campe, 1977).

Woycke, J. *Birth control in Germany 1871–1933* (London: Routledge, 1988).

Wulf, J. *Presse und Funk im Dritten Reich: Eine Dokumentation* (Frankfurt am Main: Ullstein, 1983).

Wunder, G. *Die Bürger von Hall: Sozialgeschichte einer Reichsstadt 1216–1802* (Sigmaringen: Thorbecke, 1980).

Wunder, H. Frauen in den Leichenpredigten des 16. und 17. Jahrhunderts. In *Leichenpredigten als Quelle historischer Wissenschaften*, vol. 3, R. Lenz (ed.) (Marburg a.d. Lahn: Schwarz, 1984), pp. 57–68.

Wunder, H. *Die bäuerliche Gemeinde in Deutschland* (Göttingen: Vandenhoeck & Ruprecht, 1986).

Wunder, H. Von der "frumkeit" zur Frömmigkeit: Ein Beitrag zur Genese bürgerlicher Weiblichkeit (15.–17. Jahrhundert). In *Weiblichkeit in geschichtlicher Perspektive: Fallstudien und Reflexionen zu Grundproblemen der historischen Frauenforschung*, U. Becher & J. Rüsen (eds) (Frankfurt am Main: Suhrkamp, 1988), pp. 174–88.

Wunder, H. *"Er ist die Sonn', sie ist der Mond": Frauen in der Frühen Neuzeit* (Munich: C. H. Beck, 1992; American edn forthcoming, Cambridge, Mass.: Harvard University Press).

Wunder, H. Geschlechtsidentitäten: Frauen und Männer im späten Mittelalter und am Beginn der Neuzeit. See Hausen & Wunder (eds), 1992, pp. 131–6.

Wunder, H. & C. Vanja (eds). *Wandel der Geschlechterbeziehungen zu Beginn der Neuzeit* (Frankfurt am Main: Suhrkamp, 1991).

Zank, W. *Wirtschaft und Arbeit in Ostdeutschland 1945–1949: Probleme des Wiederaufbaus in der Sowjetischen Besatzungszone Deutschlands* (Munich: Oldenbourg, 1987).

Zeman, Z. A. B. *Nazi propaganda*, 2nd edn (London & New York: Oxford University Press, 1973).

Index